D1480135

Advisory Editor: David Bayliss
Chief Planner (Transportation)
Greater London Council

Models in Urban and Regional Planning

BENJAMIN REIF
Central University of Venezuela

Intertext Educational Publishers

New York   London

DISCARDED
"UNIVERSITY OF TULSA-McFARLIN LIBRARY"
UNIVERSITY OF TULSA LIBRARY

© 1973 by Benjamin Reif

Published by Leonard Hill Books
a division of
International Textbook Company Limited

All rights reserved. No part of this publication may be reproduced,
stored in a retrieval system, or transmitted, in any form or by any
means, electronic, mechanical, photocopying, recording or otherwise,
without the prior permission of the copyright owner.

First published in the USA in 1973 by Intext Educational Publishers by
arrangement with Leonard Hill Books, a division of International
Textbook Company Limited, 24 Market Square, Aylesbury, Bucks
HP20 1TL.

Library of Congress Catalog Card No: 73-13240
ISBN: 0-7002-2443-2

Intext Educational Publishers
257 Park Avenue South
New York, New York 10010

Printed in Great Britain

HT166
.R339
1973

To my wife

CONTENTS

LIST OF ILLUSTRATIONS

ACKNOWLEDGEMENTS

This work was originally conceived and carried out by the author at the Cranfield Institute of Technology, Bedford, England in 1972, as a research project in operational research, and brought to its final stage in Venezuela. I am deeply grateful to Mr. Norman Webster, Senior Lecturer of the Operational Research Unit, for the encouragement and advice given in the course of this work. I owe a special debt of gratitude to Mr. Michael Batty of the Urban Research Unit, University of Reading, whose assistance in the early stages proved invaluable. Warmest thanks are extended to Dr. J. M. Clark of the Centre for Transport Studies, Cranfield Institute of Technology, for his helpful comments on some aspects of the work. Acknowledgement is also made to David Bayliss of the Greater London Council, for his helpful comments.

Benjamin Reif

Caracas 1973

SUMMARY

The principal aim of this book is to examine how operational research techniques and related disciplines, such as systems analysis and cybernetics, have been applied to the complex design problems of urban and regional systems. Also, it attempts to provide a framework by which interested people (especially architects and planners) may relate the new tools to the problem of planning cities and regions.

The first part outlines the underlying concepts of the 'systems approach', where the basic ideas of systems are laid down and where the usefulness of considering metropolitan and regional areas as systems is expressed. Before discussing the models of the urban spatial system, the planning process context in which they are used is briefly mentioned in Part II, and the role of mathematical or urban models assessed.

The chapters in Part III are related to models and model building, where the notion of 'model' in the general sense is outlined, and the special types of symbolic models (mathematical) and their structures are analysed. The process of building urban spatial models is also described.

Part IV is devoted to actual examples of mathematical models; first the spatial interaction submodels which generally form part of a model of the urban spatial system are described, and then some outstanding examples of models of the urban spatial structure are presented. Finally, an appraisal of the urban, spatial modelling situation is undertaken.

NOTATION

For the convenience of the reader wishing to refer to the original sources of the mathematical models described in this work, the notation employed here is the original used by the authors of each model. In some cases, in order to clarify ideas, additional or modified symbols have been incorporated in the notation.

The notation is presented at the beginning of each chapter and should only be applied to the chapter concerned. Precautions have been taken to use the same additional symbols to represent identical features in all the mathematical models described in this book.

INTRODUCTION

Operational research techniques have been available for industrial and commercial use for almost 25 years now. In this time the areas where operational research have made an impact have increased as a rate far in excess of that predicted. However, it has only been in recent years that architects and planners have begun to make use of the capabilities provided by these techniques.

These professionals expect to find in the new tools, first, a more satisfactory way of solving the problems and their particular conditions and restrictions; and second, they hope to find through an analytical process a better way of understanding the effects of their own propostions. The central feature of recent work in urban planning has been the pronounced movement towards a more scientific approach and also the desire to develop an increased analytical capability.

The environmental problems that planners face today are too complex to be solved either by a speculative approach based upon experience, intuition and imagination, or by an inductive analytic approach based on the detailed study of particular parts of the problem concerned. Probably, a better approach would be one which lies between these two extremes and which essentially is an experimental process: the scientific approach based on observation and explanation.

The scientific method involves basically three steps:

(1) Formulating a hypothesis to account for a set of isolated facts, or observations of the environment.

(2) Checking to see whether the hypothesis actually explains the known facts, which involves formulating and reformulating as many times as necessary the hypothesis in terms of the facts.

(3) Testing the validity of the hypothesis by seeing whether or not it accurately predicts events, that is, gives the correct results. We may recall that a theory is a well-tested hypothesis.

Planners have found that a scientific approach to urban systems can be usefully adopted, and it is specially beneficial when combined with new disciplines such as operational research, systems analysis and cybernetics.

Regarding cities and regions as complex systems, the urban planner is faced with the prime need of understanding the working of them, so that he can effectively diagnose problems and assess alternative designs. One facet of this revolution in approach involves the development of mathematical models which attempt to simulate the structure of land uses and activities in cities and regions. Following the fairly successful attempts to model the transport system, land-use models were built in the USA in the mid 1960s as fundamental tools in the planning process and to enable planners to deal with the complex interrelationships between land uses, traffic flows, economic and population activities, etc.

Equipped with these modelling techniques, planners should be able to predict fairly accurately the consequences of varied governmental policies on land development, or the probable impact on land uses when changes or improvements in transportation, sewerage, water systems, etc. take place. It is hoped that the new tools will help designers to be more systematic, not only during the problem diagnosis or the design stage, but also in the assessment of the impact of designs.

This work is neither a new theoretical statement nor a simple description of techniques used in urban and regional planning. Rather it is an attempt to provide a framework by which interested people may relate the new tools from operational research and other connected fields, such as systems analysis and cybernetics, to the problem of planning cities and regions.

To my knowledge, no publication is available which covers comprehensively the most relevant features of the new approach to urban and regional planning. Indeed, the literature available is generally related to specific topics and tends to be too deep for the beginner to understand; and sometimes — owing to the lack of a common terminology — some confusion arises when reading publications from different researchers on the same topic. This confusion is also extended to the possible use and role of models in the planning context. Therefore, this book sets out with the intention of bringing together some of the more recent developments in urban and regional planning where operational research techniques blended with other new disciplines have been applied. It is hoped that this work will reduce the difficulties outlined above.

In this work 'urban' is broadly defined, so that, for example, 'urban planning' can be used as a shorthand for 'urban and regional planning' unless otherwise is stated.

Because of the nature of the subject matter, the book has been divided into five parts. The first outlines the underlying concepts of the 'systems approach': Chapter 1 presents the basic concepts of the systems on which Chapter 2 is based. It lays down the systems theory basis for this study together with the role of operational research techniques in the optimization of systems. Chapter 2 recognizes the usefulness of considering metropolitan and regional areas as systems and describes the main subsystems of the urban system; emphasis is placed on the urban spatial system.

Before discussing mathematical models and techniques applied to the study of the urban spatial system, the planning process context in which they are used is briefly mentioned in Part II. Also,the role of mathematical models in the planning process is assessed.
Part III is devoted to models and model building: Chapter 4 outlines the notion of 'model' in a general sense, and its uses and advantages as well as different types are explained. Mathematical models, as used for modelling the urban spatial system, are also described and their structure analysed in this chapter. Chapter 5 refers to the process of model building, where the strategy and the basic principles of model building are described.

Part IV is devoted to actual mathematical models in use: Chapter 6 describes the most common spatial interaction submodels which generally form part of a land-use or allocation model which sets out to model the urban spatial system. Chapter 7 presents a classification for the study of models of the urban spatial structure. Chapters 8—14 describe some outstanding examples of models of the urban spatial structure based on the three dimensional classification presented in Chapter 7.

Finally, Part V presents an appraisal of the urban spatial modelling situation.

1 Systems: General Framework

1.1 Introduction

The problems that mankind face today are becoming increasingly complex owing to the number of variables involved, and commonly, by the addition of random situations or actions which add to the whole problem an incredible amount of complexity. The traditional methods of dealing with these problems have proved unsatisfactory and new methods are being adopted.

During the past three decades a new body of thought has been forming, which calls for a return to the use of rationalist-based principles for solving large-scale planning and design problems. This new body of thought has been named the 'systems approach'. Current use of reason as an understandable framework for observation of scientific phenomena is a basic principle of this new approach. Thus, we can state that the 'systems approach' has a close relationship with the empiricist school of scientific thought.

The term 'system' has meaning in every form of organized research and learning. Referring to the human body we commonly use the terms skeletal system, nervous system, digestive system, etc. In astronomy we talk about the solar system. In a business firm we refer to the production system, inventory system, etc. We also speak of the information system and decision system. In building we usually use the terms structural system, plumbing system, etc. The relationship of man to his setting can be seen also in systemic terms: i.e. ecosystem. Thus we see that the concept of system has import for every discipline that one can name.

Systems are made up of sets of components that work together for the overall objective of the whole. The systems approach means looking at each component part in terms of the role it plays in the larger system. A particular characteristic of this approach is that it attempts to arrive at decisions not only for the individual parts or elements but for their total ordering as well, through a logical, organized arrangement of steps. This involves understanding problems in terms of their detailed processes so that they can be organized for solution in a manner that can be explained and repeated. In a sense, we can say that the systems approach is simply a way of thinking and approaching problems that involves looking at the whole problem rather than concentrating on one or more parts to the exclusion of everything else. A basic objective of the systems approach is to discover those components whose measures of performance are truly related to the measure of performance of the overall system. Then, when the measure of performance of a component increases and all the others remain equal, the measure of performance of the total system should also be increased, otherwise, the component is not truly contributing to the system's performance.[1]

1.2 General systems theory

Systems are considered to have certain things in common, and these are usually studied in a discipline called general systems theory. The implication of this discipline is that it is possible to write down a general theory of system behaviour and then to apply it to, say, urban and regional systems. The use of system definitions and concepts can be seen as a useful prerequisite for investigation of concrete problems in science.

McMillan and González point out[2] that:

> In fact some hope that one day a general systems theory will exist to bind together students of all fields — biologist, mathematician, psychologist, economist, musicologist and whomever else — enabling each to describe his system in a common language, to engage in analysis such that other disciplinarians may replicate the work, and to share methodologies derived from the theory rather from the particular system under observation.

There are some obvious advantages to be gained from the general study of systems. For example it encourages discipline in the definition of systems, sub-systems, or their components, allowing their application to be quite precise. Also, the study of analogies between different systems can often help the study of a system.

According to Von Bertalanffy,[3] general systems theory itself can be classified in terms of an extension of an organismic conception of science. This organismic conception of science is based on a view that sees mental, sociological, cultural and physical phenomena as a dynamic interrelated collection of events and objects which stresses the general similarities between phenomena at different levels, and at the same time allows different phenomena to retain their autonomy and adherence to specific laws.

This conception differs radically from the mechanistic view of science as expressed by Laplace. His conception is that all phenomena are ultimately aggregates of fortuitous actions of elementary physical units. Although the mechanistic conception has allowed some notable advances in many fields of science, this 'molecular' approach is being replaced by the organismic conception. This view is stressed by Ackoff[4]:

> The tendency to study systems as an entity rather than as a conglomeration of parts is consistent with the tendency in contemporary science no longer to isolate phenomena in narrowly confined contexts, but rather to open interactions for examination and to examine larger and larger slides of nature . . . We are participating in what is probably the most comprehensive effort to attain a synthesis of scientific knowledge yet made.

When dealing with very complex systems, it is sometimes useful to break down the complex system into manageable components or subsystems to provide an analytical framework, and this is done with the help of systems analysis techniques.

1.3 Systems analysis

There are different interpretations of the term 'systems analysis'. McMillan and González[2] identify some of them and comment that:

> The most common is the one that identifies the information system of the firm and all the efforts that go into the design, improvement and maintenance of the system. Mechanically it is tied to the computer, and the payroll of the department includes programmers, machine operators, methods improvers (systems analysts), supervisors, and support personnel.

Owing to the different meanings, they add later on:

> The confusion will continue for another generation. Almost anyone is free to describe his efforts as system analysis.

For the purpose of this book, we shall follow Handler's definition[1] that systems analysis consists in clearly understanding the components of a system and their interrelationship, and viewing individual operations within the system in the light of their implications for the system as a whole. In doing so, this type of analysis puts the problem into a more formal context and enables us to understand better the parts of a problem and to derive consistent solutions.

1.4 Some terms explained

Before we attempt to define the term system with any precision, it will be helpful to explain some terms. The idea of a system is derived mainly from a branch of modern mathematics called *set theory*. Of course, no attempt can be made here to discuss this topic in full, so only a short introduction will be presented.

A *set* is any well-defined collection of objects, which are called *elements* of the set. It is only necessary to identify one property that the elements have in common to identify a set. We can thus talk of the set of all red or green objects, the set of all our friends who are married, etc. We shall represent a set by a circle, and for convenience represent the whole *universe* of all possible sets by a rectangle as shown. This diagram represents a set of elements A, and

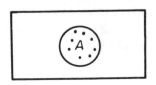

this may, of course, show any set of objects of any colour, shape or other property. Diagrams like this are called *Venn diagrams.*

Some statements and Venn diagrams, concerning sets and operations on sets, are given below:

Sets

A set is a general name for a collection of objects. There must be a rule which decides whether or not a particular object belongs to the set. This may be performed by making a list of the elements or by making a statement which describes them.

Elements

The elements of a set are the individual objects of a set. The notation used is, for example, $\{a, b, c\}$, which indicates a set of three elements.

'the element a is a member of set A' $a \in A$

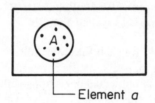

'the element a is not a member of set A' $a \notin A$

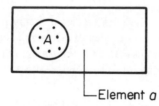

Subsets

A is a subset of B if every member of A is also a member of B.

'A is a subset of B' $A \subset B$

Union

The union of sets A and B is the set of all elements which are members of set A or set B (or both).

'union of set A and set B' $\qquad A \cup B$

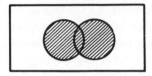

Intersection

The intersection of set A and B is the set of all elements which are members of both set A and set B.

'Intersection of set A and set B' $\qquad A \cap B$

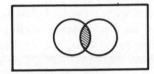

Universal sets

The universal set is the set of all elements under consideration (represented by a rectangle in our diagram).

$$\mathscr{E}$$

Empty set

The empty set is the set with no members.

$$\phi$$

Complementary sets

The complement of set A in $\mathscr{E}$ is the set of all elements of $\mathscr{E}$ which are not elements of A.

$$A'$$

1.5 Definition of system

Before describing and analysing particular systems, it is necessary to consider generally what is meant by system. Many definitions of the term system can be obtained, and one of them is given by Hall[5]: 'A system is a set of objects with relationships between the objects and between their attributes.'

Systems can consist of concrete objects like machines, switches, workers, etc., that is, material entities which exist in real time—space. Concepts or abstract objects such as equations, profit goals, processes, etc., may also comprise a system. Thus, objects are the elements, components or entities of the system, and we may say that they are the parameters of systems. As we shall see later, the kinds of entities in a system may be limitless, and so we shall consider only those which are significantly related to the system concerned.

Attributes are the properties of objects. A property is an external manifesta-tion of the way in which an object is known, observed or introduced in a process. For example, machines might have such properties as price, production rate, cost of operation, weight, colour, etc. Switches may have speed of operation and states. By listing its attributes we describe an entity or element. Although entities have many attributes, when dealing with a particular system we shall refer to a few attributes only: those which are relevant to the problem; the rest will be ignored.

Relationships that exist between and among entities and their attributes tie the system together. In economics, for example, the relationship between price and sales volume of a product is well recognized. Sales volume and accessibility to a shopping centre illustrate another common relationship. Again, relationships among entities of a system may be limitless, and we shall restrict our interest to those relationships that have a relevant effect on the system under study; that is, from an infinite number of relationships between entities, we select a set which depends on the problem at hand, where trivial and unessential relation-ships are not considered. It follows that the detection of a system is up to the researcher dealing with the problem, and so, it is in a sense a subjective matter. Chadwick[6] points out:

> Like beauty, a system lies in the eye of the beholder, for we can define a system in an infinite number of ways in accordance with our interests and our purpose, for the world is composed of very many sets of relationships. However, once we have defined our interests in terms of the objects, attributes and relationships, we can develop a rigorous analysis in line with our requirements.

According to Beer,[7] the set of relationships identified 'is not dignified by the unitary notion of a system until some unifying *purpose* is devised for it'. Thus, we may say that a system must have:

(1)   A purpose or objective, and
(2)   An established arrangements of parts or elements.

All systems are in a sense flow systems, for flows of information and/or energy and/or matter make up the relationships which are the heart of any system. Then, we may describe a system as an input—output relationship as shown in Figure 1.1.

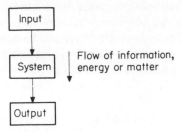

Figure 1.1 System as an input–output relationship

1.6 Definition of environment

Hall[5] defines environment in the following manner:

> For a given system, the environment is the set of all objects outside the system: (1) a change in whose attributes affects the system and (2) whose attributes are changed by the behaviour of the system.

Although by definition the environment includes all things that affect the system under study, in practice, it has to be limited to only those things that affect the system *significantly*. We may say that, in a sense, a system together with its environment makes up the universe of all things of interest in a given context. Defining the boundaries between a system and its environment is quite arbitrary and depends on the interests and aims of the researcher who defines the system. The environment of a system is taken to be those conditions that are not influenced or subjected to the control mechanism of the system concerned.

It is important to see that any system does not exist *in* an environment; it exists by *means* of it. The system may interact with its environment. The way in which this interaction may occur will depend on the properties which the system may possess as well as the manner in which the environment acts on the system.

1.7 Subsystems

From the definition of system and environment, it follows that any system can be divided into subsystems. The reason for dividing the system is for ease in handling. The idea is to break down the system into parts that display a certain richness of intercommunication, to the point where processes can be clearly identified and their parameters reduced to manageable terms within a coherent system of relationships to other processes and their parameters. For example, in a a business firm, we may identify various functional subsystems such as production, personnel, accounting and distribution. Simultaneously, we may identify other types of subsystems like the information subsystem. It is important to notice that entities belonging to one subsystem may well be part of the environment of another, or of several other, subsystems.

The difficulties related to breaking down the whole for purposes of analysis can be overcome if one knows how to subdivide the system. If one does not choose the right kind of subdivision, the whole will be destroyed. The best way is to observe the whole in action and then divide it according to whatever structural articulation is seen to operate within it.

1.8 Resolution level

We have seen that each element of a system can be considered in itself as a subsystem which contains a new set of elements, which in turn can be disaggregated into another set of elements. This implies that all systems are subsystems of the next higher system. Take for example a community as a system; the community can be described as an element within a system of communities, say a city. Then, the community can be considered as an element of a city system, and on the other hand, the community can be disaggregated into smaller units like buildings which are in turn systems (architectural systems). This change in the level of viewpoint is described as a change in resolution *level* from which an individual or group of systems can be viewed.

In the example quoted, the resolution levels are in the form of a hierarchy which is open at both ends. A change in resolution level causes a corresponding change in the viewpoint of the observer. This change of viewpoint in terms of resolution level can be seen in the different ways in which a real world situation can be viewed.

If we analyse the entities or elements of a system in the light of resolution levels, we can see that what are considered the elements of a system are the 'smallest' part of it. In the example mentioned earlier, the elements of a community system may be the individual buildings. Additionally, when viewing the community as a system, we are not interested in the structure of the buildings (elements of the system), only in their behaviour. Therefore, we consider the entities or elements as black boxes. As Chadwick[6] points out:

> In this sense, the elements of a system are black boxes (though the term may be applied to a complete system in certain circumstances): a system of whose structure we know nothing except what we can deduce from its behaviour, its input and output characteristics. A black box may be regarded as a grouping of detailed matters; a set of operations of some sort is contained by a boundary which we either cannot or do not wish to penetrate, so that our knowledge of what happens inside the boundary is missing or dissmissed.

He adds later on:

> The idea of the black box is therefore a valuable one in, as it were, putting a lower limit to the system to be considered.

1.9 Black box technique

As we have pointed out before, sometimes lack of knowledge of a system's internal structure may constitute a problem when the system is describing a real world situation. In these cases, where nothing at all is known about the way in which information, energy or matter flows inside the system, the black box approach can be applied.

Black box is a term to describe work which is concerned with manipulating the inputs and outputs of the system rather than with the system itself; that is, the interest is shifted to discovering statistical relationships between the inputs and the outputs, by manipulating the inputs. With varying inputs, records are made of corresponding outputs. These records, taken over periods of time showing a sequence of input and output states, form a set of statistical relationships which is the sole indication of the system's behaviour. In this way, although structure is inexplicable, actual events are being used to create a structure for the system: a structure designed by a set of statistical relationships.

Despite the limitations of the black box approach, this technique is and has been of considerable importance; for example, black box type experimentation with animals led Pavlov to discover conditioned reflexes.

1.10 Size of systems

The size of a system has nothing to do with the physical size of it. Chadwick[6] comments:

> As Ashby points out, we can regard the sun and the earth as an astronomical system which is very small, having only 12 degrees of freedom, whereas man's central nervous system, having 10^{10} neurons, is very large indeed. 'Size' of system is thus a matter of complexity, rather than of physical measure, and we use the concept of 'variety' in comparing the complexity of systems. Variety is simply the number of distinguishable elements within a set, but as Stafford Beer (my Reference 7) points out, the variety depends entirely on what set the elements are thought to be part of.

These concepts will become clear as we go through the stages for recognition of a system.

1.11 Stages for recognition of a system

Beer[7] indicates four stages in recognizing a system as such. To illustrate the procedure, we shall use the following example presented by Beer, where we shall consider a set of seven things from the universe represented by a circle in Figure 1.2.

A collection of dissimilars

From the universe, seven things known to be dissimilar have been separated.

Nothing more is known. The variety, that is, the number of distinguishable elements of this collection at this stage is seven. This number provides a measure of the thing's complexity. It is important to recall that the number of distinguishable elements (variety) depends entirely on what the elements are thought to be elements of. This is shown in Figure 1.2.

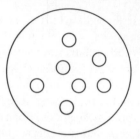

Figure 1.2 A collection of dissimilars* (Beer[7])

An assemblage of dissimilars

When these seven dissimilar things are recognized as being related, we lose interest in the things, and take notice of the relationships between them. Now, the number of distinguishable elements is given by the number of relationships between the seven entities, and corresponds to the number of lines (connections) on the diagram in Figure 1.3. The variety of this assemblage is 21; This has been obtained by the number of ways in which n things can be related in pairs:

$$\frac{n(n-1)}{2}$$

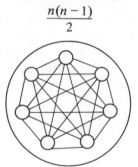

Figure 1.3 An assemblage of dissimilars* (Beer[7])

A systematic assemblage of dissimilars

When a special kind of relationship is detected between the entities, the number of connections is doubled. This is because a connection between A and B is no longer the same as a connection between B and A. This is shown in Figure 1.4 by orienting the relationship between the things. Because we have introduced more information, the variety has gone up. A greater amount of uncertainty has been removed, but at the same time, the number of possible connections

* From *Decision and Control* by Stafford Beer. Copyright © 1966 John Wiley and Sons Ltd., by permission of John Wiley and Sons Ltd.

has increased alarmingly. In the simplest case — one with oriented relationships as in Figure 1.4 — the variety is given by the formula $n(n-1)$. In this example, our variety is 42.

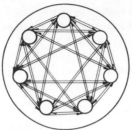

Figure 1.4 A systematic assemblage of dissimilars* (Beer[7])

A dynamic system

If we observe that this systematic assemblage of dissimilars is unified in a purposeful whole, we have identified a system. Now the set of seven entities operates. It works. It is a condition of actual operation that the relationships which exist between the entities should be capable of change. If the system itself cannot change its state (a particular relation inside the system cannot assume more than one state), then the system is not purposeful. As the states of the system are now relevant, the measure of variety of this dynamic system will be the possible states of the system. In Figure 1.5, a system of the simplest form is represented, where each relation has two states: on and off. Here, its variety is 2^{42}.

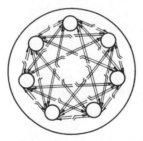

Figure 1.5 A dynamic system* (Beer[7])

Thus we have seen that every conceptual step which enriches the nature of the system, also increases the information about it, reduces the uncertainty and proliferates its variety.

1.12 Classification of systems

In developing the concept of system, it is useful to classify systems into several broad categories. To start, we may distinguish between *natural* and *man-made*

* From *Decision and Control* by Stafford Beer. Copyright © 1966 John Wiley and Sons Ltd., by permission of John Wiley and Sons Ltd.

systems. Those systems found in the field of astronomy, physics, chemistry, biology, etc., can be considered as natural systems. On the other hand, a city or a building is thought of as a man-made system even though the environment in which it operates contains natural systems.

Another useful classification is suggested by Beer[7] and is based on the criteria of complexity and determinism:

Deterministic systems   (1) simple
                                 (2) complex

Probabilistic systems   (1) simple
                                 (2) complex

As Chadwick[6] points out:

> Such a classification is helpful in that it disentangles some intuitive notions of complexity in systems; an electronic computer, for example, is complex, but deterministic: it will only perform those operations that it has been programmed to carry out; tossing a penny, on the other hand, may seem a simple problem — and so it is having only two states (i.e. a variety of 2) — but it can be described only as probabilistic, being notoriously unpredictable in outcome in any one case.

According to a system's relation with its environment, systems can be classified into two types, closed and open.

Closed systems
A system is closed if no interaction takes place with the environment. One of the uses of the concept of a closed system is to simplify the model of a physical system in order to facilitate its analysis. An example can be seen when a chemical reaction takes place in a sealed insulated container. This approach is commonly employed in conventional physics and chemistry experiments. According to Wilson[8]:

> A closed system, explicitly defined, is often a good approximation to equilibrium at a point in time, and this is true for a number of urban systems.

Open systems
An open system is one which interacts with its environment. In the human sciences, elements of a system seldom exist in isolation and usually have a rich environment with which complex interactions take place; consequently, most human science systems are open. It is important to notice that the open system plus its environment, that is, the total system, must be studied when dealing with open systems.

In architecture and urban planning, systems describing a building or city, are generally viewed as open systems. A building system exists in an environment of other related buildings with which it is interrelated from many standpoints. A city system exists in an environment which contains urban and rural areas with which the city interacts strongly.

In reality, whether a given system is open or closed depends on the amount of the universe which is included in the system and in the environment. By adjoining to the system that part of the environment with which interaction takes place, the system becomes closed.

1.13 Inputs and outputs

When dealing with open systems, we have seen that they interact with their environment. In practice, the most noticeable feature of the interaction between the system itself and its environment is that the relationships are directional: either the environment affects the system, or the system affects the environment – or both.

Thus, it is possible to divide the relationships which represent important interactions with the environment into two classes: those which affect the system called *inputs*, and those affected by the system named *outputs*. Therefore, we may say that an open system is a set of interrelated entities having properties discussed earlier, that is, separable from the rest of the universe except for two specially chosen sets of relationships with things outside, called its inputs and outputs.

The inputs can be looked upon as the stimuli which energize the system and provide it with the material for its operation. Outputs are the result of processes. We shall bear in mind that this division of relationships into inputs and outputs is arbitrary, and basically depends on the researcher and how he defines the system under study.

1.14 Systems with feedback

Certain systems have the property of reintroducing a portion of their outputs or behaviour at their inputs to affect succeeding outputs, as seen in Figure 1.6. The portion of the output fed back for purposes of control consists of information, and these systems are referred to as information-feedback systems. The term *servomechanism* defines man-made systems utilizing feedback.

An example of feedback can be seen in one of the first mechanisms illustrating this property, that is the invention by Watt of the governor. A signal indicating the speed of a steam engine is conveyed to a power-amplifying device in such a way that, when the engine accelerates, its speed is kept stable; that is, as the speed of the shaft increases, the weights fly out under centrifugal force and the sleeve to which they are attached moves up the shaft. This movement has the effect of gradually turning off the source of power until at last the shaft revolves at the required rate. It is the increase of speed of the shaft that causes the action which cuts off the power and so reduces the speed. Thus we see that the signalling arrangement is independent of energetic considerations and can be seen to feed *information* back, in order to effect speed control.

At this point it will be useful to be clear about what communication theory calls information: it is a principle of coding messages. The unit of information is called a *bit* which is the smallest amount of information required for a binary choice, for example, between 'on' and 'off'. A desirable definition of amount of

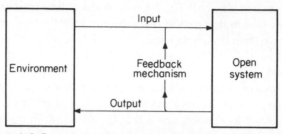

Figure 1.6 Open system, environment and feedback information

information would appear to be connected with the amount of time or the cost involved in transmitting messages. Chadwick points out[6] that 'information is a property not intrinsic to any one message, but of a *set* of messages, just in the same way that a probability is derived from a set of occurrences or events and not from one event only'. Information theory is a science which deals with the transmission of messages and not with their meaningfulness to the user.

1.15 Adaptive systems

Many systems, not only natural ones but also man-made systems, show even on a modest scale, a quality usually called adaptation. It can be said that they possess the ability to react to their environment in a way that is favourable, in some sense, to the continued operation of the system. In other words, we can call adaptive systems those systems which, on the basis of information feedback on their performance, adjust their parameters so as to improve their performance.

In the case of living systems, the improvement of their performance may be, in some cases, just the adaptation of the system to unfavourable environmental conditions with the mere purpose of survival. Adaptive systems have the ability of making a response to environmental changes which results in a new system state. In a sense, it can be said that they learn from repeated experience what is the optimal reaction or response to a particular stimulus.

1.16 System state

We may recall that a system is defined as a set of entities and their interrelated attributes. The attributes will take different values through time and so we may describe the state of the system at any point in time by indicating the actual values of those attributes. For example, in describing the state of an urban spatial system, we may list the values of such variables as population, employment, availability of different types of land, etc., at that point in time.

1.17 Cybernetics

The very birth of cybernetics came from Norbert Wiener's work carrying mathematical modelling into the field of biology, into the representation of the nervous system. Cybernetics is a science in its own right. It is '. . . the science of control and communication in the animal and in the machine' (Wiener[9]). According to Beer,[7] cybernetics is the science of proper control when the system is treated as an organic whole. It concentrates on very complex, probabilistic and adaptive systems.

Cyberneticians assume that things which act as autonomous units of adaptive behaviour do so because they possess a *control* mechanism. The control mechanism, together with what it actually controls (that is, the control and the controlled mechanisms) can be considered the two parts of any cybernetic system. Schematically, this can be represented as shown in Figure 1.7.

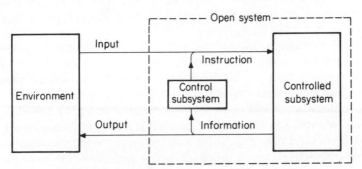

Figure 1.7 An open adaptive system and its environment

The control subsystem or controller can be considered as a natural or constructed system which interacts with its environment (in this case the controlled subsystem) to bring about a particular stability called the 'goal' or 'objective'. (Implications of this definition suggest that development control in urban planning can be seen as a control subsystem.) The feedback mechanism compares the output with standards or criteria, and so it is possible to measure and correct output when it deviates from what was planned. In a sense, it is also a means whereby objective measures of performance are methodically made (Handler[1]).

Control mechanisms are designed to make the controlled subsystems behave according to certain desired performance criteria; but this control '. . . is not a mandatory exercise in which things are coerced to operate in a desired way. Rather it is a question of coaxing a system towards optimal performance, or even better, of arranging for the system to regulate itself' (Beer[7]).

The core of cybernetics research is the discovery of the things that the control mechanisms of systems have in common. Whether they are cells, molecules, human beings, machines or business enterprises, the control subsystems must have certain things in common. Systems like the one structured

by a child driving its bicycle or the economy of a country, which has many of
the formal properties and aims of living organisms (e.g. survival), are all complex
systems which ought to respond to the same control mechanisms. These systems
can be considered cybernetic systems. Thus, cybernetics systems are characterized
by being exceedingly complex and probabilistic, where the control subsystem is
simply a homeostat. A homeostat is a control device for holding some variable
between desired limits by a self-regulatory mechanism (Beer[10]).

In order to study a system and its mode of control, we need to determine the
elements of the environment that influence the open system in order artificially
to transform the system into a closed one (Beer[7]).

The flow of information around a system, and the way in which this information is employed by the control mechanism for its purpose, is studied in cybernetics. It is important to notice that a control mechanism is an integral part of
a system, and it is almost impossible to study the control mechanism without
studying the rest of the system. Consequently, cybernetics and systems analysis
are commonly found together.

Chadwick[6] distinguishes three kinds of systems: engineering or mechanistic
systems; ecological or ecosystems, and social systems (which would seem to
include economic systems as well). He points out that the difference between
ecosystems and social systems rests in the fact that the response to change
within ecosystems occurs as a result of change external to a given animal or
community, whereas, in a social system, individual actors set their own criteria
for action. Then Chadwick adds: 'It follows, therefore, that the "control" of
ecosystems and social systems is necessarily different from that of engineering
systems, for the "controls" of the former are inside the system and are capable
of being reset or modified from within and thus only partly susceptible to
external influences. The idea of "steering" a social system, in the way that an
engineering system can be controlled, is thus not possible.'

1.18 Characteristics of systems
Systems have certain features which differentiate them from a mere collection
of things, and the study of these features helps us to understand better the
behaviour of systems. Now, we shall describe the principal characteristics of
adaptive systems, following in a way, those expressed by Goldsmith.[11]

Interrelationship
We have described a system as being an assemblage of components so connected
as to constitute a complex whole, where the degree of interconnectedness of the
parts which make up the system is very high. From this, it follows that any
alteration in the value of any of the components will affect the others and,
therefore, the system as a whole. For example, in the case of a building, where
components are put together to form spaces, we can see that the relative
positions of walls, columns, beams, etc., together with the attributes they
possess, determine the spatial, functional, aesthetic and other qualities of the

building as a whole. Thus, it is partially due to the interrelationship of the building components and their attributes that the building 'behaves' in a particular manner, and any change in these interrelationships may change the 'behaviour' of the system (Handler[1]).

In order to be able to predict the effect on a system of a change in any of its parts, generally we use a technique commonly employed in systems analysis. This technique consists in building a model of the system under consideration, which first involves carefully establishing the interrelationships between each of the elements or variables of the system. Having done this, we may alter any of the variables and observe what effect it has on the values of any of the other variables of the model and hence on the system as a whole.

We shall stress again that, because of the interrelationship between any two parts of the system, none of them can be examined in isolation, but only in terms of the whole system of which it is part.

Vertical structure

In the study of systems, the concept of level of organization is a very important one, and, although in the past it has been mainly used in biology, nowadays it is widely applied in the analysis of all systems. This concept implies what we see in the real world situation; for example, it is impossible to move from atoms to a cell without passing through the intermediate stage of molecules, nor can we pass from the individual building to a city without passing through equally essential intermediate stages, such as the communities and the neighbourhood districts.

The concept of level of organization implicitly involves the fact that a system cannot grow indefinitely. For example, there is a limit to the development of an atom, after which its development is only possible by its association with other atoms to form a molecule. In a sense, it can be said that there is a maximum size of a system which corresponds to an optimum structure, deviation from which may threaten the system's integrity.

Horizontal structure

If we analyse, for example, a business enterprise, we shall find a proportion between the different specialists — accountants, clerks, salesmen, etc. — which is optimum for that particular system. This feature indicates that a system must also have an optimum horizontal structure; that is, a correct ratio must be maintained between all the dissimilar elements of the system. If the correct proportion is not maintained, the system may become an unintegrated set of parts that will behave in a random manner compromising the correct functioning of the system. Another example can be drawn from the building industry, when a correct combination of materials is necessary to make a particular quality of concrete; if the right proportion of cement, water, sand, etc., is not maintained, the consequences may be disastrous.

Order

Goldsmith[11] points out that order 'can be defined as the influence of the whole over the parts. It is also defined as limitation of choice, for the greater the influence of the whole over the parts, the greater must be the constraints imposed on them to ensure that they behave in a way that will further the interests of the whole'. Thus, in order to ensure that each part of the system behaves in a way which benefits the activities of the system as a whole, there is a need to impose greater constraints on the parts. Referring to the cultural level, Goldsmith adds further on: 'one of the implications of this principle which we might not be too happy to accept is that permissiveness can only be regarded as another word for disorder — as the inevitable sign of social disintegration'.

Because an increase in order also increases the system's ability to deal with changes in the environment, the system tends to impose additional constraints on to its parts, which reduce the choices open to each of the parts of the system.

Goal

From the study of systems, we find that systems come into being and behave in an ordered way, not at random. This implies that they have some function to fulfil; that is, they are goal-seeking. This feature allows us to deduce from the existence of any system, that it has some operation to perform within the larger one of which it is part. Goldsmith[11] stresses that 'this principle is of the utmost importance. If one does not accept that processes are goal seeking, one must also deny the possibility of studying them scientifically. Scientific method in such conditions would then be limited to the study of purely static things, and since these do not exist, one would be denying the possibility of science.'

Chadwick[6] points out that living systems are characterized 'as showing entropic drift towards a steady state which appears to satisfy certain criteria: such criteria when applied to man's behaviour can be seen as implying goals'.

Stability

Natural systems do not have a goal that can be clearly stated. It is best described in terms of a trajectory in which disequilibria will tend to be reduced. Equilibrium can be defined in terms of system state. A system is in equilibrium if, in the absence of external stimulus, its state remains unchanged. If the system returns to an equilibrium state after being affected by an external shock, the system is stable. Thus, if the values of a system's attributes remain constant or within defined limits, the system is said to be stable or homeostatic. According to Beer,[7] the homeostat is a mechanism for achieving stability, and its sole objective is to settle the system down as quickly as possible to a stable condition after it has been disturbed. Homeostasis is a biological term denoting the principle that will bring correcting processes into play, so that the system survives and does not destroy itself by going out of control. In everyday life we may overlook the operation of this principle and notice it only when the limits are exceeded and breakdown of the system occurs.

Stability can be achieved in two ways: by increasing environmental order, that is, by modifying the environment in such a way as to reduce the disequilibrium, or by increasing cybernetic order, which corresponds to increasing the ability of the system to deal with the situation. It is important to notice that for a system to maintain equilibrial behaviour, it must have multiple contact with its environment, from where it must get abundant information.

Complexity

We have said that systems tend to become more and more stable; this tendency brings together another tendency which helps in the achievement of the desired state of equilibrium: the tendency to complexity.

We may recall that variety provides a measure of the complexity of the systems. The greater the variety, the greater the system's ability to deal with unexpected changes. For example, a balancer walking on a rope at some distance from the floor will have more stability and be better prepared to deal with environmental changes, such as winds, etc., if he uses an equilibrium rod, thus increasing the variety of the 'balancer—rope' system.

Differentiation

We have just pointed out that the greater the variety of a system the greater the system's ability to deal with an unexpected stimulus. Therefore, systems will tend to increase their variety which is obtained through a process of differentiation. Feedback mechanisms ensure that the elements of the system become more differentiated and so better adapted to varied environmental conditions. It is important to notice that systems do not grow to increase the number of elements, but to increase their variety by the differentiation of the minimum number of elements required. When the feedback mechanism does not work properly, differentiation ceases to occur and the system may become bigger but not more complex; thus surplus capacity begins to appear which may bring about the collapse of the whole system.

Economy

We have said that systems tend to increase their complexity and order to enable them to react against changes in their environment; but this increase is not without limit: the limit is imposed by the minimum necessary for the system to obtain the optimum stability or homeostasis of the larger system of which it is part. Goldsmith[11] stresses that 'In this way the complexity and order of a system will only increase when there is a need for it, or in other words, the system will display the minimum complexity and order. This means that adaptive systems are as small and decentralized as possible. This is of urgent relevance to present-day society with its seemingly uncheckable tendency towards ever greater size and centralization.'

Feedback development

We have said that for a system to adjust itself to the environment, it must be able to find out how it is performing, and this takes us to one of the basic concepts in cybernetics: the process whereby output is compared with standards or criteria and which is called feedback. Thus systems, on the basis of information feedback on their performance, adjust themselves so as to increase their homeostasis. The feedback mechanism is designed to measure and correct deviations from the planned output. This correction will take place in the opposite direction from the original divergence, and therefore will not allow the error to increase each moment: it is called 'negative feedback'. We apply negative feedback when we are driving a motor-car and the system man— driving-machine is deviating from the proposed route. 'Positive feedback' correction acts in the same direction as the existing error, thereby increasing it.

When the feedback mechanism does not exist or does not work properly, the system may go out of control. Ackoff[12] comments about the lack of the essential mechanism of feedback in architectural systems: 'The simple fact is that, in most architecture, the possibility of error is never contemplated by an architect. He designs the building so that it is there, and it's there for all time, and it frequently costs more to modify the building than it does to construct it originally. I don't think architects generally know what the costs of modification are. In every building (designed by an ordinary architect today) is incorporated a set of assumptions that the architect made about the way that people behave in an environment. The assumptions are never made explicit, nor is there a systematic effort made to find out whether the building did what the architect thought it was going to do. Currently there is virtually no feedback, so that we have a marvelous way of perpetuating our previous errors.'

Self-regulation

We have said that cyberneticians assume that for a system to adapt itself to changes in environment it must possess a control mechanism; this mechanism makes the corresponding changes in the behaviour of the system according to the information received through the feedback process. From here we see that the system is regulated from within. This is the real force of the concept of self-regulation.

The process of self-regulation will only take place if the system is continuously supplied with sufficient information and if changes in the environment remain within a reasonable range. Then, a subsystem will behave in that way which favours the stability of the whole system. Goldsmith[11] points out that: 'A self-regulating system is not free from constraints. It has just as many constraints as one controlled asystemically. *The important thing is that each individual constraint is itself subjected to the set of constraints determining the behaviour of the system as a whole.* This is precisely the difference between self-government and dictatorship. Self-regulation at all levels of organization must be the ideal towards which we strive.'

Transmission of information

Systems have the ability of communicating information through time, that is, from generation to generation, in such a way that the new generation can benefit from it. Thus they must be regarded as subsystems, just like contemporaries that need the same information that will enable them to act as temporally differentiated elements of the same system. This feature is easily seen at the cultural level. During the course of his life, an individual will acquire the information that will enable him to fulfil his function in the society of which he is a part. This, of course, is conditioned by the information he receives genetically. If this communication breaks down, the system loses its fourth dimension: time.

Probabilistic behaviour

We have said that some systems have the property that several of the states may be predicted with certainty but other states can be predicted only on a basis of probability. Thus, for each possible input to the system, there is a set of preferred outputs and so we do not know which preferred state the system will take, but we may know the probabilities associated with each of the possible reactions of the system to a particular change in the environment. Of course, some risk is taken in trying to predict the future state of the system under consideration; this risk cannot be avoided. Most of the man-made systems, especially commercial and industrial systems, have this probabilistic feature, and by use of statistical techniques the size and risk of a management decision can be known, thus allowing the manager to make better decisions against undesired happenings.

Integrity

If one starts separating parts of a system to study them, or if one insists on considering the behaviour of these parts as isolated mechanisms, the system as such will start to behave abnormally and may stop functioning. We have seen that a system behaves as an integral whole, where the elimination of any of its parts may produce the breakdown of the whole system. This is a very important characteristic of systems which has commonly been ignored, and this has consequently brought about catastrophic results. Goldsmith[11] comments that: 'This is a point which has rarely been taken into account at a cultural level. Colonialist powers have constantly interfered in the most irresponsible way with the cultures of the societies they controlled. Missionaries and colonial administrators have tampered with the delicately adjusted cultural systems of highly stable and ecologically sound societies which they regarded as "primitive" or "barbarous" and brought about their breakdown in most instances. The consequences for the inhabitants of these societies has been disastrous. They usually become rootless members of a depressed proletariat in the shantytowns we are thereby methodically creating.'

Irreversibility

According to Cowan,[13] the reversibility of a system is a relative notion and depends partially upon the time over which we observe it as well as upon its complexity. In the long run all systems are irreversible.

In the case of mechanical systems, they appear to be reversible systems if they are analysed over a short period of time, but if this period is extended, the consequences of wear, etc., will be apparent, indicating that the system is irreversible. When dealing with urban spatial systems, where the constant dynamicism is seen easily by the construction of roads, buildings, etc., we can clearly identify these systems as largely irreversible ones.

Equifinality

This concept indicates that the same final state in a system can be reached from differing initial conditions and in different ways. In a planning sense this could mean that planned intentions for an urban system can be achieved through a variety of sometimes 'unplanned' ways. Beer[7] points out that it is possible to prove in cybernetics that if a system 'is to maintain stability under disturbances not foreseen by the designer, it must behave "equifinality". This means that there must be various different ways in which it can reach a specified goal, or final state, from different working conditions.'

Rejection

This characteristic is easily found in biological organisms. Systems have a mechanism which enables them to reject any foreign entity which threatens the system's integrity. In the same way as the elimination of any of the parts of a system may produce the breakdown of it, the addition of elements to it, may generate the same catastrophic result. For example, heart transplants, which from the technological point of view have been proved to be totally feasible, are not yet a complete success because of the rejection mechanism of the recipient body to a foreign heart.

Reintegration

Once a system has disintegrated, the environment will always tend to influence the re-creation of a new system which will emerge with a better capacity of adaptation to the environment. In relation to this feature of systems, Goldsmith[11] points out: 'At a cultural level, individuals find it difficult to survive when deprived of that highly structured environment consisting of a family and a home, a community and a village, fields and forests, enemies and their strongholds, and unknown areas inhabited by dreadful supernatural creatures, that is, an environment displaying the required distribution of order. In the absence of such an environment, they will be forced to seek short-term substitutes to satisfy those of which they have been deprived. These substitutes will include taking drugs, drinking, cheap entertainments, anything in fact that will render their unenviable lot slightly more tolerable. At the same time, they will be particularly susceptible to new doctrines that might enable them to re-establish new social structures, and hence that environment to which they have been adapted by millions of years of evolution.'

Identity

In the same way as the characteristics of systems outlined here help us to differentiate them from a mere collection of things, we have to agree that a system has its own characteristics which differentiate it from other systems. For example, a motor-car system has its own characteristics which differentiate it from a bicycle or a horse. That is, a system has to be invariable in some way, so that it may be recognized again by the same unchanged features. This is the real feature of the characteristic of identity in systems.

Law of optimum value

Under the assumption that all the parts of the system can be quantified, this law states that every part of the system must have an optimal value, which is determined by the other parts. It is clear from the interrelationships between entities that any of the elements of the system can alter its value between certain limits — the limits allowed by the other elements of the system — deviation from which may only lead to total disintegration of the system. The optimum value is given by the element's ability to fulfil its specific function within the system of which it forms part.

Optimizing a subsystem with respect to its objectives is called suboptimization, and the optimization of all subsystems of a system does not guarantee an optimum system, because of interactions.

1.19 Operational research

In recent years, owing to advances in technology, man-made systems have become more and more complex, and specialization has produced a tendency for decentralization which has created the division of the enterprise into departments or subsystems. Each of these subsystems began to develop its own objectives. In many cases the objectives of these subsystems conflicted, and the optimum production or value for each department was not necessarily the optimum for the system as a whole. For example, in architecture, Handler[1] comments: 'In the organization of the process of designing and producing buildings, as well as in the organization of the building itself, each of the units or subsystems has its own objectives. Frequently, these are unrelated to, or inconsistent and in conflict with, the objectives of the others. It becomes necessary to find solutions which balance components and overall objectives such that the goals of the former are not given up in the interests of the whole, but an overall optimum is sought through their coordination. It is characteristic of the building industry that the whole, the building itself, tends to be lost sight of in the production of components. In the opposite direction, it is all too easy to find architectural solutions which fail to meet necessary components' objectives in the presumed interest of the total organization of the building.'

To face problems of this kind and others dealing with systems, new techniques were needed, and so, operational research (OR) techniques entered into the problem of control of systems – *to help optimize performance.*

Churchman, Ackoff and Arnoff[14] give the following definition of operational research:

> OR is the application of scientific methods, techniques, and tools to problems involving the operations of a system so as to provide those in control of the system with optimum solutions to the problems.

Handler[1] commenting about operational research applied to architectural systems says: 'it has relevance not only to the process of planning, designing and producing buildings, but also to the building itself conceived as an organization. In the former case, it would seek to organize an effective operation for the production of buildings and other facilities. In the latter, it would try to achieve an organization of components into a building which would operate effectively for the uses and objectives for which it was designed. He adds later on: Applied to the design of buildings, this would mean the development of methods and techniques for the effective solution of architectural problems.'

The increasing recognition that the new and complex problems cannot be solved effectively within the boundaries of any discipline has generated the need for organizing interdisciplinary teams.

In the context of the systems approach, where an organization is seen as an interconnected complex of functionally related components, in which the effectiveness of each part depends on how it fits into the whole and the effectiveness of the whole depends on how the parts are functioning, three related disciplines are commonly used to manipulate systems: systems analysis, cybernetics and operational research.

Researchers from these disciplines and many other sciences commonly combine their knowledge, experience, etc. and work together as a team, attempting to solve very complex problems or systems. In a sense, they are part of the control subsystem of the system concerned. The common procedure of the team (generally called the OR or systems team) is to study the situation, construct a scientific model of it, experiment on it, obtain or choose the best solution and recommend it to the decision mechanism of the system (the decision maker).

The process of reaching the best decision is known as *optimization* and the corpus of theoretical knowledge which bears on this process is called *decision theory*. Decision theory comprises a large number of mathematical techniques, e.g. queueing theory, mathematical programming, critical path analysis, statistical quality control, etc. We may say that decision theory is primarily devoted to finding optimum procedures for making decisions involving variables subject to random variation.

References
1 HANDLER, A. B. *Systems Approach to Architecture*. American Elsevier Publishing Co. Inc., New York, 1970.
2 McMILLAN, C. and GONZALEZ, R. F. *Systems Analysis: A Computer Approach to Decision Models*. Richard D. Irvin Inc. December, 1971.
3 BERTALANFFY, L. VON. *General Systems Theory*. George Braziller, New York, 1968.
4 ACKOFF, R. L. 'Games, decisions and organisation'. *General Systems*, 1959, vol. 4, pp. 145 − 150.
5 HALL, A. D. *A Methodology for Systems Engineering*. D. Van Nostrand Company, Inc., Princeton, New Jersey, Reprinted 1968.
6 CHADWICK, G. *A Systems View of Planning*. Pergamon Press, Oxford, 1971.
7 BEER, S. *Decision and Control*. John Wiley and Sons, Ltd., Chichester, 1966.
8 WILSON, A. G. *Entropy in Urban and Regional Modelling*. Pion Limited, London, 1970.
9 WIENER, N. *Cybernetics*. The MIT Press, New York, 1948.
10 BEER, S. *Cybernetics and Management*. The English Universities Press Ltd., London, 1970.
11 GOLDSMITH, E. 'Bringing order to chaos'. *The Ecologist Magazine*, 1970, vol. 1, part 2, pp. 16−19.
12 ACKOFF, R. L. *Progressive Architecture*. August 1967.
13 COWAN, P. 'On irreversibility'. *Architectural Design*, 1969, September, pp pp. 485−6.
14 CHURCHMAN, C., ACKOFF, R. and ARNOFF, E. L. *Introduction to Operations Research*. John Wiley and Sons, Inc., New York, 1968.

2 Urban Systems

2.1 Cities as systems

A careful analysis of the structure of a city demonstrates that it is not possible to study any of its parts in isolation, because they are strongly related to other elements of the city structure. For example, it is not possible to study the location of a shopping centre without analysing the transportation facilities and the number of potential customers. Additionally, any variation in these two factors may influence the first. From here we see that, for example, a good solution to the transportation problem in this case may depend on the location of the retail centres and residential areas. Economic factors also influence the situation: any variation in the income level may affect the size of the shopping centre, the mobility of the people, the residential location, etc. In fact the income level may also alter the whole situation.

The examples given above show us the inadequacies of considering parts of the urban system independently. A more useful approach would be to consider cities and regions as systems, that is a systems approach to urban problems.

We may recall that a system is not the real world, it is just a way of looking at it, and therefore the definition of systems depends in part on the objectives of the researcher and the purposes which they are intended to fulfil.

2.2 Identification of the urban system

In order to attempt to define the urban system, we must try to identify the components or entities of the system or of the subsystems which form part of the urban system.

Snell and Shuldiner[1] define some basic entities of the urban system which can be classified under four groups as indicated in Figure 2.1.

Entities from these various classes can be grouped together to generate the subsystems of the urban system. To do so, we shall recall the stages for recognition of a system and we must remember that care must be taken to account for interrelationships between the elements or entities of the system, especially in relation to the 'causal' structure. In this sense, systems are structured by the entities relevant to the function of the system in question.

For example, we could generate a system by grouping together the following entities: population, residing, working, houses, factories, transportation and its corresponding land. Another system (or subsystem of the urban system) can be formed by grouping population, shopping, shops, transportation and its corresponding land. In these two examples, we see that some entities (e.g. population) form part of both subsystems. This feature partly explains the

Objects
Population
Goods
Vehicles

Activities
Residential
Working
(Shopping) retail trade
Education
Production of goods and services
Recreation

Infrastructure
Buildings:
  houses
  schools
  shops
  factories
  offices
Transport facilities:
  roads
  railway lines
  airports
  ports, etc.

Land
Land in different uses

Figure 2.1 Basic entities of the urban system (Snell and Shuldiner[1])

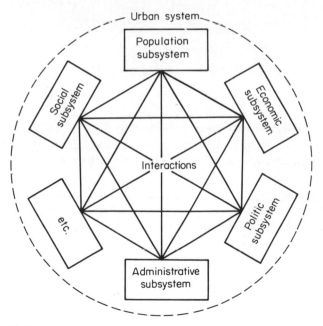

Figure 2.2 The urban system can be considered structured by several subsystems

strong interrelationship found between the different subsystems of the urban system.

The urban system can be considered to be structured by several parts or subsystems. Figure 2.2 shows some of the subsystems which form the urban system and their interrelationship. It also represents the urban system as a closed system. When we are studying a particular subsystem of the urban system, the other subsystems interact both with each other and with the one under study, thus influencing its behaviour. Consequently, we can identify all the other subsystems as the *environment* of the subsystem concerned, which is then regarded as an open one (see Figure 2.3).

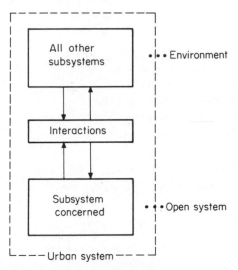

Figure 2.3 The subsystem concerned as an open system

Owing to the difficulties and lack of knowledge surrounding many relationships between elements of the urban system, researchers have tended to isolate artificially the different subsystems with the hope that further research on the subsystems will provide more insight into the relationship between subsystems and consequently between *all* the elements of the urban system.

2.3 Subsystems of the urban system

Convenient urban subsystems have been generated around the entities in Figure 2.1, and the following subsystems (which in the future will be called systems because this is just a relative term) have received more attention from the researchers:

At a high level of spatial aggregation:

(1)   Urban population system
(2)   Urban economic system

At a low level of spatial aggregation:

(3)   Urban spatial system
(4)   Urban transportation system.

Urban population system

The urban population system is always related to a high level of spatial aggregation; that is, the area under study (the city or region) is considered as being formed by one larger zone where the population activities take place.

The urban population system can be broken down into activities such as:

(1)   Residential activity
(2)   Industrial activity
(3)   Retail trade (shopping) activity
(4)   Recreational activity, etc.

From here we can see that this system is organized around some entities which appear in Figure 2.1, such as population and those entities under the heading 'activities'. Each unit of population (person or family) can be additionally classified according to its age, sex, income level, car ownership, etc.

One of the prime studies which planners must perform is that of population projection from which estimates of labour force can be made. Projection involves two studies in itself: those of population growth and migration. Numerous methods for projecting population growth are at present available, including mathematical and graphical methods (Isard[2]), ratio and apportionment method (Chapin[3]), migration and natural increase method (Isard[2]) and cohort-survival methods (Chapin[3]). Matrix models are now being introduced both for population growth as well as migration studies (Rogers[4]).

When a variety of assumptions about birth rates and possible migration are made, generally a range of population is forecast rather than a single set of figures.

Urban economic system

The urban economic system is built around the entities 'goods and services' indicated in Figure 2.1. As in the urban population system, this system is related to a high level of spatial aggregation, that is, economic activities for an entire city or region which is considered as being formed by one large zone where the economic activities take place.

Analysis of economic activity and economic projection have been described as being as difficult as, if not more difficult than, population projection. Reasons for the difficulties include the complexity of the subject, the lack of satisfactory exploration, economic phenomena and reliable data.

In the planning context there are a number of methods which, with varying degrees of accuracy, are of use in the prediction of employment, capital, trade and income levels. These methods include the simple extrapolation (Isard[2]), forecasts including the study of productivity (Beckerman[5]), economic base method (Tiebout[6]), ratio and apportionment methods (Chapin[3]), input–output analysis (Stone[7] and Leontieff[8]), and the most recently developed methods which are still in embryonic stage (Hirsch[9]) called 'social' or 'regional' accounts methods.

Urban spatial system

When we introduce spatial disaggregation into the urban system, that is, when the city is divided into a number of sub-areas or zones, we realize the need to relate the population activities to zones of the system, and consequently to the physical infrastructure which contains these activities (e.g. land, buildings, roads, etc.).

The term 'spatial refers to a direct concern for spatial pattern, i.e. for the pattern in which culture, activities, people and physical objects are distributed in space. Conversely aspatial refers to a lack of such concern.' (Foley[10]).

In order to define the urban spatial system, we must identify its components and their interrelationships. The introduction of physical subdivisions into the urban system emphasizes the distinction of activities in relation to the level of adherence to places. Within the vast range of human activity, there is a continuous gradation between those activities that are strongly *place-related* and those that are totally random with respect to place (McLoughlin[11]). An activity like working in an office can be considered as strongly place-related, while a hobby such as taking photographs can be regarded as a very weak place-related activity.

We can attempt to identify as the elements of the urban spatial system those activities presented in Figure 2.1 that take place *within-place*; that is, those that are strongly place-related (e.g. residential, industrial, shopping, etc.) together with the physical infrastructure or *adapted spaces* where these activities take place. It is important to notice that adapted spaces do not necessarily mean physical constructions, and so they can be houses, parks, factories, etc.

Having identified population activities and their corresponding adapted spaces as the elements of the urban spatial system, our next step is to identify what ties the system together or what are the relationships. The interrelationships between the activities of the urban spatial system are the *communications*. The communications enable the various activities to interact according to their needs by means of flows of information, people, goods, transactions, etc. That is, the interactions between the population activities and the environment take place by means of these connections. Communication involves many types of interactions: from the information transmitted by radio, which is unrelated to place, to the flow of people and goods, which can be strongly related to the network of roads. The transactions or interactions between willing buyers and willing sellers, which according to Lowry[12] determines the spatial organization of urban activities, may be considered also as part of the communication links.

It is useful to recognize the flow of goods and persons (material interaction) as a subsystem of communication (transportation). We shall deal with this very important subsystem in a later section (p. 36).

The physical infrastructures where communications occur are called *channel spaces*. They group the transportation and other communication networks, such

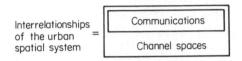

as roads, rivers, pipelines, etc. Thus, we may conclude that the urban spatial system is structured by activities and their related places linked by communications.

The environment, as we may recall, influences the behaviour of the corresponding system, and in a sense the environment of the urban spatial system is structured by all the *other* systems of the urban system (e.g. economic, political, social, etc.) at the corresponding level of spatial aggregation. This is represented in Figure 2.4.

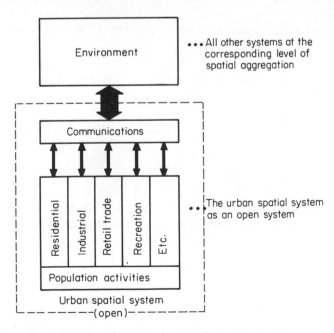

Figure 2.4 The urban spatial system as an open system

As has already been pointed out, owing to difficulties and complexities in handling the systems of the urban system, the system most commonly used (with some degree of understanding) as part of the environment of the urban spatial system is the economic system which provides the level of employment, trade, etc., for the region under study. Of course, interactions take place at the corresponding or equivalent level of spatial aggregation.

Urban transportation system

Planners dealing with urban problems from the physical side have always been trying to discover and understand the patterns of urban location; all their efforts have been towards the study of the urban spatial organization, which can be defined as the outcome of a process which allocates population activities to sites.

Webber[13] has stated:

> The activities generated by a piece of land cannot be understood in terms of the land alone but must be seen as part of the system of urban activities linked by functional relations through time.

We mentioned earlier that there is a wide range of activities and we also identified within-place activities as one example of them. We could now recognize other activities like travelling, etc., which take place between zones, and so we may classify population activities into two categories:

(1)   Within-place activities
(2)   Between-place activities.

It is clear that between-place activities take place in channel spaces, and so we may classify spaces into two classes:

(1)   Adapted spaces
(2)   Channel spaces.

There is a simple correspondence between activity and space types, as can be seen in Figure 2.5. As we have said before, the urban spatial structure is the outcome of a process which allocates population activities (both within and between places) to sites (adapted and channel spaces), and consequently physical planners attempt to understand the structure of population activities and land uses.

We should emphasize here that in all the models of the urban spatial structure that we shall describe in this work, there is a strong relationship between activities and land uses; in other words, the location of activities among the zones of the area under study correspond to the 'assignation' of zones to the activities performed in the area being modelled. To explain this feature, we shall refer to

Figure 2.6 which indicates several population activities which are going to be related to zones.

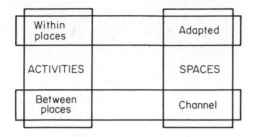

Figure 2.5 Correspondence between activity and space types

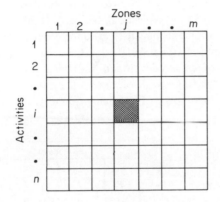

Figure 2.6 Relation between activities and land uses

We could allocate activity i to zone j; but we may also obtain the same result by assigning zone j to activity i. Thus, for example, residential activity can be allocated to zone j, but we may also say that zone j has been assigned to a residential activity, and consequently zone j has a residential *land use*.

If we expand Figure 2.6 and apply it hypothetically to a city with n population activities and m zones or sites, we may obtain a table like the one shown in Figure 2.7. In this we may see, for example, that the industrial activity of the city is located in zones j, k and l, and consequently the land corresponding to zones j, k and l has an industrial use.

Recently, interesting research has been carried out on the process of urban spatial organization in order to understand the different aspects of urban location behaviour. Owing to the complexity of the urban spatial system, few attempts have been made to deal with all the activities simultaneously, and the commonest approach has been to break down the urban spatial system into sub-systems dealing with individual activities. The subsystems most frequently studied are:

(1)   Residential activity subsystem
(2)   Industrial activity subsystem
(3)   Retail trade activity subsystem.

Other activities and land uses have been almost totally neglected, although they are of major importance in metropolitan planning:

(4)   Office activities
(5)   Agriculture and extractive activities
(6)   Construction activities
(7)   Public services activities, etc.

To understand the urban system's spatial structure, researchers have been trying to develop quantitative models which attempt to simulate the structure of land uses and activities in cities and regions. In the early 1950s, the notion of inter-relationships between elements began to influence transportation engineers. Instead of dealing with individual traffic questions, the idea of a road system, a network of links and roads, has developed. Individual problems were seen as sub-problems within the framework of an overall system whose behaviour as a whole influenced the many parts. The conception of traffic at this time also

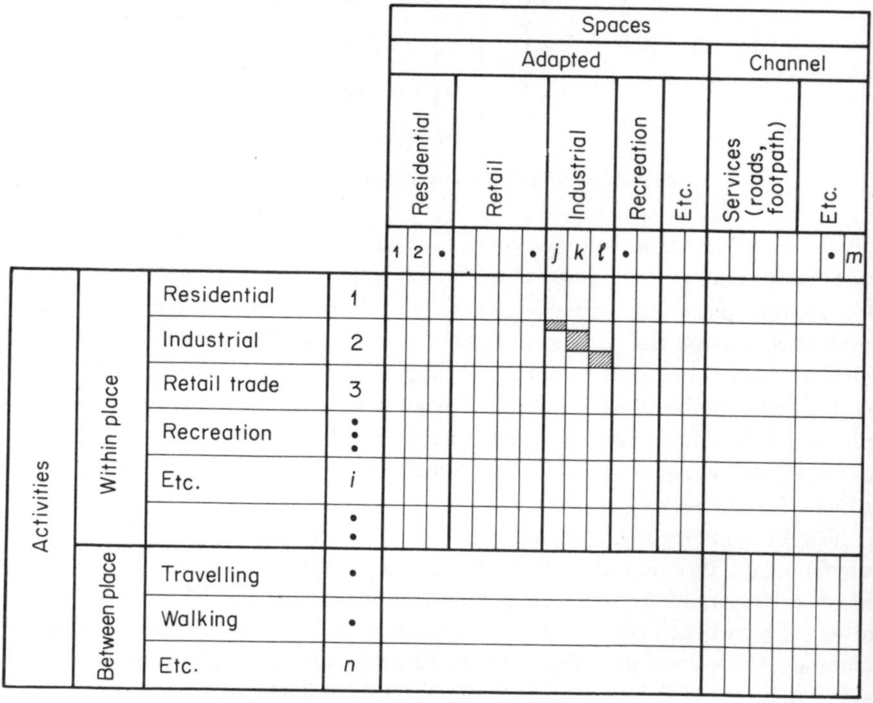

Figure 2.7 Relation between activities and sites

changed. In a major work,[14] Mitchell and Rapkin stated the idea that traffic was a function of land use. Journeys were seen as part of the way in which activities were connected through the flows of people and goods. Estimates of future flows of these commodities based on predicted forms of land use would allow calculations of future traffic volumes and hence needs. Future road networks would then be based on these projected needs. At that time, although techniques to deal with transportation problems were well developed, land use prediction, a prerequisite for the new approach, was difficult. Aside from simple extrapolation of existing land use trends, no serious methods were available. Then work was undertaken to fulfil this need for predicting land use and especially to avoid basing sophisticated traffic models on inputs of land use data which were produced in a very rudimentary way.

A number of models are in operation which deal with specific activities or land uses such as residential, industrial, retail, office, etc., corresponding to the various subsystems of the urban spatial system. Some models deal with more than one activity or land use simultaneously. Usually, both the regional and town scale models operate in terms of activities, although in the case of town scale models, the activities are converted to land use which is measured in terms of floorspace.

A common point of confusion arises from the various names that models of urban spatial structure receive from different authors. Some are:

> Urban spatial structure model
> Urban development model
> Land-use model
> Activity model
> Location or allocation model
> Model of the ecosystem
> Land-use allocation model.

All of course attempt to simulate the structure of land uses and activities in cities or regions.

It is worth while to mention here that Lowry[12] proposes a very interesting method for classifying existing models according to their emphasis on land-use, location, land-use succession or on migration patterns, and so we may find location oriented models, activity oriented models, etc., although basically they deal with the urban system's spatial structure.

Residential activity subsystem
The common problem in residential location involves building a model which predicts the residential location of the working population based on the information obtained about the workplace location, attractiveness of the residential areas, transport facilities, cost of travel, etc.

Examples of residential models would be the 'Probabilistic model for residential growth' by Chapin and Weiss,[15, 16] and the 'Penn–Jersey regional growth model' by Herbert and Stevens.[17] Hansen[18] has designed a very interesting model 'How accessibility shapes land use'. Other models are 'An opportunity-accessibility model for allocating regional growth' of Lathrop and Hamburg,[19] and the 'San Francisco C.R.P. model' of Little.[20]

Industrial activity subsystem

The location of industrial activity is commonly analysed together with other activities. For example, in the 'EMPIRIC model' of Hill,[21] the industrial activity is treated together with the residential and retail trade activities. Schlager's 'A land use plan design model'[22] accounts for almost all urban land uses, including industrial.

Retail trade activity subsystem

The central problem which confronts all retailing studies is basically locational, that is, one of allocating or distributing a person's present and future spending between various competing shopping centres. Also, we could say that we are interested in knowing how much of a centre's turnover derives from (and will derive from) the potential customers of any area.

Lakshmanan and Hansen's 'A retail market potential model' specifically attempts[23] to explore the possible equilibrium distribution for large retail centres in sub-regional scale. Retail trade is commonly found in more general models[24] like Lowry's 'A model of metropolis' which at the same time deals with the location of residential activities. Other models like Hill's 'EMPIRIC model'[21] and Schlager's 'A land use plan design model'[22] deal with retail location and other activities.

In reality, office activities have received very little attention from researchers, although Cowan[25] has done some study in this field. No specific models exist for recreation, open space, civic or public utility uses. However these activities and land uses can be considered in a sense, incorporated into Schlager's model.[22]

It should be stressed that this list names just a few of the many models that have been produced during recent years and is by no means a comprehensive review. For this we may refer to several interesting papers. The more general literature is usefully reviewed in a paper by Nancy Leathers,[26] Wilson,[27] Harris[28] and Lowry[12] also give valuable reviews. A series of interesting models has been published by the *Journal of the American Institute of Planners* in May 1965, and Batty[29] presents a very comprehensive review of British research.

Urban transportation system

It has been found that subsystems with a high level of interaction with other subsystems may sometimes be better analysed if they are treated separately. This is the common approach applied by planners to the transportation sub-system, which we have already distinguished as a subsystem of communications which deals with the flow of goods and persons (material interaction between activities of the urban system).

In a sense, urban transportation models are the most developed form of urban spatial models, probably because they were the pioneers in modelling the urban spatial organization. As we said before, during the early period of development and research, the transportation network of a city was studied in almost complete isolation from the land use or activities that it was supposed to communicate with and bypass. Only when the interdependence between transportation and land use was realized and the relationship between them found to be one of circular causality, did the building of models of land use or activity location start.

The circular causality may be explained by an example: Suppose that an urban spatial model has allocated land zones to various uses for some future period. Based on this land allocation, a transportation model would then allocate traffic volume between zones. The predicted traffic volume will probably require new highways which once constructed may alter the pattern of land use. Thus, one cycle has been completed.

Again, although physical planners have found it useful to study the transportation subsystem separately (but now strongly interrelated with the others), it is nevertheless a part of the urban spatial system from which it has been separated for technological or administrative reasons.

A great variety of transportation models have been built, some of them sometimes too sophisticated for their necessary use in combination with models of the urban spatial structure.

Trip distribution techniques can be divided into two major groups (Richards[30]):

(1) 'Inter-area travel formulae' which cover:
    (a) Basic gravity model (Carrothers[31])
    (b) Intervening opportunities model[32]
    (c) Competing opportunities model (Tomazinis[33])
    (d) Multiple regression model (Osofsky[34])
    (e) Entropy maximizing method[35]
(2) Growth factor or 'analogue' techniques. Of these the most widely used in the UK is probably the Furness[36] method.

Many models have been developed using the techniques mentioned above. The simpler models attempt only to allocate flows to interzonal trips, while the more sophisticated ones predict many transportation variables such as route choices, modal split, etc. Two very interesting models developed in Britain are the General Transport Model[37] and the SELNEC Transport Model.[38]

2.4 Limiting the scope

In this chapter, we have outlined some of the systems and subsystems which make up the urban system. For the purpose of this book we shall attempt to restrict the scope of this study to the urban *spatial* system and to give special emphasis to land use or activity location models. We shall stress that evaluation models such as cost-benefit analysis and others are omitted from this study. Thus, in the remainder of this work, all the effort will be concentrated into the physical problems of cities and regions and especially into the different mathematical models developed to aid planners in the control of cities.

References

1 SNELL, J. and SHULDINER, P. 'Analysis of urban transportation research'. North Western University Research Report, 1967.
2 ISARD, W. *Methods of Regional Analysis*. Cambridge, Mass., 1960.
3 CHAPIN, F. S. *Urban Land Use Planning*. Urbana, Illinois, 1965.
4 ROGERS, A. 'Matrix methods of population analysis'. *Journal of the American Institute of Planners*, 1966 January.
5 BECKERMAN, W. and ASSOCIATES. *The British Economy in 1975*. Cambridge, 1965.
6 TIEBOUT, C. M. *The Community Economic Base Study*. The Committee for Economic Development, New York, 1962.
7 STONE, R. *Mathematics in the Social Sciences*. Chapman and Hall, London, 1965.
8 LEONTIEFF, W. *Input-Output Analysis*. Oxford University Press, 1967.
9 HIRSCH, W. Z. *Elements of Regional Accounts*. Baltimore, Md., 1964.
10 FOLEY, D. L. 'An approach to metropolitan spatial studies', in *Explorations into Urban Structure*, Philadelphia, 1964.
11 McLOUGHLIN, J. *Urban and Regional Planning*. Faber and Faber, London, 1970.
12 LOWRY, I. S. 'Seven models of urban development: A structural comparation'. Special Report 97, Highway Research Board, Washington D.C., 1968.
13 WEBBER, M. M. 'Order in diversity: community without propinquity' in WINGO (ed.) *Cities and Space: The Future Use of Urban Land*, Baltimore, Md., 1963, pp. 23–54.
14 MITCHELL, R. B. and RAPKIN, C. *Urban Traffic: A Function of Land Use*. New York, 1954.
15 CHAPIN, F. S. Jr. and WEISS, S. F. 'A probabilistic model for residential growth'. *Transportation Research*, 1968, vol. 2, pp. 375–390.
16 CHAPIN, F. S. Jr. 'A model for simulating residential development'. *Journal of the American Institute of Planners*, 1965, May, pp. 120–136.
17 HERBERT, J. D. and STEVENS, B. H. 'A model for the distribution of residential activities in urban areas'. *Journal of Regional Science*, 1960, (Fall) 2/2, pp. 21–36.
18 HANSEN, W. G. 'How accessibility shapes land use'. *Journal of the American Institute of Planners*, 1959, vol. 25, May, No. 2, pp. 73–76.
19 LATHROP, G. T. and HAMBURG, J. R. 'An opportunity-accessibility model for allocating regional growth'. *Journal of the American Institute of Planners*, 1965, May, pp. 95–103.

20 LITTLE, A. D. 'Model of San Francisco housing market'. San Francisco Community Renewal C65400, Cambridge, January 1966.

21 HILL, D. M. 'A growth allocation model for the Boston region'. *Journal of the American Institute of Planners*, 1965, May, pp. 111–120.

22 SCHLAGER, K. J. 'A land use plan design model'. *Journal of the American Institute of Planners*. 1965, May, pp. 103–111.

23 LAKSHMANAN, T. R. and HANSEN, W. G. 'A retail market potential model'. *Journal of the American Institute of Planners*, 1965, May, pp. 134–143.

24 LOWRY, I. S. *A Model of Metropolis*. Rand Corporation, Santa Monica, California, 1964.

25 COWAN, P. 'The accommodation of activities'. *Arena*, 1967, April, pp. 256–259.

26 LEATHERS, N. J. 'Residential location and model of transportation to work: A model of choice'. *Transportation Research*, 1967, vol. 1, August No. 2, pp. 129–155.

27 WILSON, A. G. 'Models in urban planning: A synoptic review of recent literature'. *Abstract in Urban Studies*, 1968, November, pp. 249–276.

28 HARRIS, B. 'Quantitative models of urban development: Their role in metropolitan policy-making', in PERLOFF, HARVEY, S. and WINGO, LOWDON Jr., *Issues in Urban Economics*, Baltimore; Johns Hopkins, 1968.

29 BATTY, M. 'Recent developments in land use modelling: A review of British research'. Urban Systems Research Unit, Department of Geography, University of Reading, 1970.

30 RICHARDS, M. G. 'Applications in transportation planning'. Gravity Models in Town Planning, Department of Town Planning, Lanchester College of Technology, Coventry, October 1969.

31 CARROTHERS, G. 'An historical review of the gravity and potential concepts of human interaction'. *Journal of the American Institute of Planners*, vol. 22, No. 2, pp. 94–102.

32 CHICAGO TRANSPORTATION STUDY. 'Final report'. vol. II, 1960.

33 TOMAZINIS, A. R. 'A new method of trip distribution in an urban area.' *Highway Research Board Bulletin*. 1962, No. 347.

34 OSOFSKY, S. 'The multiple regression method of forecasting traffic volumes.' *Traffic Quarterly*, 1959, July, vol. XIII.

35 WILSON, A. G. 'A statistical theory of spatial distribution models'. *Transportation Research*, 1968, vol. 1, No. 3, pp. 253–270.

36 FURNESS, K. P. *Traffic Engineering Practice*. E. DAVIES, (ed.) Spon, London, 2nd edition, 1968.

37 LANE, P. and PRESTWOOD SMITH. *Analytical Transport Planning*. Duckworth.

38 WILSON, A. G., HAWKINS, A. F., HILL, G. J. and WAGON, D. J. 'Calibration and testing of the SELNEC transport model.' *Regional Studies*, 1969, vol. 3, pp. 337–350.

3   The Planning Process

3.1   Definition of planning

We have identified the urban spatial system as a very complex and probabilistic system in which changes in activities or communications and in their related adapted and channel spaces, respectively, result in repercussions which alter the system and its behaviour.

From cybernetics, we may recall that a controller is a natural or constructed system which interacts with its environment (in this case the controlled system) to bring about a particular stability called the 'goal' or 'objective'. Implications of this definition suggest that development control in urban spatial systems can be seen as a control mechanism and planning may be regarded as part of it.

Although 'planning' is a generic term which is applicable to a wide variety of situations, in the context of the urban spatial system, with which we are dealing here, planning is the regulation of the use and development of land and of communications. Because planning is essentially oriented to the future, planners attempt to devise policies which can influence the development in desired directions according to the possibilities of the community as a whole.

The systems approach to urban and regional problems has had a significant effect on the traditional method of planning, which was based on the narrow conception of land use manipulation through the production of a *static* overall development master plan. This view of planning has been changing, and now it is regarded as an essentially *dynamic* process. This view was confirmed in Britain by the Planning Advisory Group (PAG), which was set up in 1964 to assist the Ministry of Housing and Local Government and the Ministry of Transport in a general review of the planning context. A move towards the study of cities and regions as systems and acknowledgement of planning as a dynamic process were the underlying concepts of the new approach.

In dealing with controllable systems, the Law of Requisite Variety is the main tool in understanding the way in which systems can be controlled. This law is stated by Ashby:[1] 'only variety destroys variety'. This means that the variety of the control mechanism must be equivalent to the controlled part of the system. Beer[2] gives a very interesting example to illustrate this law: Suppose that we have 15 men in striped shirts and give them an odd-shaped ball and instructions to place the ball between a set of upright posts some distance away: How can we control the system? We could find many alternatives to control it but soon we may realize that the best way would be to get 15 other men (in differently striped shirts) and instruct them to do the same thing, but moving in an opposite direction to the first set. Here we see that the variety of the control system is equal to the variety of the controlled system.

This requisite variety has to be present in the planning process if we try to control a very complex system such as the urban spatial system. Partly, this requisite variety is obtained by considering planning as a dynamic process where every major variation in the system is analysed and evaluated with the help of models. If we accept Meier's definition[3] of urban system as 'A sequence of states of an interacting population, each state being a function of preceding states', we have to agree that it is practically impossible to control a dynamic system with a static development master plan; we may conclude that planning should be seen as a continuous cyclic process. Chadwick[4] points out that:

> Planning is a conceptual general system. By creating a conceptual system independent of, but corresponding to, the real world system, we can seek to understand the phenomena of process and change, then to anticipate them, and finally to evaluate them; to concern ourselves with the optimisation of a real world system by seeking optimisation of the conceptual system.

3.2 Stages of the planning process
The following stages can be identified in the planning process:

(1) Review and understanding
(2) Goal formulation
(3) Problem formulation
(4) Possible courses of action
(5) Evaluation
(6) Selection
(7) Implementation and control.

Review and understanding
This facet of the planner's activity requires the ability to understand the urban spatial system in terms of a system framework, i.e. the way in which the planner can view the composition of the urban system, the way in which particular subsystems behave, and also the way in which the results of previous planning policies affecting urban subsystems can be examined.

Definition of urban activities and entities within a system framework, as well as analysis of such defined subsystems, form the tasks which the planner is required to carry out at this stage in the planning process. In order to understand the system and describe the relationships between the relevant factors, planners generally use descriptive models.

Goal formulation
Having identified the system, the next task is the design of plans to correct system deficiencies, but this can only be possible by evaluating the problems in

terms of deviation from planners' and community goals, and so we must first enumerate the goals of the various sections of the community.

Young[5] has stated that:

> A goal is an ideal and should be expressed in abstract terms . . . an objective is capable of both attainment and measurement, its inherent purpose is implicit rather than explicit.

Because the goals of the different sections of the community are generally very different and often incompatible with each other, and because money and time budgets are constrained, the simultaneous attainment of all the goals is not possible, and a set of weights has to be assigned to the different goals until clarification and definition of goals is obtained. Chadwick[4] makes very interesting comments about this point:

> Because the real world is constantly changing, planning must be concerned with continual change, and this means that the goals of planning will change with time — and thus the policies necessary for optimisation will also change; . . . the goal of politicians may be simply: to stay in power; that of entrepreneurs: to maximise profit. How can the socially-motivated planner reconcile his implied aims with goals such as these? . . . The hard truth is that goal formulation is a difficult art, both technically, and politically: it is nonetheless essential, and the difficulties have to be faced — sometime — if a rational approach to the planning process is intended.

As we have already said, goals are somewhat vague and general, and the progress towards a goal requires the attainment of objectives which are more clear and precise. Then, once the goals are formulated, the objectives must be clearly stated, because it is practically impossible to decide the course of action that must be chosen without a clear definition of goals and objectives. Thus, we may say that goals are ends toward which processes are directed, the purposes for which the system has been organized and the end towards which everything is aimed.

Problem formulation

The design of plans to correct systems deficiencies can only be done once the problem has been identified by comparing the actual state of the system and the proposed state expressed by the goals and objectives.

In addition to new goals formulated by the government, community and planners would also impose changes in the planner's system objective and hence require the formulation of new plans for the particular system or subsystem concerned.

Possible courses of action
Alternative solutions to the problem are prepared because they are means of displaying and exploring the different possibilities open to the planner. In a sense, the generation of alternatives is implicitly a learning and exploring process which helps in understanding the consequences of each of the possible alternatives. The generation of alternative solutions, or possible courses of action, requires a model of the system which will show how the real system would behave through time under varying conditions.

We know that activities performed in any one zone of the area under study will have repercussions in other zones and activities sectors; with the help of models, we can represent the relationships between them and simulate the repercussions. Thus, at this stage, models are used as predictive and explorative techniques, to elaborate and explore alternatives of action.

Evaluation
The evaluation stage provides a set of weights to relate the different alternatives developed and to compare them. These weights should be given by the planner after analysing the changing needs and preferences of the whole community, which will be affected by the possible action. But, as Wilson[6] says:

> This is, of course, a much idealised representation of what happens now. In fact, the weights are usually supplied by different 'government' groups making value judgement and in varying degrees this will continue for the foreseeable future.

In some cases, when a full set of compatible objectives has been difficult to specify during the goal formulation stage, tentative objectives are formulated and followed until this stage, when the consequences are explored and informally evaluated. Then we return to stage two, in order to formulate the objectives more precisely. Elaboration and evaluation of the modified alternatives take place more formally, and this process continues until the various alternatives are well documented and evaluated. Thus, a process of learning is performed.

The elements of the plan that are going to be used in the evaluation process depend directly on the goals and objectives identified, and although there are several evaluation techniques that have been developed, such as cost-benefit analysis (Prest and Turvey[7]), planning balance sheet method (Lichfield[8]) and Hill's goals-achievement matrix,[9] there are considerable problems of measuring costs and especially benefits. According to Cordey-Hayes:[10]

> Formal evaluation techniques exist, but these are of strictly limited applicability, partly because they do not distinguish clearly between economic efficiency and broader socio-economic considerations, but also because of the difficulty of specifying a full set of objectives as required by the techniques of cost-benefit and effectiveness analysis.

Selection
Once the various alternative plans have been formally evaluated, the one which optimizes the proposed objectives and goals is chosen.

Implementation and control
At this stage, action is taken to implement the plan which has been chosen at the selection stage. We must recall that the urban system is a dynamic one, and that changes are occurring constantly through time. To control these constant changes, a control mechanism which is also continuous must be set up. This control mechanism makes judgements on proposals for changes with reference to models of the system.

The proposed changes in the urban spatial system presented by developers, industries, etc., are introduced into the model of the system in order to estimate their probable effect in the system and see in which way the new proposals alter the current plan. In this way, planners can assess the impact of public and private proposals and how they deflect the system from the course charted for it in the plan. The same models used under 'Possible courses of action', above, are again used here.

As time passes, the needs and desires of the community change and the actual

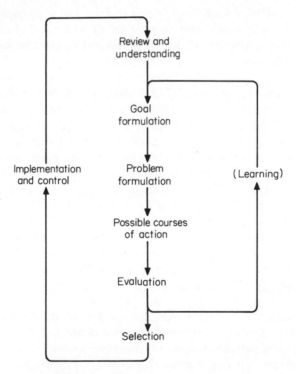

Figure 3.1 Planning as a cyclic process

performance of the system is not necessarily the one planned, because we are dealing with probabilistic systems whose behaviour cannot be defined with certainty. Consequently, the plans for the region under study must be reviewed to cope with the new situation, and so we must return to stage one and start the cycle again. This cycle process is represented schematically in Figure 3.1.

3.3 The place of models in the planning process

Urban system models are now beginning to play an important part in the urban planning process, and their use can be of assistance in almost all stages of this process. The understanding of urban systems and their analysis by models which simulate urban behaviour, or facets of it, can indicate where problems are arising or where they exist.

Urban models expressed mathematically provide a systematic statement of relationships between the different elements of the region under study, and hence improve our concept of the forces associated with community growth and transportation requirements. The use of models allows planners a better insight into the system being controlled and increases rigour and order in the thought process.

The advantages and disadvantages of the various alternative plans can be assessed more easily with the help of models. Equipped with modelling techniques, a planner should be able to predict fairly accurately the consequences of various alternatives of land development. Models are the means by which planners can evaluate the probable impact that improved transportation services, zoning laws, extension of water systems, etc., would have on land development. Models have been developed to describe and predict location of employment, residences, services, etc., which when linked together can provide a framework for the study and planning of a whole region or city.

We have already pointed out that one of the greatest difficulties in the use of models lies in the evaluation of alternative plans. The measurement of benefits is still very difficult to carry out. Models are much more than straight forecasting procedures; they are tools which can help planners during the implementation stage when estimating the possible effects of new developments.

Systems modelling, and techniques predominant in the systems approach to planning, should merely be seen as methods and techniques useful in any form of planning where the role of planners and the objectives of the process are fully considered, and they should be used with caution at the present time, until they are fully tested and justified empirically. Models are just a useful technique for clarifying planning problems.

One final use of these models need to be recognized: the use of such models for educational purposes. As Lowry[11] points out:

> Above all the process of model-building is educational. The participants invariably find their perceptions sharpened, their horizons expanded, their professional skills augmented. The mere necessity of framing

questions carefully does much to dispel the fog of sloppy thinking that surrounds our efforts at civic betterment.

Models should evolve as 'teaching machines', so that a planner can acquire a common image of the organization and environment of the system he is trying to understand and study. One of the values of these models is to improve human judgement; thus their preparation is essentially an educational enterprise.

Batty[12] in his interesting review of British research in land use modelling stresses the educational purposes of models and comments that:

> The model built for Merseyside (*my Reference 13*) was developed primarily for educational purposes involving the teaching of elementary finite mathematics and computer programming. The Central Lancashire model (*my Reference 14*) was also initially developed as an educational device for use alongside a subregional planning project. Finally, the model of Cambridge (*my Reference 15*) built by sixth year architectural students at the University of Cambridge was conceived as an educational program. Because the different variants of the model are so easy to build, there is tremendous potential for the development of these techniques in a teaching context, where such models can be used to demonstrate the effect of planning policies and the process of model design.

Thus, we may say therefore that, to some extent, all models can be considered as educational. Some, however, have been devised purely for teaching purposes. Typically these represent the planning system as a series of operators with simple objectives and a series of simple rules; characteristic of these is the Cornell Land Use Game (CLUG), which in form lies somewhat between a 'real' planning model and a game of *Monopoly*.

3.4 Computers and the planning process

The tool which is being used in the planning process, with the hope that it will relieve the planner of some of the problems associated with decision making and design, is the computer. There are two basic capabilities that the computer offers to the planner: the first is related to the large amount of information that is usually handled regarding activities, land, buildings, etc. and which must be stored and retrieved. The second and equally important capability refers to the computation process itself which allows very large arithmetical and logical calculations to be performed at very high speed.

These two basic capabilities of computers allow them to deal simultaneously with the large number of variables and interrelationships that take place in comprehensive planning, and which are unmanageable to the human planner. Planners can delegate to computers the hard and tedious mechanical work and dedicate themselves and their time to do more of the thinking and creative work necessary in the planning process. Harris[16] has enumerated the possible roles of the computer in planning:

They can, first of all, be used to obtain, process, store and retrieve information. Second, they can be used in the analysis of information. Third, they can be used to make predictions. Fourth, they can control systems in the real world or, more correctly, they can generate control signals. Finally, it is believed that computers can find solutions to problems. I shall suggest that there are serious limitations on the fourth or fifth of these models of computer operation, and that the others are not exactly as represented. I believe, however, that this relatively trite and well-known list of computer functions is in many ways thoroughly applicable to the planning process.

It is important to stress that planners will not be replaced by computers, and in a very simple way we could say that regardless of time and reliability, men can do any job that the computer does, but that the converse is not true.

References

1 ASHBY, W. R. *An Introduction to Cybernetics.* Chapman & Hall Ltd. and University Paperbacks, London, reprinted 1970.
2 BEER, S. *Decision and Control.* John Wiley and Sons Ltd., Chichester, 1966.
3 MEIER, R. L. *A Communication Theory of Urban Growth.* Cambridge, Mass. M.I.T. Press, 1962.
4 CHADWICK, G. *A Systems View of Planning.* Pergamon Press, Oxford, 1971.
5 YOUNG, R. C. 'Goals and goal setting'. *Journal of the American Institute of Planners*, 1965, August, pp. 186.
6 WILSON, A. G. 'Models in urban planning: A synoptic review of recent literature'. *Abstract in Urban Studies*, 1968, November, pp. 249–276.
7 PREST, A. R., and TURVEY, R. 'Cost-benefit analysis: a survey'. *Economic Journal*, 1965, vol. LXXV, December, pp. 683–735.
8 LICHFIELD, N. 'Cost-benefit analysis in city planning'. *Journal of the American Institute of Planners.* 1960, November, pp. 273–279.
9 HILL, M. 'A goal-achievements matrix for evaluating alternative plans'. *Journal of the American Institute of Planners*, no. 34, pp. 19–29.
10 CORDEY-HAYES, M. 'Structure plans and models'. *Architectural Design*, 1970, July, pp. 362–363.
11 LOWRY, I. S. 'A short course in model design'. *Journal of the American Institute of Planners*, 1965, May, pp. 158–166.
12 BATTY, M. 'Recent developments in land use modelling: A review of British Research'. Urban Systems Research Unit, Department of Geography, University of Reading, 1970.
13 MASSER, I. 'Notes on an application of the Lowry model to Merseyside'. Unpublished paper, Dept. of Civic Design, University of Liverpool. 1970.

14 BATTY, M. 'Models and projections of the space-economy'. *Town Planning Review*, 1970, vol. 41, 2.

15 CAMBRIDGE UNIVERSITY. 'Cambridge: the evaluation of urban structure plans'. Land Use and Built Form Studies, WP 14. Cambridge, July 1970.

16 HARRIS, B. 'Computer and urban planning'. *Socio-Economic Planning Sciences*, 1968, July, pp. 223–230.

4 Models: General Framework

4.1 Models in general

Introduction
Man has been using models in every phase of life, and it can be said that a model in itself is man's oldest intellectual tool. A mental image used in thinking is a model. A written description is a model. Toys, pictures, films and words are all various kinds of models.

Definition of model
A model of a situation is simply a representation of our understanding of the corresponding real world situation. In this context, a situation may be an object, event, process or system. Models are idealized in the sense that they are less complicated than reality and hence easier to use for research purposes. Recalling that variety is the number of distinguishable elements within a set, we may point out that the creation of a model involves reducing variety from the high level of the system being modelled to the much lower of the modelling system.

The simplicity of models compared with the reality of the situation being modelled lies in the fact that only the relevant properties of the real world are represented; that is, all the major features of the situation, suitably transformed, will be found in the model of the situation. For example in a road map, which is a model of part of the earth's surface, vegetation is not shown because it is not relevant to the use of the map.

This selective attitude to representing only the features that are useful, will depend, as we have seen in the road map example, on the intention of the model maker, who in a sense reduces the number of properties of reality which are going to be represented in the model.

As Haggett and Chorley[1] say:

> Models can be viewed as selective approximations which, by the elimination of incidental detail, allow some fundamental relevant or interesting aspects of the real world to appear in some generalised form.

The construction of a model presupposes the use of a theory which explains parts or the whole of the relationships established in the model. Consequently, the predictions and solutions derived from the model are deduced consequences of the theory. As Harris[2] says 'A model is an experimental design based on a theory.'

During the renaissance, Kepler observed the planets in motion and built up a mass of data on their positions at various times of the year. Then, by testing various hypotheses against these data as to the nature of their orbits, he concluded that elliptical orbits nearly fitted the observed data. He thus built up a model which explained planetary motion and, furthermore, allowed predictions to be made about all future positions of the planets. This method of observation and hypothesis has stimulated scientists from different disciplines to find equivalent predictive models for other particular phenomena.

Functions of models

Models have multiple uses, but by far the most important ones are related to the function of understanding and explaining the real world system, and once this is performed to satisfaction the model is generally used to predict the future. This last function is probably the most outstanding of all, because, if the model maker produced an effective model of the system, he would be able to know how the system would react to different sets of possible eventualities, and so he would be capable of evaluating the likely performance of the system modelled.

Haggett and Chorley[1] give an extensive analysis of the function of models:

Psychological function: in enabling some group of phenomena to be visualized and comprehended which could otherwise not be because of their magnitude or complexity.

Acquisitive function: in that the model provides a framework wherein information may be defined, collected and ordered.

Organizational function: with respect to data.

Fertility function: in allowing the maximum amount of information to be squeezed out of the data.

Logical function: by helping to explain how a particular phenomenon comes about.

Normative function: by comparing some phenomenon with a more familiar one.

Systematic function: in which reality is viewed in terms of interlocking systems.

Constructional function: in that they form stepping stones to the building of theories and laws.

Cognitive function: promoting the communication of scientific ideas.

A comprehensive outline of the uses of modelling in connection with theory has been given by Apostel.[3] These uses include the following:

(1) The case where no theory is known about a certain group of facts. Instead of studying this group of facts another group of facts about which a theory is well known and which show several important characteristics with the field under investigation is modelled. The model is then used to develop a theory from near-zero hypotheses. Examples of this have occurred in neurology where the central nervous system is modelled via an analogue computer programmed to show certain neurological peculiarities.

(2) The case where a well-developed theory about a group of facts is known but where mathematical solutions prove difficult with present techniques. Using a model the fundamental conceptions of the theory are simulated in a way in which the simplifying assumptions can express the same assignment. Under these simplifying assumptions the equation becomes soluble. In physics the theory of harmonic oscillators in the study of heat conduction is an example of such a procedure.

(3) The case where two theories are unrelated. One theory can be made the basis of a model whose behaviour simulates the other theory, or else a common model can be introduced interpreting both and thus relating one theory to the other.

(4) The case where a theory is well-confirmed but incomplete. Here a model can be assigned whereby the theory may be completed through study of the model and its empirical output.

(5) The case where new information about a certain group of facts becomes available. To ensure that the new and more general theory still conforms to the original group of facts, this original group is constructed as a model of the later theory, and possibly it is shown that all models of this theory are related to the original group of facts, constructed as a model, in a specific way.

(6) The case where, even if a theory is available about a set of facts, explanation of these facts may be uncertain. In some such cases models have provided explanation (model-use in experimental work on wave theories of light).

(7) The case where it is impossible to experiment directly with a system because of size, etc. A conceptual model system is constructed and experiments are performed which can be considered sufficiently representative of the original system to yield the required information.

(8) The case where the theoretical level is far away from the observational level; that is, concepts cannot be immediately interpreted in terms of observation. Models are constructed to constitute a bridge between the theoretical and observational levels.

Beer,[4] referring to operational research models, says:

> When a manager sets out to apply one of these remedies to a complex problem, he will certainly attempt to foresee the outcome. In fact, various alternative courses of action will be open to him. Before choosing one, he will want to predict and compare these outcomes − to know in a word, which is the least vulnerable to a malignant future. This is what the OR model is for.

Types of models

The following classification of models will be used here:

Physical	(1) Iconic models
	(2) Analogue models
Conceptual	(3) Verbal models
	(4) Symbolic models.

According to the means chosen to represent the real world system, models can be grouped into two classes: physical and conceptual.

'With the physical model, the physical characteristics of reality are represented by the same or analogous characteristics in the model' (Echenique[5]). These types of models can be divided into two categories:

(1) *Iconic models* 'They represent the relevant properties of the real thing by those properties themselves, with only a transformation in scale,' (Ackoff[6]).

For example, an architectural drawing of a house represents distances and relative positions of walls, doors, windows, etc., and with respect to these properties the drawing differs from the real thing only in scale. Other examples of this class of models are architectural models, maps, photographs, etc., and they are 'generally difficult to use to represent dynamic situations', (Churchman, Ackoff and Arnoff[7]).

(2) *Analogue models* In these models 'one property is used to represent another, and hence the necessity of a legend' (Ackoff[6]). For example, when we want to show elevation on a map and we do not want to produce a three dimensional one, we may use colour or shading and supply an appropriate legend which explains the transformation of properties. Slide rules, graphs, etc., are also analogue models. Another case is the representation of an electrical system by a hydraulic system.

'With the conceptual model, the relevant characteristics are represented by concepts (language or symbols)' (Echenique[5]). This type of model can be divided into two classes:

(3) *Verbal models* The description of reality is in logical terms using spoken

words. These models are of limited help in predicting or precisely specifying the state of a system.

(4) *Symbolic models* In these models, the properties of the real world system are represented and expressed symbolically. Models in which the symbols employed are quantitative terms are called *mathematical models*. A mathematical model of a system consists of a set of equations whose solution explains or predicts changes in the state of the system; they have an important role to play in urban and regional planning especially because they are highly abstract, subject to manipulation and precise in terms of the information gained from their use.

4.2 Urban mathematical models

Introduction
In recent years, researchers and planners of urban systems have come to the conclusion that through mathematical representation it is possible and advantageous to describe the process which determines the use of urban land. Since then, mathematical models have been used to represent urban systems, and they express the elements of the system as symbols and their relationships in equation form. In this context, a comprehensive definition of a mathematical model is given by Broadbent:[8]

> Mathematical model is a simplified and abstract view of some aspect of the urban system embodied in an explicit mathematical form, usually through a set of equations. These equations, operating on a massive set of urban data through the use of a computer, help us to simulate the likely growth and development of a city — and in particular, facilitate testing and evaluation of alternative sets of plans.

In urban planning modelling, the model builder is accepting that the city is a system, that is, the city is an organized entity displaying certain patterns. The theory of city development underpinning a model is supposed to represent the model maker's understanding or assumptions of the pattern and order by which the urban system actually works; consequently, models are built to test how well the pattern identified by theories fits the real world situation. We can conclude that a model is no better than the theory on which it is based.

Mathematical models can be classified as probabilistic and deterministic according to the degree of probability. Systems that deterministic models represent are devoid of uncertainty, and changes of state can be perfectly predicted. By definition, probabilistic models are those that include stochastic processes. In relation to urban systems, Harris[2] says:

> We must clearly recognize that there will always be a probabilistic element in the simulation of metropolitan phenomena, based on the fact that

individual behaviours do indeed contain elements of free will, which are inaccessible to us for analysis and prediction.

And he adds that the object of probabilistic models

Would be to discover the range of variation to be expected from constrained random decisions in the overall pattern of metropolitan development.

Systems described on a large level of aggregation and categorization often behave in a more deterministic and less probabilistic way.

Purpose of urban models

Classification
Echenique[5] has provided a very comprehensive classification of models, according to the intentions of the model maker and the purposes for which the model is designed. Four main types of models can be distinguished:

(1) Descriptive models
(2) Predictive models
(3) Explorative models
(4) Planning or decision models.

The theoretical relationships between them and reality can be observed in Figure 4.1.

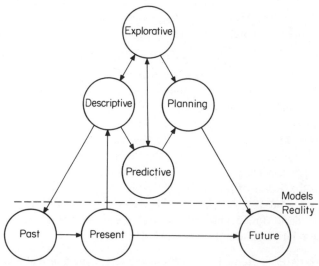

Figure 4.1 Ideal process of model making in relation to the reality (Echenique,[5] 1968)

Descriptive models

These models are orientated towards the need for understanding the mechanisms which govern the structure and behaviour of cities and regions. The builder of a descriptive model has the limited objective of trying to replicate the relevant features of an existing urban environment.

The value of these models lies in the fact that they reveal much about the structure of the urban environment, reducing the apparent complexity of the observed situation to the coherent and rigorous language of mathematical relationships.

Models of this type are logically essential to any other type, because it is not possible to predict, explore or plan without a previous description of the reality under study. In any case, this step is usually necessary as the first part of the model-building process, to establish the nature of the relationships between variables. They do not directly satisfy the planner's need for information about the future, nor help him to choose between alternative policies. They simply explain, in some sense, the present situation in an urban area. They help us in understanding how the urban system works.

Predictive models

These models are designed to help in forecasting the future states of city and regional systems. They must be time related, for a prediction is meaningless unless it states the time dimension to which it relates. We can distinguish two classes: extrapolative and conditional.

The predictive extrapolative models forecast by assuming, in some sense, the continuation of present trends which have already been established in the descriptive model.

In the predictive conditional models, the mechanisms of cause and effect governing the variables are specified; that is, the model may be allowed to respond in the form 'if x occurs, then y must follow', without explicitly asserting the likelihood of the occurrence of x. A special case of this class of model is called 'impact analysis', where the interest lies in the consequences that should be expected to follow a specified exogenous impact — change in x — if the environment were otherwise undisturbed. In the predictive model, as Echenique[5] says:

> Alternatives are left out, either because they have not been discovered or because they do not fit the theory that describes the phenomena.

Explorative models

According to Echenique,[5]

> The main intention with the explorative model is to discover by speculation other realities that may be logically possible by systematically varying the basic parameters used in the descriptive model.

In addition to helping us to explore alternative allocations of activity and the forms of the city which result, this type of model helps us assess the feasibility of these alternatives.

Planning or decision models

In this class of models, a measure of performance is introduced and the model objective is to determine the optimum solution under certain conditions.

In a general context, this class of models should always take the following special form (Ackoff[6]):

$$V = f(x_i, y_j) \qquad (4.1)$$

where V = the measure of the value of the decision that is made

x_i = the variables which are subject to control by the decision maker; the decision variables define the alternative courses of action

y_j = the factors (variable or constant) which affect performance but which are not subject to control by the decision maker within the scope of the problem as defined; these we shall call 'parameters'

f = the fundamental relationship between the independent variables and constants, x_i and y_j, and the dependent variable V.

Then, the purpose of constructing this type of model of a problem situation (in a general context), is to enable us to determine what values of the controllable variables (x_i) provide the best measure of performance (V), under conditions described by the parameters (y_j). Therefore, we want to determine what values of x_i either maximize or minimize V, according to the requirements laid down.

A model of a general situation problem has two essential characteristics:

(1) At least one of the input variables has to be controlled by the decision maker. This means that there should be at least one decision variable x_i.

(2) The output variable V must have some kind of measure expressing the value of the outcome. This means that from the measurement of the output variable, the decision maker is able to choose the best values of x_i — the ones that he will then use.

The value of the solution depends on how adequately the model represents the problem situation; that is, the adequacy of the solution depends on the adequacy of the model. In the urban planning context, this technology is not far developed, although the best known planning models follow, in a sense, the procedure outlined for general situation models by means of linear programming techniques.

Lowry,[9] in order to overcome the difficulties of a lack of a direct procedure (in this type of model for urban systems) proposes the following essential steps:

(1) Specification of alternative programmes or actions that might be chosen
(2) Prediction of the consequences of choosing each alternative
(3) Scoring these consequences according to a metric of goal achievement
(4) Choosing the alternative which yields the highest score.

Broadbent[8] stresses that:

> The particular model developed will always depend partly on the political and institutional context pertaining. The type of model actually used in practical planning will depend upon the perceived problem — and the acceptability of such a model to those who have the responsibility of allocating resources for its development.

Function of urban models

Classification

Urban models perform three basic functions (Kilbridge, O'Block and Teplitz[10]): projection, allocation, and derivation.

A model's purpose is the outcome of one or more of these functions in varying combinations. Most models do not deal with only one of these functions, because generally they perform composites of them. For example, a model of the urban structure that performs these three functions may project an activity, say population, into the future and then allocate it to different zones. Or it may first allocate the population to zones and then project the allocated parts of the population individually. The derivation of a new activity, as for example employment, from the population, may be performed before or after the allocation of population takes place, depending on the model's structure.

Projection

Projection is the estimation of the future state of a model's activity. The input data to the model describe the activity at the beginning of the projection period; a set of functional relations converts these inputs into output data that describe the activity at the end of the projection period.

Allocation

Allocation is the distribution of a model's activity amongst subclasses of use or demand for it, at a point in time. For example, given the total population in a town, models can be built to allocate or locate this population to zones of the town.

A pure allocation model distributes the activity concerned by dividing it according to some theory of the relationship of the parts to the whole and to each other. An example of this type of model is 'A probabilistic model of residential growth' (Chapin and Weiss).[11,12]

Derivation

Derivation is the process by which a model derives activities of the urban system, given other activities. For example, given employment, models can be built to derive population. It is important to notice that derivation takes place at a point in time, and not over time. Commonly, derivation is found associated with allocation or projection, and so it is difficult to find in practice a pure derivation model. For example, Lowry's 'Model of Metropolis' is an allocation-derivation model.[13]

Structure of mathematical models

Components

For obvious reasons, in the rest of this work, the word 'model' will refer to 'mathematical model' unless otherwise stated.

A model can be considered to constitute of: variables, parameters, structural relations, and an algorithm.

Variables

> The activities of the urban system which the model tries to represent are called variables. These are quantities which vary over space and time (Batty).[14]

The purpose of the model and the intentions of the model maker determine which variables the model is going to refer to. In urban spatial models, variables will usually refer to zones. Examples are: land, population, employment, income, housing, labour force participation rate, etc.

Some variables, such as distance or journey time, may connect zones. A variable conceived in general terms (as for example income) must be related to an available statistic. The source of the data and the nature of the variable itself should be carefully analysed, to be sure that its role in the model is not weakened. As an example, suppose that for income, which is a person variable, in the model we use the average of the distribution of income of the population concerned. It is not difficult to imagine that if the spread of the distribution is very wide, the mean of the distribution may be a poor measure of the effect that it is being tried to detect in the model.

In some cases, 'A variable included in the model because of its theoretical significance may not be directly observable in the real world, so that some more accessible *proxy* must be chosen' (Lowry[9]). An example can be found when we need 'location rents' (defined as that portion of the annual payment to an owner of a parcel of land which is attributable to the geographical position of the parcel), but we are only able to obtain empirically 'contract rents' (defined as the total contractual payment of tenant to landlord).

Variables are usually of two types:

(1)   Independent variables (also called exogenous variables): whose values
       are given as input to the model.
(2)   Dependent variables (endogeneous variables): their values are
       determined by the model, and given by the model as output.

Parameters
Parameters are quantities which do not vary within the model; that is, they are
numerical constants. Parameters are programmed for periodic revisions to reflect
changes in the environment of the system. 'They can be regarded as special
quantities which adjust the general structure of the model to the particular
structure of the world' (Batty[14]). For example, the parameters of a population
projection model are mortality and fertility rates, which are specific to the
region being studied.

Structural relations
The heart of the model is the set of structural relations between the parameters,
the dependent and the independent variables, generally presented as equations.
The underlying theory of the model is represented by these structural or
functional relations.

Algorithm
This is the computational method or the procedural steps for the solution of
the model's problem which is generally programmed for the computer. To
construct the algorithm means devising a sequence cf steps which, when
processed, evaluated or worked out, will operate on the data in such a way as to
solve the problem or produce the desired output.

    Diagrammatically, the structure of a model can be represented as shown
below:

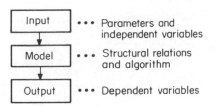

References
1 HAGGET, P. and CHORLEY, R. J. 'Models, paradigms and the new
   geography', in *Models in Geography*. London, 1967, pp. 19–41.
2 HARRIS, B. 'Quantitative models of urban development: their role in
   metropolitan policy-making', in PERLOFF, HARVEY, S. and WINGO,
   LOWDON Jr. *Issues in Urban Economics*. Johns Hopkins, Baltimore,
   1968.

3 APOSTEL, L. 'Towards the formal study of models in the non-formal sciences', in *The Concept and Role of the Model in Mathematics and Natural Science*, ed. H. FREUDENTHAL. Dortrecht, Holland, 1961.

4 BEER, S. *Decision and Control*. John Wiley and Sons, Ltd., London, 1966.

5 ECHENIQUE, M. 'Models: a discussion'. Land Use and Built Form Studies, WP, 6, March 1968.

6 ACKOFF, R. L. *Scientific Method*. John Wiley and Sons, Inc., New York, 1968.

7 CHURCHMAN, C., ACKOFF, R. and ARNOFF, E. L. *Introduction to Operations Research*. John Wiley and Sons, Inc., New York, 1968.

8 BROADBENT, T. A. 'An urban planning model: what does it look like? *Architectural Design*, 1970, August, pp. 408–410.

9 LOWRY, I. S. 'A short course in model design'. *Journal of the American Institute of Planners*, 1965, May, pp. 158–166.

10 KILBRIDGE, M. D., O'BLOCK, R. P., and TEPLITZ, P. V. 'A conceptual framework for urban planning models'. *Management Science*, 1969, vol. 15, February, No. 6.

11 CHAPIN, F. S. Jr. and WEISS, S. F. 'A probabilistic model for residential growth'. *Transportation Research*, 1968, vol. 2, pp. 375–390.

12 CHAPIN, F. S. Jr. 'A model for simulating residential development'. *Journal of the American Institute of Planners*, 1965, May, pp. 120–136.

13 LOWRY, I. S. *A Model of Metropolis*. Rand Corporation, Santa Monica, California, 1964.

14 BATTY, M. 'Introductory model-building problems for urban and regional planning'. Urban Systems Research Unit, Department of Geography, University of Reading, 1970.

5 Building Mathematical Models

5.1 Introduction

The art of model building is above all the art of simplifying complicated problems (Lowry[1]).

Since it is not possible with the present state of the art to prepare a manual of instructions for model building, we shall just outline the various basic constituents for a future methodology for this purpose. We should note that intuition, insight and other mental operations play an important role in the process of model building. According to Lowry:[2]

> The first principle of model building is internal coherence; beyond that, the choice of abstractions is guided in part by the experience of others who have worked in the field, in part by 'hunch' (primitive theory), and in part by a sense of analytical style (say), a preference for mathematical elegance or massive generalization.

5.2 Simplification of reality

One of the most important problems that the model builder has to face deals with the difficulty of obtaining a good balance between accurate representation and mathematical manageability. Lowry[2] says:

> To be useful, the model must replicate those features of the real world which are relevant to the experiment, and abstract those that are irrelevant or of only minor import.

Chadwick[3] stresses that,

> Like all models, of course, spatial models are low-variety representations of high-variety situations: variety is destroyed in the modelling process, but can be re-invoked by retracing the path via models of sub-systemic aspects of the larger system which has been followed in the crystallisation of overall system modelling.

In order to reduce the complexity of the system under study and consequently reduce to a manageable size the mathematical model, the researcher has to simplify the real world situation. The simplification of reality can be obtained by (Ackoff and Sasieni[4]):

(1) Omitting relevant variables
(2) Changing the nature of variables
(3) Changing the relationship between variables
(4) Modifying constraints.

Omitting relevant variables
Some controlled and uncontrolled variables may only have a very small effect on the system's performance while contributing a great deal toward the mathematical complexity of the solution. These variables may be deliberately omitted only after a rigorous analysis is performed which truly justifies doing so.

Changing the nature of variables
To simplify its handling, the mathematical characteristics of the variables may be changed. This may be done in many ways; the most common are:

(1) A continuous variable may be treated as discrete and vice versa
(2) A variable may be treated as a constant.

Changing the relationship between variables
A model may frequently be simplified by modifying the functional form of either the entire model or parts of it. It is very common to approximate non-linear functions by linear functions in order to simplify their manipulation; in other words, to treat the non-linear relationship as linear over a short time, i.e. mathematically representing the curve of the former by its tangent for a short interval. This has to be done with caution because sometimes it can be very dangerous. This simplification is performed in many applications of linear programming techniques.

Other functional simplifications, like assuming a function is continuous when it is discontinuous, are often found in practice. Also, discrete distributions (e.g. the binomial and Poisson) are sometimes approximated by continuous ones. It should be stressed here that fitting a function to a set of data is to a great extent an estimation procedure and hence an approximation.

Modifying constraints
Constraints may be added, substracted or modified so as to simplify the model. If solving a model with constraints is difficult, it is common practice to solve the problem ignoring the constraints and to see whether the solution obtained satisfies the constraints. If it does not, constraints are added one by one in order of increasing complexity, until a solution which satisfies all the constraints is found.

In some cases, problem situations are so complicated that it is impossible to construct one model of the entire situation. In these cases, the system of interest may be broken into parts so that each part can be modelled separately, but special care must be taken when doing so. Additionally, specifications of the interactions between the partial models must be carefully stated.

5.3 Strategy of model building

Lowry[5], referring to the strategic alternatives of model design, says that they are choices open to the model builder

> which demand all his skill and ingenuity, since they bear so heavily on the serviceability of his model to its predetermined purposes. Typically, these decisions must be made in an atmosphere of considerable uncertainty with respect to problems of implementation and eventual uses, and there are no clear canons of better and worse.

The following strategic alternatives are of particular interest:

(1) Theoretical approach
(2) Level of aggregation and categorization
(3) Solution methods
(4) The treatment of time.

Theoretical approach

General framework
Theory can be defined in many ways, and one of them is given by Harris:[6] 'Theory is a general statement about the real world'; since theories consist of statements about the real world, their degree of correspondence with this reality can be tested. In terms of scientific methods, models are used to test theories or hypotheses about the system under consideration; consequently, behind all modelling activities lie theories about how a system behaves.

Analysis begins with observation of a system or event. From observation, familiarization and thinking about the system comes the formulation of hypotheses which are possible explanations of the system behaviour. The construction or invention of a theory involves in essence a precise statement regarding formal relationships, usually including relationships of cause and effect. Very often the link between theory and model may appear tentative, but it must be remembered that theories sometimes have to be simplified before they can be modelled. As we shall see, models are usually based on quasi-theories, that is, theories which do not qualify as formal theories, but give some degree of explanation of the relationships which occur in the real world.

The explanation of the relationships between subsystems or elements of the urban spatial system in a model of it can take place in a number of ways:

The use of an economic or *behaviourist approach* (sometimes called a micro-analytic approach) is one way. One, or a combination of several behavioural theories may be used in this approach.

Another organizing principle on which a model operates is the *social physics approach* (also called the macroanalytic approach).

If both approaches are carried out properly, they should ultimately give the same results. In some cases, both approaches are integrated into a social physics/behavioural approach.

Behaviourist approach
The behaviourist approach is a method of theory building where it is assumed that larger groups will act in ways which can be derived from an understanding of the individual unit.[3] This approach attempts to think in terms of the market model, in which resources are allocated or events determined through competitive interaction of optimizing individuals whose behaviour is based on a theory of rational choice. As an example, the location of industry can be explained as being motivated by economic incentives such as the optimization of some function of cost or profits.

Lowry[2] referring to this approach (which he calls economic location theory) says:

> The literature of location theory includes a number of fragmentary analyses of the problem of locational choice from the viewpoint of a business enterprise or a household; we are told what considerations should, on *a priori* grounds, enter into a rational choice, and how they should be weighted against each other.

Harris[7] appears to take the position that models based on a behaviourist approach (he calls them disaggregative models), in any event, may be more satisfactory than models based on the social physics approach (which he calls aggregative models):

> I cannot, however, pursue this argument to the point where it may be contended that aggregative models are apt to be intrinsically more accurate than disaggregative models. This may in fact be the case if the measure of accuracy is taken as the fit for an observed situation in the present or recent past. If, however, we take the view that one of the major sources of future change will be changes in mix of the underlying population, then the dangers of overaggregation in relation to prediction become apparent. The process of aggregation itself, especially where the proper roles of aggregation would be nonlinear or discontinuous, effectively debars the model from adjusting properly to future changes in mix. The use of aggregative models therefore inevitably freezes some portions of the present mix of population attributes and behaviours. Disaggregation tends

to reduce this mix and its attendant dangers, and microanalytical might completely eliminate it except insofar as the mixture is inherent in the behaviour of decision units themselves.

The major problem of the behaviourist approach is that a model based on the theory of rational choice can be implemented only if the chooser's system of relative values can be specified in considerable detail.

As Lowry[5] has pointed out, the search for an empirical technique to achieve the detailed specification required by the behaviourist approach has frustrated generations of economists, and approximations to data are both crude in detail and based on highly questionable operating assumptions. A second problem of this approach is the implementation of a comprehensive market model — one embracing the entire range of transactions which substantially affect the pattern of urban development and land use.

Social physics approach
The social physics approach, also called the macroanalytic approach, is a method of theory building where the behaviour of the individual is deduced as being typical of group behaviour (Chadwick[3]). In this approach, the researcher attempts to simulate in a very empirical manner the statistical regularities of what he observes in the geographical distribution of population — which in reality results from the combination and/or competition between the many different forces and individuals operating within the urban system, without specifying these forces directly; in other words, without asking why things occur.

The principal criticism of the social physics approach is that it consists in most part of descriptive generalizations which lack an explicit causal structure. Lowry,[5] commenting about models based on the social physics approach, says:

Thus, a macro-model of residential mobility may consist essentially of a set of mobility rates for population subgroups classified by age, sex or family status, rates based on historical evidence of the statistical frequency of movement by the members of such groups. For purposes of prediction, one may assume that these rates will apply to future as well as past population; but since the reasons people move are not explicit in such a model, the assumption of continuity in behaviour cannot be easily modified to fit probable or postulated future changes in the environment of this behaviour.

A second objection to this approach is that it is not easily reducible to a single metric system, for example money, that will facilitate the distinction between better and worse policy alternatives.

A limitation in the social physics approach to model building can be seen in connection with the selected level of aggregation and categorization. So much depends in this approach on the drawing of empirical regularities from the interrelationships between variables or entities of the urban system. At increasing levels of detail (i.e. low level of resolution), highly disaggregated, difficulties occur in obtaining regularities due to the 'emerging uniqueness' of a particular local facet of the system. For this reason no satisfactory urban model at present exists for dealing with, say, local spatial planning. Most models presently in operation usually operate at middle and higher resolution levels, e.g. city, subregional, regional, national and international levels.

Analogies with models used by other sciences are generally employed in the formulation of urban models. An example of this approach is the inter-action concept based on Newton's Law of Gravitation.

Analogy

As Wilson[8] has stated very clearly:

> The study of analogies between different systems can often bring about a situation where the study of one system helps the study of another.

Owing to the widespread use of this approach in model building, the process of formulating a model by analogy will be outlined here.

At this point, we shall explain some terms which will be used in the formulation of models by analogy. Let us suppose that we have two finite sets of elements: one is a set whose elements are the 26 letters of the English alphabet and the other set consists of the natural numbers $1-26$ inclusive. If these two sets are placed in correspondence with each other, we will obviously find that there is one number for each letter, or in other words, there is a *one-one* correspondence. The process of making this correspondence is called a *mapping*.

When we undertake a mapping process, we need the rules for changing the elements of one set into those of the other. Thus, it is then necessary to specify a *transformation*. For example, if the set $1, 2, 3, 4, 5, \ldots$ is to be mapped into the set $5, 10, 15, 20, 25, \ldots$ the mapping is specified by the transformation $b = 5a$. We can identify this example as a *one-one* correspondence. If the same set $1, 2, 3, 4, 5, \ldots$ is mapped into the set composed only of the number 5, the transformation may be identified by $b = (5 + a) - a$, which then defines a *many-one* correspondence.

According to Beer,[9] *isomorphism* 'is a special name for mapping which not only involves a one-one correspondence of elements, but which also preserves operational characteristics'; *homomorphism* refers to a mapping which involves a many-one correspondence and where certain operational characteristics concerning the relationship of elements are preserved.

The process of formulating a model by analogy can be considered as consisting of three stages:

(1)   Formulation of analogous conceptual models

(2) Formulation of the corresponding homomorphic models
(3) Generalization in a scientific model.

These stages are represented diagrammatically in Figure 5.1.

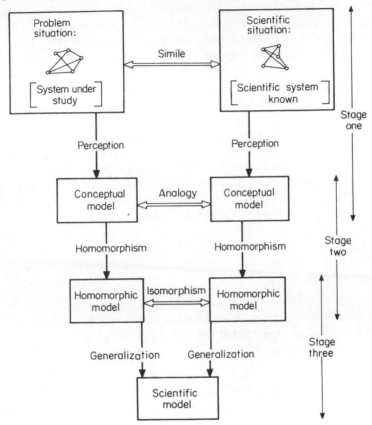

Figure 5.1 Process of formulating a model by analogy* (based on Beer's 'The nature of a scientific model'[9])

Stage one: Formulation of analogous conceptual models
Once a conceptual model of the system under study has been formulated, it is compared with existing conceptual models of the different branches of science, which are believed to have marked resemblances to the problem situation.

The model of any one system stands in some sort of correspondence with the model of any other system: the question is only whether the correspondence is greater or smaller — and therefore more useful or less useful (Beer[9]).

* From *Decision and Control* by Stafford Beer. Copyright © 1966 John Wiley and Sons Ltd., by permission of John Wiley and Sons Ltd.

By analysing the extent to which the behaviour of the one system throws light on the behaviour of the other, possible agreements between the conceptual model of the system under study and each of the different conceptual models of the various scientific disciplines considered are related.

It is possible that every aspect of the problem situation is represented by a different scientific model. For example, one may represent growth, another efficiency, another interrelationship, etc. If so, several scientific conceptual models are required to represent the totality of the system under study.

Stage two: Formulation of the corresponding homomorphic models
In this stage, an attempt to establish a mapping between the conceptual model of the problem situation and the scientific conceptual model is performed. Using the languages of mathematics, statistics and logic, the researcher is engaged in a process of formulating them more precisely, mapping each conceptual model into a neutral scientific language, that is, the researcher produces homomorphic models which may well be isomorphic with each other. During this process some of the conceptual richness will be lost, but in return, the researcher will obtain a more precise unambiguous model.

Stage three: Generalization in a scientific model
The scientific model equally represents the different situations expressed by the homomorphic models.

A scientific model is a homomorphism on to which two different situations are mapped, and which actually defines the extent to which they are structurally identical (Beer[9]).

Example of the process of formulating a model by analogy
A classical example of this approach is the gravity model, commonly used in transportation planning, to calculate the number of trips between two cities.

Stage one
When dealing with urban spatial systems, the *attraction* between cities may be considered an analogous situation to the *attraction* of bodies in the physical science, and consequently the problem situation of the urban spatial system and the scientific situation of a physical system may be mapped into conceptual models which are analogous. This activity is carried out at this first stage.

Stage two
Now, each conceptual model is mapped homomorphically onto a rigorous mathematical formulation, that is, onto homomorphic models which are isomorphic in relation to each other. The homomorphic model related to physics is expressed by Newton's Law of Gravitation:

The force of interaction between two bodies is proportional to the product of their masses and inversely proportional to the square of the distance between them.

The law can be expressed by the equation

$$F = g\frac{M_1 M_2}{d^2}$$ (5.1)

where F = force of interaction between the two masses
M_1 and M_2 = masses of the bodies 1 and 2 respectively
d = distance between the masses
g = constant.

The homomorphic model related to the urban system can be expressed by:

The number of trips between concentrations of population is proportional to the product of the population of the two centres and inversely proportional to the square of the distance between them.

Mathematically, this can be expressed as follows:

$$I = K\frac{N_1 N_2}{d^2}$$ (5.2)

where I = number of trips between the two centres
N_1 and N_2 = population of the centres 1 and 2 respectively
d = distance between the two centres
K = constant.

We can see the isomorphism between equation 5.1 and equation 5.2.

Stage three
These two homomorphic models are embedded in a scientific model represented by a generalization of any of the homomorphic models, and so the gravity concept or model equally represents the two situations.

Entropy maximizing method
In the social physics approach, the researcher attempts to simulate in a very empirical manner the statistical regularities of what he observes, without asking why things occur. Generally, in the formulation of urban models, analogies with models used by other sciences are employed. An example of this approach is the interaction concept based on Newton's Law of Gravitation.

The principal criticism of the social physics approach is that it consists largely of descriptive generalizations that lack explicit causal structure.

The work of Wilson[10] has produced an outstanding advance in urban modelling by supplying a new approach for deriving theories of urban interaction. This approach draws heavily from concepts and techniques in statistical mechanics linked to the social physics approach.

Statistical mechanics is a branch of physics developed to study the state of a system, without having to refer to the behaviour of each element.

Conceptually, entropy is a measure of uncertainty used in information theory which is concerned with the problems of deriving maximum useful information from a given signal. If the 'given signal' is considered to be the data which partially describes the urban system, the information theory provides a framework for analysing the data in such a way as to extract from them the least biased description of the state of the urban system as a whole (LUBFS[11]).

Wilson's entropy maximizing method is based upon a definition of the micro-states and macrostates which characterize the system of interest. A microstate of the system can be defined as a complete description of the system under study; while a macrostate is less than complete in terms of information, and, as we shall see, many microstates can give rise to the same macrostate.

The method establishes that the most probable macrostate of any system is the one which satisfies the known constraints and which maximizes its entropy.

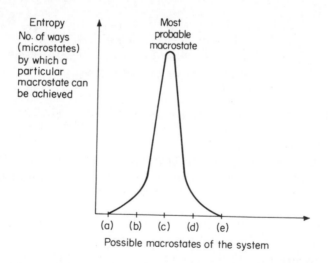

Figure 5.2 Diagrammatic representation of the statistical theory

Maximum entropy is achieved by the macrostate which can be arrived at, in the maximum number of ways (microstates). Figure 5.2 gives a diagrammatic representation of the statistical theory, where the degree of uncertainty is given by the spread of the distribution.

Illustrative example

In order to clarify these concepts, we shall consider a very simple example: Let us imagine a shop which sells only three types of article at the following prices:

Type of article	Price
I	£2
II	£3
III	£4

We know that on a particular day only three customers A, B and C entered the shop and each of them bought one article. We also know that at the end of that day the shop's total sales were £9. Our interest lies in knowing, within the constraints imposed by the available information, how many articles of each type were sold during that day. It is clear that we are not concerned with who were the customers for each article; in fact, we may say that we are interested in knowing the most probable distribution of customers (as totals, not as individuals) amongst the available articles.

We can define the constraints of the system as follows:

(1)   Number of one-article customers: 3
(2)   Total sales: £9

In this example, the system of interest can be specified by a table of the following form:

Articles type

Three customers (A,B,C)

I	II	III

To start with, we are going to enumerate all possible assignments of customers to articles, together with the amount that the shop would have received had that particular assignment taken place:

Assignment No.	I	II	III	Total amount (£)
1	ABC	—	—	6
2	—	ABC	—	9
3	—	—	ABC	12
4	AB	C	—	7
5	AC	B	—	7
6	BC	A	—	7
7	AB	—	C	8
8	AC	—	B	8
9	BC	—	A	8

Assignment No.	I	II	III	Total amount (£)
10	–	AB	C	10
11	–	AC	B	10
12	–	BC	A	10
13	A	BC	–	8
14	B	AC	–	8
15	C	AB	–	8
16	A	–	BC	10
17	B	–	AC	10
18	C	–	AB	10
19	–	A	BC	11
20	–	B	AC	11
21	–	C	AB	11
22	A	B	C	9
23	A	C	B	9
24	B	A	C	9
25	B	C	A	9
26	C	A	B	9
27	C	B	A	9

It is important to notice that cases like the following ones

I	II	III
AB	C	–
BA	C	–

are identical, because customers A and B have each bought an article type I, and customer C has purchased an article type II. From the point of view of the trader, he also considers these two cases identical because he has sold the same number of articles of each type in both cases. But assignments like the following ones:

I	II	III
AB	C	–
AC	B	–

are considered by the system as different ones. Although the trader has sold the same number of articles of each type in both cases, customers B and C have purchased different articles in each case. Thus, from the trader's point of view, these two different assignments form the same distribution, which can be described as:

I	II	III
2	1	0

Here we can see that two different assignments give rise to the same distribution. We also notice that an assignment gives a complete description of the system, thus, according to our definition, an assignment can be considered a microstate of the system.

A distribution can be identified as a macrostate of the system, as it is less than complete in terms of information and, as we have seen, the same distribution is obtained in two ways (microstates).

Now, these 27 microstates (assignments) give rise to 10 different macrostates (distributions) as follows:

Assignment no.	Distribution	Total amount (£)
1	(a) (3, 0, 0)	6
2	(b) (0, 3, 0)	9
3	(c) (0, 0, 3)	12
4, 5, 6	(d) (2, 1, 0)	7
7, 8, 9	(e) (2, 0, 1)	8
10, 11, 12	(f) (0, 2, 1)	10
13, 14, 15	(g) (1, 2, 0)	8
16, 17, 18	(h) (1, 0, 2)	10
19, 20, 21	(i) (0, 1, 2)	11
22, 23, 24, 25, 26, 27	(j) (1, 1, 1)	9

The total sales constraint (£9) restricts the probable distributions of the system to distributions (b) and (j):

Assignment no.	Distribution	Total amount (£)
2	(b) (0, 3, 0)	9
22, 23, 24, 25, 26, 27	(j) (1, 1, 1)	9

We may notice that distribution or macrostate (j) can be achieved by six different assignments (microstates), while distribution (b) can arise in only one way. Then, assuming that all microstates of the system occur with equal probability, we may conclude that the most probable macrostate of the system is (j), that is, that distribution where the shop has sold one article of each type. Graphically this result can be represented as shown in Figure 5.3.

Although the concept of entropy and likelihood are not precisely the same, the reader will find it useful to go through some examples related to the principle of maximum likelihood presented in the paper cited in Reference 11, which will help to explain the relevance of both.

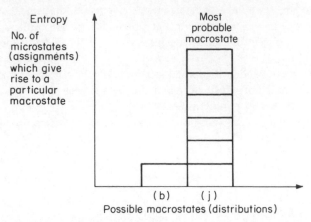

(b)   (j)
Possible macrostates (distributions)

Figure 5.3 Diagrammatic representation of the statistical distribution obtained

Application to origin–destination problem

Now that we have a basic understanding of the entropy maximizing method, we shall consider an example from the social sciences, used by Wilson[8] to explain his methodology.

Our system of interest is going to be the flow of workers from residences to jobs; that is, we are interested in knowing the number of people living in zone i who go to work in zone j. This system can be specified by an origin–destination table as shown below:

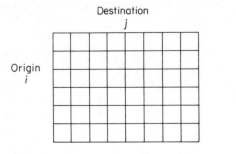

We can define the constraints of the system from the information assumed to be given:

(1) Number of workers living in zone i
(2) Number of jobs available in zone j
(3) Total expenditure on trips in the system.

Then, our interest lies in knowing, within the constraints imposed by the available information, how many workers living in zone i go to work in zone j; in other words, which is the most probable distribution of workers amongst the available jobs.

According to the definition given earlier, a microstate of the system is an assignment of individual persons to the origin–destination table which does not violate any of the constraints. A macrostate of the system is a distribution of movements regardless of the individual persons. This distribution of trips to work can be expressed in matrix form, where a number of trips is assigned to each cell of the origin–destination table, that is, a matrix distribution $\{I_{ij}\}$.

Wilson[10] has shown that the number of microstates (assignments) associated with any distribution $\{I_{ij}\}$ is as follows:

$$W(\{I_{ij}\}) = \frac{\sum\limits_{i=1}^{n} \sum\limits_{j=1}^{m} I_{ij}!}{\prod\limits_{i=1}^{n} \prod\limits_{j=1}^{m} I_{ij}!} \quad (5.3)$$

where I_{ij} = number of workers living in zone i and working in zone j

$W(\{I_{ij}\})$ = number of microstates associated with the matrix of distribution $\{I_{ij}\}$; that is, how many microstates give rise to a particular macrostate of the system expressed by the matrix distribution $\{I_{ij}\}$.

Batty,[12] referring to Wilson's methodology applied to residential location, makes the following comments:

A fundamental idea emerges from this work, for Wilson is able to demonstrate that by viewing location models as summations of inter-actions, new insights can arise in the modelling of spatial structure and behaviour.

Level of aggregation and categorization

Introduction

In order to deal with the level of aggregation and categorization in urban models, a brief review of the question of resolution level and hierarchical order of sub-systems will be outlined here. This is done because it is against these backgrounds that the level of aggregation and categorization in urban models can be seen.

Resolution level

The example of a city as an urban system can be described by considering it as an element within a system of cities. With one city as a system, all other cities form the environment of the system. At a national level, the individual city systems can be viewed as elements in a national urban system. This change in the level of viewpoint is described as a change in *resolution level*. From this level an individual system or group of systems is viewed.

In the example quoted, the resolution levels are in the form of a hierarchy which is open at both ends. Resolution level and the hierarchy concept are illustrated in Figure 5.4. The inverted branching tree analogy is used to show differing levels. It should be remembered that each element is a system which contains the elements indicated at the next lower resolution level or vice versa.

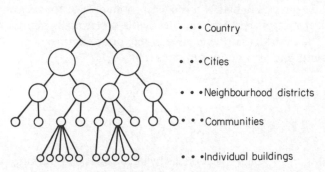

Figure 5.4 System resolution level and hierarchies

A change in the resolution level causes a corresponding change in the view-point of the observer. This change of viewpoint in terms of the resolution level can be seen in the different ways in which urban phenomena can be viewed.

If we analyse the entities or elements used in the urban spatial system, a hierarchy in terms of increasing generality or increasing detail can be made. The level in the hierarchy which the model considers can then be termed the degree of aggregation or categorization. Aggregation however can occur not only in a vertical sense but also at a horizontal level in terms of different characteristics of an element at a particular level of resolution.

Level of aggregation
The level of aggregation has usually been taken to mean the level of *spatial* aggregation, or the size of zones in the model.

A wide variety of choices is possible. For example, some models use city blocks as their basic unit, while others use square miles or large units. In the 'Econometric model of metropolitan employment and population growth',[13] the plan area is divided into only the central city and the metropolitan ring. On the other hand, models like the San Francisco CRP model[14] divide the city into 4980 two-acre zones.

Level of categorization
The level of categorization is generally referred to as the degree of stratification of the variables other than land which are present in the model. For example, the population variable is frequently categorized into some of the following classes:

Income level
Household size
Car ownership
Sex
Age, etc.

Often, the degree of population categorization is directly related to the level of aggregation; the greater the level of disaggregation of space, the greater the population stratification.

The most common categorization of economic activity is by types of employment, as for example:

Industrial
Retail trade
Office workers.

There is a common but unnecessary relationship between the underlying theory of the model and the degree of aggregation and categorization employed. Most behavioural models tend to be quite disaggregate, while models based on a social physics approach generally employ aggregate measures.

The extent to which a model builder can and should disaggregate the variables used in the model, will depend upon:

(1)   The structure and texture of the plan area.
(2)   The availability and quality of data. It is no use defining a set of very small zones if all the available data refer to very much larger ones.
(3)   Storage and process limitations of the computational method used.
(4)   The nature of the question to be answered, that is, the stated objectives of the model.

The choice of a particular resolution level and degrees of aggregation and categorization can therefore be seen as presenting thousands of different possible urban systems, and this shows the importance of the model builder's objective.

Solution methods
There are several procedures to determine values from mathematical models, but three general methods are prominent; the choice between them largely depends on the degree of logico-mathematical coherence of the model itself:

Analytical method
Numerical method
Simulation method.

Analytical method

According to Lowry,[5] the analytical method 'is the neatest and most elegant method'; he continues, 'ordinarily, it is applicable only to models which exhibit very tight logical structures and whose internal functional relationships are uncomplicated by non-linearity and discontinuities'.

This procedure consists of a numerical evaluation of a solution that has been obtained analytically; in other words, we do not consider any particular set of values of the controllable variables; we just proceed directly to the solution by solving the equations by the use of calculus or other means.

Numerical method

According to Lowry,[5] this method is 'used by models lacking complete logical closure or whose structures are overburdened with inconvenient mathematical relationship'.

In this method, a set of numerical values of the controlled variables are tried out by inserting them into the model, and the outcome is calculated by normal arithmetical operations. By trying a number of possible solutions, the best (or approximately best) can be identified and selected. Using this method, the solution itself is directly obtained in numerical (rather than abstract) form.

The selection of a set of output values which satisfy all the equations of the model may be achieved in several ways. There are two common approaches:

(1)   By a heuristic approach, that is, by a trial-and-error procedure. Frequently, with the help of graphical plots, one can more rapidly determine the neighbourhood of the optimum and concentrate one's trials in the region. One of the disadvantages of this approach, is that it fails to signal the existence of alternative solution sets.

(2)   By an iterative procedure, which is a process for calculating a result by performing a series of trials repeatedly, and in which successive approximations tend to approach an optimal solution. An example of this technique is linear programming.

Other approaches have been proposed, as Ackoff[15] points out; 'Recently there has been another development which may make numerical procedures even more accessible. It involves the use of logical techniques (Boolean algebra) to reduce the number of possible solutions which must be considered.'

Simulation method

Before we describe the use of this technique as a solution method, an analysis of the general technique of simulation will be presented.

Simulation is a way of manipulating a model so that it imitates reality; in other words, it is a way of using a model in order to obtain a motion picture of reality. It will be stressed that models tend to *represent* the real world and by the process of simulation they attempt to *imitate* this world (Ackoff and Sasieni[4]). Simon[16] says:

> Generally, we now call the imitation 'simulation', and we try to under-
> stand the imitated system by testing the simulation in a variety of
> simulated or imitated environments'.

The technique of simulation always involves the manipulation of a model, and consequently the benefits of this technique cannot be separated from the advantages of working with models.

Some of the advantages of simulation are (Beer[9]):

(1)   It provides artificial experience of the real system very much more quickly than it could be otherwise obtained.
(2)   The experience is gained without running any risks.
(3)   It is even possible to alter the system as it now is, to see what would be likely to happen to it under a new kind of regime.

According to Ackoff:[15]

> In principle, everything that can be accomplished by simulation can be
> accomplished by experimenting directly on the phenomena involved in the
> problem. In practice, however, it may be impossible or impractical to
> experiment on the phenomena themselves.

Beer[9] makes the following comments:

> The whole virtue of simulation is that it explores the influence of the
> difficult features of real life. Having run a simulation and procured a set of
> results, it is possible to postulate influences which were not originally
> taken into account – and to run the simulation again. This is a full scale
> experimental method.

We can deduce that simulation is a powerful technique for producing conditional forecasting because, when employed in urban models, it allows the planner to work out (generally in the computer laboratory) the behaviour of an urban system under varying conditions. Of course, this technique is widely used to analyse business enterprises, hospitals, airports and other systems. For example, a model of a production system can be processed to deduce the effect of different machine loading, scheduling and dispatching procedures, and so avoid the cost of trying out new scheduling procedures in the real system. Also, several months of activity of a large airport can be simulated in a matter of minutes, so testing alternative operating or design plans.

A simulation model typically consists of four major components (Kilbridge, O'Block and Teplitz[17]):

(1)   Status variables
(2)   Exogenous variables
(3)   Functional relations
(4)   Output.

Status variables
We may recall that the set of attribute values at any point in time defines the state of the system, and that the attributes of system entities may change through time; thus, we may call them state or status variables. In urban spatial systems, they either describe the state within the urban area at the beginning of the period (such as land-use pattern), or they describe constraints (such as existing zone regulations) on the operation of the model during the period.

McMillan and González[18] comment that,

> State variables . . . must be given an initial value, but relationships in the system are periodically evaluated so that the system model is said to generate values for these variables. And (not to add to the confusion) we might point out that because these values are generated within the model, and depend on what happened earlier in the simulation, these values − or rather the variables to which the values are assigned − are called endogenous variables.

Thus, we shall use the following terms interchangeably: status, state and endogenous variables.

The output obtained from running the model for one time period, frequently becomes part of the status variable input for the subsequent period.

Exogenous variables
These are those which, for reasons of convenience or cost, are not built into the basic statement of the model. By far the most important type of exogenous variable is that used for impact analysis. For example, to test the potential consequences of public policies on the system represented by a model, alternative policies can be programmed and inserted independently as exogenous variables.

Functional relations
The set of functional relations are the heart of the model which attempts to depict the real-life system being modelled. The practical usefulness of the model depends largely upon how successful its designers have been in capturing the real world in these statements.

The value of such parameters, exponents or coefficients, can be changed from one run to the next, the value used characterizing a variable of the system during that run. In this way, the exact nature of the functional relationships can be tried out and, in effect, the underlying theory of the model tested.

Output

The model's output describes the state of the activity at the end of the period; output data may, in turn, become status variables for the next period.

Machine simulation with intervention

Although simulation models can be designed to operate autonomously in a computer from beginning to end of their cycle, many are structured for human intervention. In a man—machine simulation, the computer processing of input data is periodically interrupted and the intermediate state of the system is read off for examination by a human participant.

There are two common reasons for the existence of machine simulation models with intervention (Lowry[5]). The human participant is ordinarily included for educational reasons — to give him practice in responding to planning problems. On occasion, the human participant is there simply because the model builder does not fully trust his model to behave 'sensibly' under unusual circumstances.

Simulation as a solution method

Having explained the scope of the simulation procedure, we will analyse the way in which this technique is used as a solution method for obtaining results from models.

The principal use of simulation, in deriving or testing solutions from decision or planning models, occurs when the model contains stochastic expressions that are difficult or impossible to evaluate analytically; that is, when probability distribution cannot be analytically expressed, or cost and computational complexity become excessive.

The evaluation or testing of a proposed solution to a decision or planning model by simulation consists of running the system (generally in a computer) for a set of values of the controlled variables in order to generate enough instances of outcomes for their distribution to be determined.

Simulation for this use normally involves large amounts of computation; hence this procedure has been stimulated by the advent of high-speed electronic computers. The association of simulation exclusively with computers is wrong, because their use is not essential to the procedure.

Random sampling of a variable's possible values is the basis of simulation in this kind of problem. Therefore, to carry out a simulation, random numbers are required and they must be converted into random variables from the relevant distribution. This application of sampling is called the *Monte Carlo* procedure. According to Churchman, Ackoff and Arnoff,[19]

The Monte Carlo technique is a procedure by which we can obtain
approximate evaluations of mathematical expressions which are built up
of one or more probability distribution functions;

and in essence

consists of simulating an experiment to determine some probabilistic
property of a population of objects or events by the use of random
sampling applied to the components of the objects or events.

The treatment of time
The behaviour of a system depends on the change in the states of the system
through time. The manner in which this change in state occurs is therefore of
considerable importance. According to the treatment of time, we can make a
distinction between: static models and dynamic models.

The choice involves the model builder's perceptions of (Lowry[5]):

(1)   The self-equilibrating features of the world represented by his model
(2)   Empirical evaluation of response-lags amongst his variables
(3)   His interest in impact analysis.

Static models
They are also called comparative static, static equilibrium, or 'one shot' models.
These models attempt to simulate an equilibrium pattern of spatial structure at
one point in time; that is, they usually represent a cross-section of the urban
system at some date. As Batty[12] says 'the temporal element, which contains the
sequence of causes and effects which compose the behaviour of such systems,
is not within the ambit of these models'.

The process by which the system moves from its initial to its terminal state
is unspecified in these models; they are not particularly concerned with how the
terminal state is reached. Basically, models of this type would be used for
testing the feasibility of future sketch plans of town configuration and can
especially be used for impact analysis, assuming that the future form of a city
or region could reach an equilibrium condition. These models imply a
'conviction that the system is strongly self equilibrating, that is, that the
endogenous variables respond quickly and fully to exogenous changes' (Lowry[5]).

As McLoughlin[20] states, referring to these models: 'The logic of this approach
is to regard the city at the present time as a system in unstable equilibrium which
is then "disturbed" by the addition of a number of elements of change'. A
typical example of this type of model is Lowry's 'Model of Metropolis'.

Dynamic models
Most of the real decision problems faced in urban systems are related to the
dynamic characteristics of the metropolitan areas rather than to static optimal

(equilibrium) conditions. This approach deals implicitly with change and with trends of development, and so it focuses attention on the process of change, rather than on the terminal state of the system at a specified date.

In these models, self-equilibration is not a necessary assumption; but if the system is self-equilibrating, the values of its variables should be the same as those obtained by a static model. Dynamic models tend to answer the question of how development will actually take place, considering that private decision makers take a relatively short view and tend to inspect closely only conditions which exist at the time of their decisions.

The ideal way to formulate dynamic models can be as a system of differential equations or difference equations, that is, in an analytical form (analytical dynamics). This approach requires that all variables except time are endogenous (complete closure). But as Harris[7] says, referring to the formulation of dynamic models in terms of differential equations or difference equations,

> It is generally somewhat unusual to find a model explicitly formulated in one of these manners, owing to the analytic complexity of metropolitan relationships. We find instead, the use of recursive sets of models in which the changes taken place in a given period depend on the state of the system at the beginning of this period, and hence indirectly on the changes of the preceding periods and the states at earlier times.

These recursive models show the stepwise sequences through which the spatial form of the urban system could pass. Examination of recursive models shows the following necessary characteristics:

(1) The model must possess a causal chain, logical in terms of models methodology.
(2) The modelling process may vary in the number of stages before initial input becomes final output. The model may contain a number of interrelated parts or submodels each with its own sequence of operation. These submodels are connected since output from one submodel will be input for another.
(3) The model can operate through varying periods of time. The time period considered for the model operation may vary.

Figure 5.5 illustrates a model in two stages, possibly two submodels. The recursive nature of the model is seen in the feedback loops indicated. Within the submodel of stage two, the feedback loops allow triple iteration which takes place during the period $t_2 - t_4$. In other models, submodels may be coupled in parallel or in a combination of series and parallel with differing iterative characteristics.

According to Batty:[12]

> Difficulties in the collection of time-series data have meant that dynamic models have not been forthcoming, although at present it is gradually

being realised that time is an extremely important dimension in land use modelling.

Of course, dynamic models are of great utility in making realistic decisions about the impact of policy and the feasibility of development programmes; but clearly, both dynamic models and static models have a role to play in the planning process.

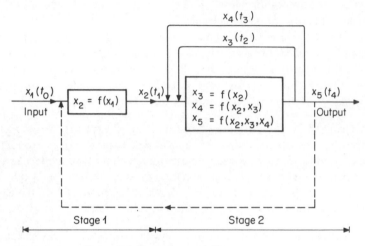

Figure 5.5 Recursive modelling: two stages

It should be stressed at this point, that very interesting research is being carried out to simulate urban systems as dynamic ones. A fundamental work in every sense is Forrester's *Urban Dynamics*,[21] where difference equations are also used. Urban systems as other complex systems, such as a corporation, an economy, a government, etc., are seen by Forrester as feedback processes having a specific and orderly structure. One of the basic elements invoked by his model is a feedback relationship which allows interrelationships between different subsystems, provision for delays, implication of multiple goals, etc. to take place; thus, permitting the characteristics of complex systems such as the urban system to be simulated.

The city represented by Forrester's model — although it occupies 100,000 acres — has no spatial dimension; that is, there is no physical accommodation or allocation of activities to land space. Additionally, as a consequence of the absence of a spatial dimension, there is no specific transport sector.

Forrester[21] points out that:

It has become clear that complex systems are counterintuitive. That is, they give indications that suggest corrective action which will often be ineffective or even adverse in its results. Very often one finds that the policies that have been adopted for correcting a difficulty are actually intensifying it rather than producing a solution.

also, complex systems

... have a high sensitivity to changes in a few parameters and to some changes in structure. If a policy at one of these points is changed, pressures radiate through the system.

Chadwick[3] comments about Forrester's urban dynamics model:

The model has attracted criticism both for its advocacy of unpopular (some would say, unfounded) policies, and for some of its technical points, especially regarding the sensitivity of its parameters. On the first score, it may be that Forrester has drawn too sweeping conclusions from too little evidence, evidence based on perhaps on inadequate data. Data for real cities, especially long time series, may be hard to come by, but the results of using a real case study might seem to carry more potential value as a policy test-bed. On the other hand, it *is* true that most remedial urban policies have been invented from a very simple cause-and-effect view of urban phenomena (not "urban systems") whereas real urban systems, because of feedback complexity, as Forrester points out, are counter-intuitive, and simplistic analogies are unlikely to be helpful. On the second point, of parameter sensitivity, it seems highly probable that Forrester is right: such systems may well be insensitive to all but a few parameter changes.

5.4 Basic principles of model building

The basic principles of model design described here are based on general principles outlined by a number of authors (Harris;[7] Lowry;[5] Wilson;[22]), and are grouped under the following sub-headings:

(1) Definition of the problem
(2) Variables
(3) Data availability
(4) Strategic alternatives
    (a) Theoretical approach
    (b) Level of aggregation and categorization
    (c) Solution methods
    (d) Treatment of time
(5) Calibration methodology
(6) Evaluation of performance.

Definition of the problem

'Firstly, it is necessary to be clear-minded about the purpose of the model: what questions is the model trying to answer?' (Wilson[22]). Logically, in the case of urban spatial systems, the questions will differ from city to city and with the city size. In some cases, emphasis should be placed on the provision of an adequate transport network, or on a housing development plan. All these situations need different types of models.

Variables

The purpose of the model and the intentions of the model builder determine which variables the model is going to refer to. It is also necessary to investigate which of these variables can be (at least partially) controlled by the planners.

A distinction can be made between observed and constructed variables. According to Batty:[23] 'Observed variables are directly measured quantities in the urban system, such as *population* and *employment*' and constructed variables '. . . are not directly observed but are computed from observed variables. They can be sums of observed variables or ratios or weighted averages, or much more complicated quantities, but in all cases they are derived from algebraic manipulations of observed variables' (Seidman D. R.; in Batty[23]). Examples of constructed variables are densities, activity rates, etc.

Young[24] points out:

> In practice the choice of variables is influenced by the availability of data, by the range of conceivable real-life changes to stocks of buildings and land, by the importance attached to greater or lesser detailed consideration of different amenities and other factors, by the desired level of detail of any results of the model and by the constraints to be used. The choice will be dependent to some extent on whether or not a computer is available and even on the type of available computer.

Data availability

To produce a model of the system under study, urban planners require a comprehensive knowledge of the area which they are planning, and so the relevant data must be available to allow them to do so. Ideally, the data required for a particular model should be specially collected in new surveys, but in practice this is not possible, for reasons of time and cost. The main sources of data are the censuses, the large scale transportation studies and a variety of other local sources.

One of the major problems faced by planners is on the subject of information, that is, to decide the type and the amount of information required and the reason for it. Large amounts of money and time are spent in obtaining data which are never used, while in many cases the necessary data are lacking. Data are sometimes confused with information, which is said to result from the processing of data, so that information derives from the assembly, analysis and/or summarizing of data into meaningful form.

The use of computers has facilitated the obtaining, processing, storage and retrieval of information, and, as computerization increases, facilities for handling data will improve and there have been serious developments towards the concept of an urban data bank.

The urban system is a dynamic one, and so data collected about it at one moment in time are a static representation of it; to overcome this limitation, it is necessary to re-collect data periodically. Thus, we see that the availability of data plays a very important role in the process of model building.

In relation to data availability, Forrester[21] makes very interesting comments:

> In the social sciences failure to understand systems is often blamed on inadequate data. The barrier to progress in social systems is not lack of data. We have vastly more information than we use in an orderly and organized way. The barrier is deficiency in the existing theories of structure. The conventional forms of data-gathering will seldom produce new insights into the details of system structure.

Further on he adds:

> A shortage of information is not a major barrier to understanding urban dynamics. One can say the same for other complex systems. The barrier is the lack of willingness and ability to organize the information that already exists into a structure that represents the structure of the actual system and therefore has an opportunity to behave as the real system would.

Strategic alternatives

The decisions related to the following important questions are referred to here as strategic alternatives in model building:

(1) What theories about the system under study are we trying to represent in the model? (theoretical approach)
(2) How are the variables going to be categorized, and what is the size of the area unit to be used? (level of aggregation and categorization)
(3) What solution procedure is the model going to employ? (solution methods)
(4) How is the time factor going to be treated? (the treatment of time).

These strategic alternatives have been already described under 'Strategy of model building' (see page 63).

Calibration methodology

Introduction

'Calibration is the process of finding the parameter values of the model which make it fit the real world in the best possible way' (Batty[25]). The fitting of parameters is necessary for two reasons (Lowry[5]):

> One: theoretical principles and deductive reasoning therefrom are seldom sufficient to indicate more than the appropriate sign (positive or negative) and probable order of magnitude for such constants.
>
> ... and two: since these constants are measures of relationships between numerical variables, the precise empirical definition of the variable affects the value of the parameter.

For example, the age of the population concerned affects among other factors the value of the parameter 'labour force participation rate'.

Methods

The methods for obtaining estimates of the various parameters may vary considerably. The following methods are the most commonly used:

(1)   Analytical method
(2)   Heuristic method
(3)   'Human' method.

Analytical method

Parameter fitting by the analytical method is a highly developed branch of statistical analysis. The most common tool is regression analysis.

In the case of linear equations, precise estimating techniques have been developed in statistics to obtain the values of such parameters, as for example the least squares method. Sometimes, with non-linear equations, it may be possible to carry out some transformation to make the equations linear and apply the simple procedure mentioned earlier.

Heuristic method

When the model is too complex for analytical solution or for some other reasons, trial and error methods are adopted. A range of parameter values is specified and each one of these is put in the model, the model is run, and its performance assessed. The parameter value which gives the best performance is then adopted.

'Human' method

According to Lowry,[5] model builders sometimes despair of finding the values of parameters and resort to 'human' parameters:

At the appropriate point in the operation of the model, intermediate or preliminary results are scanned by persons of respected judgment, who are asked to alter these outputs to conform to an intuitive standard of plausibility based on their experience in the field. The altered data are then fed back to the computer for further processing.

Alternatives

Parameters can be fitted either in the context of the system itself or outside the system, that is, independently.

When the fitting of parameters takes place inside the context of the system, the parametric values are chosen in such a way as to optimize the performance of the system as *a whole* for a given set of data. If the model can be formulated as a set of simultaneous linear equations, the analytical method of solution can be easily applied. In most cases, a formulation of this kind is not possible, and in order to obtain the best fit for the parameters in the system as a whole, a heuristic method based on an iteration procedure is generally applied, in which combinations of parameter values are tested. The main disadvantage of this procedure is its cost because, where there are x values for each parameter and y parameters, the model has to run x^y times. Thus, the computer time increases exponentially with the number of parameters.

In the alternative case, when the parameters are fitted independently, that is, outside the context of the system, the model is partitioned into smaller systems of equations (some may only contain a single parameter) in such a way that the parameters of each subsystem can be fitted independently. This approach is common in model building, since the systems of equations used by the larger models are too complex to allow them to obtain a 'best fit' for all parameters of the system. This approach has been used by Lowry[2] in his 'A Model of Metropolis' where he comments:

There is no guarantee that such an assemblage of independently-fitted components will function smoothly together; but if they do, at least the performance of the system can not be dismissed as merely reflecting built-in circularity.

The fitting of parameters outside the framework of the model is considered by Batty[12] as:

... highly unsatisfactory for they ignore the interdependencies between parameter values in the model.

In conclusion, none of the approaches is completely satisfactory and further research is needed in calibration methodology.

Evaluation of performance

The many factors which have been described can be seen as the vocabulary for the model builder in the design and production of models of the urban spatial structure. It is imperative that these models be vigorously evaluated before there is a widespread introduction of them in the planning process.

The testing of a model is the procedure by which the model maker evaluates how adequately the model represents the real world situation. Although part of the model is tested simultaneously with its construction, once it is completed, the model has to be tested as a whole. It is this phase of testing with which we are primarily concerned here. The aspects of the evaluation as well as of model construction itself are: (1) determination of whether the model contains the relevant variables and parameters; (2) whether these constants and variables are evaluated appropriately, and (3) whether the functional form is proper. Ackoff[15] indicates the way in which a model can fall into error:

(1) The model may contain variables which are not relevant; that is, have no effect on the outcome. Their inclusion in the model, then, makes the predicted outcome depend on factors on which it has no dependence in reality.

(2) The model may not include variables which are relevant; that is, ones that do affect the outcome.

(3) The function *f*, which relates the controllable and uncontrollable variables to the outcome, may be incorrect.

(4) The numerical values assigned to the variables may be inaccurate.

Builders of models of the urban spatial structure, find it extremely difficult to establish clear and objective standards of performance, and according to Lowry,[5] the appropriate test of a model depends on its predetermined function. It is obviously illogical to expect a descriptive model to make a prediction or a predictive model to find an optimal solution.

In a descriptive model, where the model simulates features of a 'real system' through supplied information inputs, evaluation can take place by direct comparison with the real system. Changes in information input may be wherever they are found to be deficient.

Problems may arise when attempting to fit a model's structure and behaviour to a particular time- (and place-) dependent real system in descriptive models. Fitting the model in this case may cause a lack of generality, usually as a result of particular exogenously supplied inputs or constraints which become inapplicable when used in modelling an alternative time- (and place-) dependent system.

In the case of predictive models, the appropriate test usually involves running the model, obtaining a prediction, and verifying this prediction against the real urban system situation. This is usually done by calibrating the model for past periods and obtaining a prediction of present time conditions.

The test of a planning or decision model can be performed by checking on the ability of the model to select an optimal solution from several alternatives. Lowry[5] indicates the reason why this model may fail to do so:

(1) Short-cut methods may eliminate as suboptimal some outcomes which have more promise than they immediately show;

(2) The evaluation of outcomes may be very sensitive to engineering estimates of cost or imputation of benefits, and these are intrinsically nebulous;

(3) The criteria of selection may be poorly stated, so that an outcome which would in fact be acceptable to the client is classified as unacceptable by the model.

Obviously, an effective evaluation of a model cannot be obtained if the model is tested against the same data which were used to obtain values for the parameters and estimates for the functional form. Generally, when possible, the available data are divided into two parts: one is used for the process of obtaining estimates of the parameters and functional form, and the other half of the data is used for testing the model.

An alternative means of evaluation can be performed using the mathematical methods of 'sensitivity analysis'. This method provides an indication of the strength of the model design, in terms of the model characteristics, as opposed to accuracy in description, prediction and optimization. Lowry[5] describes this method as follows:

By varying the value of a single parameter (or even of an input variable) in successive runs of the model, one can measure the difference in outcome associated with a given parametric change. If the model's response to wide differences in parametric values is insignificant, this may be an indication that the parameter − and the associated network of functional relations − is superfluous. On the other hand, extreme sensitivity of outcomes to parametric changes indicates either that the parameter in question had better be fitted with great care, or that some further elaboration of this component of the model is in order − on the grounds that the analogous real world system must in fact have built-in compensations to forestall wild fluctuation in outcome.

Generally, the model is compared with the real-world situation by comparing values of the outcome given by the model with actual outcomes, when these can be determined with little or no error. Commonly, to show the fit between these two results, the correlation of determination (R^2) and the chi-square are used. It is important to notice that in some cases, high levels of the coefficient of determination or low levels of chi-square do not necessarily imply high accuracy or reliability of the model. In other cases, by examining carefully not only the statistical measures used in the model, but the structure of the model itself, some possible inconsistencies and contradictions may be found, which will lower the value of the coefficient of determination for the period of calibration, but which will increase its reliability.

References
  1 LOWRY, I. S. 'Seven models of urban development: a structural comparation'. Special Report 97, Highway Research Board, Washington D.C., 1968.
  2 LOWRY, I. S. *A Model of Metropolis*. Rand Corporation, Santa Monica, California, 1964.
  3 CHADWICK, G. *A Systems View of Planning*. Pergamon Press, Oxford, 1971.
  4 ACKOFF, R. L. and SASIENI, M. W. *Fundamentals of Operations Research*. John Wiley and Sons, Inc., 1968.
  5 LOWRY, I. S. 'A short course in model design'. *Journal of the American Institute of Planners*, 1965, May, pp. 158–166.
  6 HARRIS, B. 'The use of theory in the simulation of urban phenomena'. *Journal of the American Institute of Planners*, 1966, September, pp. 258–273.
  7 HARRIS, B. 'Quantitative models of urban development: their role in metropolitan policy-making', in PERLOFF, HARVEY, S. and WINGO, LOWDON JR. *Issues in Urban Economics*, Johns Hopkins, Baltimore, 1968.
  8 WILSON, A. G. *Entropy in Urban and Regional Modelling*. Pion Limited, London, 1970.
  9 BEER, S. *Decision and Control*. John Wiley and Sons Ltd., Chichester, 1966.
 10 WILSON, A. G. 'A statistical theory of spatial distribution models'. *Transportation Research*, 1968, vol. 1, no. 3, pp. 253–270.
 11 LAND USE AND BUILT FORM STUDIES. 'Urban system studies, demostrations and seminars'. University of Cambridge, 1972, July.
 12 BATTY, M. 'Recent developments in land use modelling: a review of British research'. Urban Systems Research Unit, Department of Geography, University of Reading, Whiteknights, Reading, 1970.
 13 NIEDERCORN, J. H. *'An Econometric Model of Metropolitan Employment and Population Growth*. RM-3758-RC, Rand Corporation, Santa Monica, California, 1963, October.
 14 LITTLE, A. D. *Model of San Francisco Housing Market*. San Francisco Community Renewal C65400, Cambridge, 1966, January.
 15 ACKOFF, R. L. *Scientific Method*. John Wiley and Sons, Inc., New York 1968.
 16 SIMON, H. A. *The Sciences of the Artificial*. The M.I.T. Press, 1969.
 17 KILBRIDGE, M. D., O'BLOCK, R. P., TEPLITZ, P. V. 'A conceptual framework for urban planning models'. *Management Science*, 1966, vol. 15, February, no. 6.
 18 McMILLAN, C. and GONZALEZ, R. F. *Systems Analysis: A Computer Approach to Decision Models*. Richard D. Irvin Inc., 1971, December.

19 CHURCHMAN, C., ACKOFF, R. and ARNOFF, E. L. *Introduction to Operations Research.* John Wiley and Sons Inc., New York, 1968.
20 McLOUGHLIN, J. *Urban and Regional Planning.* Faber and Faber, London, 1970.
21 FORRESTER, J. W. *Urban Dynamics.* The M.I.T. Press, Cambridge, Mass., 1969.
22 WILSON, A. G. 'Models in urban planning: a synoptic review of recent literature'. *Abstract in Urban Studies,* 1968, November, pp. 249–276.
23 BATTY, M. 'Spatial theory and information systems'. Urban Systems Research Unit, Department of Geography, University of Reading, 1970.
24 YOUNG, W. 'Planning – A Linear Programming Model'. *GLC Intelligence Unit Quarterly Bulletin,* no. 19, 1972, June.
25 BATTY, M. 'Introductory model-building problems for urban and regional planning'. Urban Systems Research Unit, Department of Geography, University of Reading, 1970.

6 Spatial Interaction Models

6.1 Framework

Planners have always been interested in the spatial structure of the urban system, that is to say, in the way in which elements are located in space and their spatial interaction.

Generally, models of the urban spatial structure contain one or more interaction models, according to the number and types of activities dealt with in the system under study. It is for this reason that interaction models are generally considered as submodels in the sense that they are always part of a more comprehensive model.

A considerable amount of research has been carried out into models and theories which describe the interaction of movement between sets of activities. Here will be described the most important and commonly used concepts of human interaction.

6.2 Gravity models

This group of models was the earliest kind of interaction model used and was developed by analogy with Newton's Law of Gravitation expressed by the formula

$$F = G \frac{M_1 M_2}{d^2}$$

where F = force with which each mass pulls the other
M_1, M_2 = size of masses concerned
d = distance between them
G = universal constant, the pull of gravity.

Carrothers[1] has stated the basic gravity concept of interaction:

The gravity concept of human interaction postulates that an attracting force of interaction between two areas of human activity is created by the population masses of the two areas, and a friction against interaction is caused by the intervening space over which the interaction must take place.

In other words, interaction between two centres of population concentration or focal points varies directly with some function of the population size (N) of the two centres and inversely with some function of the distance between them. This relationship can be expressed mathematically as follows:

$$I_{ij} = \frac{f(N_i, N_j)}{f(d_{ij})} \qquad (6.1)$$

where I_{ij} = interaction between centre i and centre j
N_i, N_j = population of zones i and j respectively
d_{ij} = distance between centre i and centre j.

Later developments of the basic concepts have introduced other key variables in place of population N and distance d, and to cope with these adjustments, a more general expression for this formulation will be used here:

$$I_{ij} = K \frac{O_i D_j}{T_{ij}} = K O_i D_j T_{ij}^{-1} \qquad (6.2)$$

where I_{ij} = interaction between an origin zone i and destination zone j. It may be measured in terms of person flows, sales, etc., depending on the activity being considered.

O_i = level of demand requirements generated or produced at the origin zone i. Henceforth this variable will be called 'production' variable. The measure of demand depends on the activity considered and can be expressed as the total number of workers within a residence zone, or available expenditure for shopping generated within a residence zone.

D_j = level of opportunities in zone j, that is the attractiveness of the destination zone. Then, this variable will be called the 'attraction' variable. The opportunity levels may be measured by the number of jobs available in zone j, the size of shopping centre, etc., depending on the activity concerned.

T_{ij}^{-1} = generalized travel function. Gives a general measure of impedance between zone i and zone j. Although physical distance was the obvious measure to use in the early gravity models, other factors like time and cost have been recently incorporated to the models.

K = constant of proportionality.

It will be pointed out here, that when O_i and/or D_j can not be independently estimated (are not given), they can be represented by I_i and I_j respectively, where

$$I_i = \sum_{j=1}^{n} I_{ij} \qquad (6.3)$$

$$I_j = \sum_{i=1}^{n} I_{ij} \qquad (6.4)$$

In cases where the identities expressed by equations 6.3 and 6.4 cannot be applied, O_i and D_j can be replaced in equation 6.2 by proxy variables $W_i^{(1)}$ and $W_j^{(2)}$, respectively, to which O_i and D_j are thought to be related. For example, suppose that in a shopping model, we have an independent estimate of the shopping trips leaving zone i, that is, we know O_i, but we do not know the total number of trips attracted by the service centre j (D_j), then, we can use some proxy variable $W_j^{(2)}$, such as the number of shops in zone j, in substitution of D_j in equation 6.2. Now, we can estimate the number of total trips attracted by centre j by summing up all trips reaching zone j, that is, applying equation 6.4. This value I_j, not independently estimated, replaces D_j in any further calculation.

Depending on whether constraints are incorporated into the gravity model, two basic cases can be distinguished: the unconstrained case, and the constrained case.

Unconstrained case

According to Carrothers,[1] this kind of interaction model is the earliest known and was developed by H. C. Carey during the first half of the nineteenth century. This group of models can be further classified as:

(1)   Those concerned with measuring the total interaction between two focal points
(2)   Those concerned with measuring the attractive force exerted by a single focal point in competition with one other on an intermediate point.

Unconstrained case type (1)

This type of interaction model is concerned with measuring the total interaction between two zones by means of equation 6.2,

$$I_{ij} = KO_i D_j T_{ij}^{-1}$$

and no constraints are considered. The early models of this type generally used population size as a measure of production O_i and attraction D_j. The generalized travel function was expressed by physical distance raised to some power, $d_{ij}^{-\alpha}$.

The most important limitation of the unconstrained case of the gravity model is that, in predicting, it overestimates interaction. Thus, if we double the value of the input variable O_i and D_j, we get a quadrupling of interactions rather than a more appropriate value as we would expect. This case gives I_{ij} as n^2 quantities, when n is the number of zones.

Examples of this case in practice are the flows of goods from factories not location-constrained (nor production-constrained in any other way) to uses in destinations also not constrained to particular locations.

Unconstrained case type (2)

This type of gravity model has been applied most extensively in the marketing field, where the owner of a retail establishment has been interested in determining the effectiveness of his business in competition with similar traders in other service centres in the area around him.

Probably, the most well-known model of this type is that of Reilly.[2] In 1929, he postulated his 'Law of Retail Gravitation' which approaches the gravity concept from a rather different direction. According to this formulation,

> A city will attract retail trade from an individual in its surrounding territory in direct proportion to the population size of the service centre and in inverse proportion to the square of his distance away from the centre.

The point of equilibrium x on the line joining any two cities where competitive influence is equal, is expressed mathematically by Reilly in the following equation:

$$\frac{N_i}{d_{xi}^2} = \frac{N_j}{d_{xj}^2} \qquad (6.5)$$

where N_i, N_j = population of cities i and j, respectively
x = point of equilibrium on the line joining i and j
d_{xi} = distance from city i to point x
d_{xj} = distance from city j to point x
$d_{ij} = d_{xi} + d_{xj}$.

Manipulation of equation 6.5 gives the break point or equilibrium point x in distance units from city j:

$$d_{xj} = \frac{d_{ij}}{1 + \sqrt{\left(\frac{N_i}{N_j}\right)}} \qquad (6.6)$$

The break point is the point where the probability of trade going to one city is equal to the probability of it going to the competing city.

The effect of this straightforward modification to Reilly's formula (extensively used by Converse[3]) is to define areas over which each competing shopping centre is dominant. These catchment areas tend to suggest that spheres of influence are mutually exclusive, whereas research on shopping habits suggests that most households patronize a variety of shopping centres for different types of goods.

The improved version of the 'catchment area' approach to retail activities recognizes this complexity in shopping patterns by defining catchment areas at several levels of hierarchy, and in this way, the largest centres compete at all levels. One of the advantages of this method used to define catchment areas is its manual application.

Constrained case
Wilson[4] has pointed out the need to introduce constraints in order to avoid the limitations imposed by the unconstrained case; and more recently, Wilson[5,6] has shown that a whole family of spatial interaction models can be derived by defining different types of constraints. Two of these will be introduced at this stage:

$$\sum_{j=1}^{n} I_{ij} = O_i \qquad (6.7)$$

$$\sum_{i=1}^{n} I_{ij} = D_j \qquad (6.8)$$

An alternative explanation of these two equations is that the specified (input) and calculated (output) total production and attraction respectively, balance for individual zones.

Depending on the fact that one or both constraints are incorporated to the model, three distinct cases can be distinguished:
(1) Production constrained case
(2) Attraction constained case
(3) Production–attraction constrained case.

Production constrained case
In this case the constraint

$$I_i = \sum_{j=1}^{n} I_{ij} = O_i \qquad (6.7)$$

must be satisfied and I_i is independently estimated (given as O_i). The spatial interaction model only estimates $n^2 - n$ quantities I_{ij}, since the n identities given by equation 6.7 are known. This constraint equation states that the sum of all flows between a particular origin i and all destination zones j sum to the known demand generated at that origin. The use of this constraint also implies that the spatial system is considered as a 'closed' system in the sense that no flow leaves the area under study.

An example of this case is the shopping model, because available expenditure is constant and the sales at the service centre are unconstrained. In this example, I_{ij} may represent sales in a shopping centre j by the residents of zone i; and O_i may be the expenditure power available at i.

Since in this single constrained case, an independent estimate of D_j is not available, the attraction variable D_j is replaced in equation 6.2 by its proxy $W_j^{(2)}$. In our example, proxies that have been used to index attractive power may be number of shops, number of retail remployees, shopping floor space and retail sales themselves.

Then $\qquad\qquad I_{ij} = KO_i W_j^{(2)} T_{ij}^{-1} \qquad (6.9)$

and substituting in equation 6.7 we have

$$\sum_{j=1}^{n} KO_i W_j^{(2)} T_{ij}^{-1} = O_i$$

This constraint can only be satisfied if a set of proportionality constants $K_i^{(1)}$ replaces the single constant K.

Then
$$K_i^{(1)} = \frac{1}{\sum\limits_{j=1}^{n} W_j^{(2)} T_{ij}^{-1}}$$
(6.10)

and so

$$I_{ij} = K_i^{(1)} O_i W_j^{(2)} T_{ij}^{-1} = O_i \frac{W_j^{(2)} T_{ij}^{-1}}{\sum\limits_{j=1}^{n} W_j^{(2)} T_{ij}^{-1}}$$
(6.11)

Potential concept

This form of equation is readily understood by considering an alternative approach based on a 'potential' concept. This concept may be thought of as a measure indicating the intensity of the possibility of interaction. The basic principles underlying potential models can be formulated as follows (Carrothers[1]):

At a given location i, the potential influence, or possibility of interaction with respect to an individual at i, which is generated by the attractiveness of any given area j, will be greater as the attractiveness of j is larger and will be smaller as the distance between i and j increases. Then, according to this formulation, the accessibility of an origin zone i to attractions in the destination zone j, can be expressed by the basic equation:

$$U_{ij} = \frac{K W_j^{(2)}}{T_{ij}} = K W_j^{(2)} T_{ij}^{-1}$$
(6.12)

where U_{ij} = potential at i of the attractiveness of zone j
$W_j^{(2)}$ = attractiveness of zone j
T_{ij}^{-1} = generalized travel function
K = constant.

To develop the potential formula, an example will be used. If we consider that equation 6.11 gives us the number of trips between i and j (I_{ij}), then, to get the proportion of trips from zone i to any zone j (P_{ij}), we have

$$P_{ij} = \frac{\text{no. of trips from } i \text{ to } j}{\text{no. of trips from } i \text{ to all zones}}$$
(6.13)

$$P_{ij} = \frac{K W_j^{(2)}/T_{ij}}{\dfrac{K W_1^{(2)}}{T_{i1}} + \dfrac{K W_2^{(2)}}{T_{i2}} + \dfrac{K W_3^{(2)}}{T_{i3}} + + + \dfrac{K W_n^{(2)}}{T_{in}}}$$
(6.14)

$$P_{ij} = \frac{K W_j^{(2)}/T_{ij}}{K \sum\limits_{j=1}^{n} \dfrac{W_j^{(2)}}{T_{ij}}} = \frac{W_j^{(2)} T_{ij}^{-1}}{\sum\limits_{j=1}^{n} W_j^{(2)} T_{ij}^{-1}}$$
(6.15)

This proportion can be also considered as the probability that destination zone j will be chosen from the origin zone i.

The number of trips from zone i to zone j can be found by multiplying the number of trips generated in zone i (O_i), by the proportion of them going to zone j, that is

$$U_{ij} = O_i P_{ij} = O_i \frac{W_j^{(2)} T_{ij}^{-1}}{\sum\limits_{j=1}^{n} W_j^{(2)} T_{ij}^{-1}} \qquad (6.16)$$

Comparing equation 6.16 with equation 6.11, we see that they are identical. Here we can see how a different concept of interaction, called potential, can be formulated as constrained gravity models. This fact is precisely one of the relevant conclusions of Wilson's approach. Cordey-Hayes and Wilson[7] comment that:

It does not make sense to talk of a unique gravity model that is generally applicable, but that is more fruitful to explore the underlying hypotheses and to recognize that there is a family of related models of spatial interaction that can be used to represent different situations in different sectoral subsystems.

From equation 6.12, the total possibility of interaction between zone i and all zones of the study area can be derived in the following form

$$U_i = K \sum\limits_{j=1}^{n} \frac{W_j^{(2)}}{T_{ij}} = K \sum\limits_{j=1}^{n} W_j^{(2)} T_{ij}^{-1} \qquad (6.17)$$

where U_i = total potential at i.

This model was used by Lowry[8] in his 'A model of metropolis'.

Attraction constrained case
In this case the constraint

$$I_j = \sum\limits_{i=1}^{n} I_{ij} = D_j \qquad (6.8)$$

must be satisfied and D_j is independently estimated, that is, D_j is available. This constraint equation states that all flows between all origin zones i and a particular destination zone j sum to the known level of opportunities of the destination zone.

This model only estimates $n^2 - n$ quantities I_{ij}, since the n entities given by equation 6.8 are known. The use of this constraint also implies that the spatial system is regarded as 'closed' because no flow comes from outside the study area. An example of this case is the elementary residential location model where I_{ij} can represent the number of people residing in zone i and working in zone j; and D_j the number of jobs available at working zone j. Then, the constraint equation (6.8) states in this example that the number of people residing in all zones and working in zone j cannot exceed the number of jobs available in zone j.

Since an independent estimate of O_i is not available, the production variable O_i is replaced in equation 6.2 by the proxy variable $W_i^{(1)}$. In our example, $W_i^{(1)}$ could be indexed by house price or the number of houses already developed in the zone i. Then equation 6.2 becomes

$$I_{ij} = KW_i^{(1)}D_jT_{ij}^{-1} \tag{6.18}$$

and substituting in equation 6.8 we have

$$\sum_{i=1}^{n} KW_i^{(1)}D_jT_{ij}^{-1} = D_j \tag{6.19}$$

To satisfy this constraint the constant K must be replaced by a set of constants $K_j^{(2)}$ given by

$$K_j^{(2)} = \frac{1}{\sum_{i=1}^{n} W_i^{(1)}T_{ij}^{-1}} \tag{6.20}$$

then

$$I_{ij} = K_j^{(2)}D_jW_i^{(1)}T_{ij}^{-1} = \frac{D_jW_i^{(1)}T_{ij}^{-1}}{\sum_{i=1}^{n} W_i^{(1)}T_{ij}^{-1}} \tag{6.21}$$

This model is illustrative and has been little used in practice, but in any case, to obtain the number of residents in zone i, we just sum over all j:

$$I_i = \sum_{j=1}^{n} I_{ij} \tag{6.3}$$

Production–attraction constrained case
In this case both constraints,

$$I_i = \sum_{j=1}^{n} I_{ij} = O_i \tag{6.7}$$

$$I_j = \sum_{i=1}^{n} I_{ij} = D_j \tag{6.8}$$

must be satisfied and there are independent estimates of the total demand generated at origin i and of the total opportunities at destination zone j. This model only estimates $n^2 - 2n$ quantities I_{ij}, since equations 6.7 and 6.8 give $2n$ entities which are known.

The use of this model is limited to those cases where we are only concerned in estimating the volume of interaction between zones, such as traffic distribution, or in certain limited cases of residential behaviour where both homes and workplaces are fixed.

In the case of a 'journey to work' model, O_i is the number of employees residing in zone i, and D_j is the number of jobs in the destination zone j. I_{ij} is the number of workers who live in i and work in j. Because no proxy variable is used, the gravity equation is the original one:

$$I_{ij} = KO_iD_jT_{ij}^{-1} \qquad (6.2)$$

The constant K in equation 6.2 must be now replaced by a product $K_i^{(3)}K_j^{(4)}$, so that both constraint equations can be satisfied. This gives us a new estimate of I_{ij}:

$$I_{ij} = K_i^{(3)}K_j^{(4)}O_iD_jT_{ij}^{-1} \qquad (6.22)$$

Substituting equation 6.22 into the constraint equations 6.7 and 6.8 we obtain

$$K_i^{(3)} = \frac{1}{\sum_{j=1}^{n} K_j^{(4)}D_jT_{ij}^{-1}} \qquad (6.23)$$

and

$$K_j^{(4)} = \frac{1}{\sum_{i=1}^{n} K_i^{(3)}O_iT_{ij}^{-1}} \qquad (6.24)$$

The equations for $K_i^{(3)}$ and $K_j^{(4)}$ are solved iteratively normally by initially putting $K_j^{(4)} = 1$ in equation 6.23 and then substituting the calculated value of $K_i^{(3)}$ in equation 6.24. This is repeated until a satisfactory convergence is obtained.

6.3 Intervening opportunities model

Introduction

This kind of model differs from the gravity model in the sense that spatial separation is measured not in terms of the absolute travel time, cost, or distance between one zone and the other, but rather in terms of the number of intervening opportunities; thus, interzonal impedance does not appear explicitly in this model, but possible destination zones away from an origin zone i have to be ranked in order of increasing impedance from i.

This model was originally proposed by Stouffer[9] in a simple form, assuming that the number of trips from an origin zone to a destination zone is proportional to the number of opportunities at the destination zone, and inversely proportional to the number of intervening opportunities. Schneider[10] developed this model in an extended form.

The intervening opportunities model utilizes a probability concept which in essence requires that a trip should remain as short as possible, lengthening only as it fails to find an acceptable destination at a lesser distance. The underlying assumption of the model is that the tripper considers each opportunity, as reached, in turn, and has a definite probability that his needs will be satisfied. An equal area-wide probability of acceptance for any origin is defined for all destinations in a given category.

During the model's operation, the first opportunity considered is the one closest to the origin and has the stated area-wide probability of acceptance. The next opportunity has the same basic probability of acceptance; however, the actual probability is reduced by the fact that the trip being distributed has a chance of already having accepted the first opportunity. The procedure continues with each successive opportunity having, in effect, a decreased probability of being accepted.

The model will be derived here in the form developed by Schneider:[10]

j_μ is the μth destination in the rank list from a particular origin i.

Q_{ij_μ} is the probability that an individual has not been satisfied with these first μ opportunities, that is, the probability that the individual will proceed beyond the μth destination.

L is the probability that an individual will be satisfied by a particular opportunity.

D_{j_μ} is the number of opportunities at the μth destination.

Derivation of the model

Verbally, if $\mu = 1$, we can formulate the following equations:

Q_{ij_1} = probability that an individual will proceed beyond the first destination (6.25)

In probability terms, this is the same as:

Q_{ij_1} = probability that an individual *is not* satisfied with the first destination (6.26)

The last statement can also be expressed as:

Q_{ij_1} = 1 − probability that the individual *is* satisfied by the first destination (6.27)

Now,

probability that the individual *is* satisfied by the first destination
= probability that the individual is satisfied by an opportunity (L)
x number of opportunities at the first destination (D_{j_1}) (6.28)

Then, equation 6.27 can be expressed mathematically as

$$Q_{ij_1} = 1 - LD_{j_1} \qquad (6.29)$$

When $\mu = 2$,

Q_{ij_2} = probability that an individual will proceed beyond the second destination (6.30)

This equation can also be stated as:

Q_{ij_2} = probability that the individual is not satisfied with the *first two* destinations (6.31)

Equation 6.31 can be expressed as a combined probability:

Q_{ij_2} = probability that the individual *is not* satisfied with the first destination (Q_{ij_1})
x probability that the individual *is not* satisfied by the *second* destination (6.32)

Now, we know that

probability that the individual *is not* satisfied by the second destination
= 1 − probability that the individual *is* satisfied by the second destination
= $1 - LD_{j_2}$ (6.33)

Equation 6.33 is obtained following the same reasoning expressed in equations 6.28 and 6.29.

Substituting equation 6.33 in 6.32, we have, in mathematical terms, the following equation:

$$Q_{ij_2} = Q_{ij_1}(1 - LD_{j_2})$$ (6.34)

When $\mu = 3$, and following the same procedure, we obtain

$$Q_{ij_3} = Q_{ij_2}(1 - LD_{j_3})$$ (6.35)

and so on. In general:

$$Q_{ij_\mu} = Q_{ij_{\mu-1}}(1 - LD_{j_\mu})$$ (6.36)

This equation can be written

$$\frac{Q_{ij_\mu} - Q_{ij_{\mu-1}}}{Q_{ij_{\mu-1}}} = -LD_{j_\mu}$$ (6.37)

If V_{j_μ} is the number of opportunities passed up to and including zone j_μ, then

$$D_{j_\mu} = V_{j_\mu} - V_{j_{\mu-1}}$$ (6.38)

and therefore equation 6.37 becomes

$$\frac{Q_{ij_\mu} - Q_{ij_{\mu-1}}}{Q_{ij_{\mu-1}}} = -L(V_{j_\mu} - V_{j_{\mu-1}})$$ (6.39)

This equation can be written, with the assumption of continuous variation, as

$$\frac{dQ}{Q} = -L \, dV$$ (6.40)

$$\frac{dQ}{dV} = -LQ$$ (6.41)

which integrates to give

$$\ln Q = -LV + \text{constant} \tag{6.42}$$

$$Q = K \exp(-LV) \tag{6.43}$$

so that in discrete notation

$$Q_{ij_\mu} = K_i \exp(-LV_{j_\mu}) \tag{6.44}$$

where K_i is a constant. This equation states that the proportion of trippers proceeding beyond j_μ varies exponentially with the cumulative number of opportunities.

The number of trips from zone i to the μth destination away from i is obtained as follows:

I_{ij_μ} = total number of trips originating at i (O_i)
    x probability that a trip will remain at the μth destination   (6.45)

We know that,

probability that a trip will remain at the μth destination
= probability that a trip will proceed beyond the $(\mu - 1)$th destination
    $(Q_{ij_{\mu-1}})$
− probability that a trip will proceed beyond the μth destination
    (Q_{ij_μ}) (6.46)

Thus, equation 6.45 can be expressed mathematically as

$$I_{ij_\mu} = O_i(Q_{ij_{\mu-1}} - Q_{ij_\mu}) \tag{6.47}$$

Substituting equation 6.44 into equation 6.47 gives

$$I_{ij_\mu} = K_i O_i [\exp(-LV_{j_{\mu-1}}) - \exp(-LV_{j_\mu})] \tag{6.48}$$

This is the usual statement of the intervening opportunities model.

Although further research is required before full integration is obtained, the intervening opportunities model can be derived using entropy maximizing methods; and as Cordey-Hayes and Wilson[7] point out,

> There is a common theoretical base to all models of spatial interaction and the difference between the models appears to be essentially one of emphasis and approach.

In certain critical states the intervening opportunities model approximates to the gravity model.

6.4 Elements of interaction models

Interaction
Interaction is the end product of most interaction models. In the transport

field it is a measure of the movements of goods, persons or vehicles. In the retailing field, interaction can usually be interpreted as being the probable extent to which customers will patronize one shopping centre as opposed to another.

Production variable

In most models, this is the passive variable, the location in the field of influence of one or more focal points which is the recipient of their attractive powers. It can represent the zone of origin of journeys or of retail spending power. The number of journeys or the spending power usually being a function of the population in that zone.

Attraction variable

Population has been extensively used as a measure of attractiveness in many fields, but lately, other types of units have been employed: In the transportation field, the level of employment in an industrial or office area is a common measure. In the retail field, fashion good sales figures (Converse[3]) and retail floorspace (Huff[11]) are now in common use.

A paper from Manchester University, in a revision of a study for a regional shopping centre,[12] has suggested the use of the formula:

$$F = a + bf + cP + dW + eA \qquad (6.49)$$

where F = attractive power of the shopping centre
           f = square feet of durable goods floorspace
           P = number of car parking spaces
           W = number of people working in the central area
           A = some measure of other activities associated with the central shopping area, such as cinemas, theatres, etc.
    a to e = constants derived from a multiple regression analysis of observed data.

Parry-Lewis and Trail[13] have suggested that the attraction factors should be weighted by a constant to reflect the increased competitiveness achieved by concentration; that is one centre with two department stores is more competitive than the sum of two centres with only one department store each.

Spatial separation

Physical distance was the obvious measure to use in the early interaction models. Casey[14] suggested that time distance would be a more appropriate measure. With further increases in mobility, other factors may assume a greater importance as a deterrent to travel, for example cost (Tanner[15]), as well as other non-quantifiable elements such as safety, etc.

Distance or time alone cannot be considered a satisfactory measure of zonal separation, and a combined effect of these two factors can be expressed as a generalized cost function. Probably, the simplest form of cost function can be expressed:

$$c_{ij} = a_i + a_j + \lambda d_{ij} + \delta d_{ij} \qquad (6.50)$$

where c_{ij} = total journey cost

a_i = origin terminal cost

a_j = terminal cost at the destination zone (may include costs due to time spent waiting and walking)

d_{ij} = distance between zone i and zone j

t_{ij} = time separation of zones i and j

λ, δ = constants.

Generalized travel function

Users of the gravity model have traditionally described the deterrent effect of spatial separation by raising the actual distance d_{ij} to a power α, and, in dealing with specific problems, values of α have to be found which give calculated interzonal flows comparable to those observed. In transport models, the exponent can be varied to reflect the varying economic and social conditions in the zones of origin and destination of journeys.

Huff,[11] using time instead of distance, suggests a range of exponents varying with the type of shopping goods being considered, reflecting the willingness of people to travel more readily for fashion goods and furnishings than for groceries or other day to day goods. In practice, the deterrence function or generalized travel function has been chosen empirically on the basis of which function gave the best fit of predicted variables to actual measures of variable. Cripps[16] has pointed out that the deterrence function has varied from:

$$T_{ij}^{\ 1} = f(c_{ij}) = c_{ij}^{-\alpha} \text{ (inverse power)} \qquad (6.51)$$

$$T_{ij}^{-1} = f(c_{ij}) = \exp(-\beta c_{ij}) \text{ (exponential)} \qquad (6.52)$$

$$T_{ij}^{-1} = f(c_{ij}) = \exp(-\beta c_{ij}) c_{ij}^{-\alpha} \qquad (6.53)$$

The earlier and traditional approach where $d_{ij}^{-\alpha}$ was used, can be readily identified with the expression indicated in equation 6.51. The exponential function of the form $\exp(-\beta c_{ij})$ is commonly used. β is a constant derived through calibration. Tanner[15] derives the expression $\exp(-\beta c_{ij}) c_{ij}^{-\alpha}$, where β and α are constants and determined through calibration. This expression has two special cases:

(1) If $\beta = 0$, it behaves as the traditional inverse power of c_{ij} (equation 6.51)

(2) If $\alpha = 0$, it behaves as the exponential function described above (equation 6.52).

The exponential function $\exp(-\beta c_{ij})$ decreases more rapidly than the inverse power function $c_{ij}^{-\alpha}$ as c_{ij} increases, and therefore describes more accurately the normally observed deterrent effect of spatial separation. When the trip is short, that is c_{ij} is small, the exponential function $\exp(-\beta c_{ij})$ does not always serve to describe the deterrent effects. In order to overcome this, Tanner[15] proposed the expression $\exp(-\beta c_{ij})c_{ij}^{-\alpha}$. If very short trips are prevented by the form of zoning, then the expression $\exp(-\beta c_{ij})$ is most probably sufficient. Wilson,[4] using his maximum entropy model, has shown that the most probable form of the deterrence function $f(c_{ij})$ is $\exp(-\beta c_{ij})$.

Proportionality constants
In the early interaction models, the K factors were used to allow the results that were obtained from variables used empirically to be calibrated against a real measured situation; and generally, to allow for factors other than simple spatial separation which affect the interchange between specific pairs of zones. Wilson,[4] stressing the relevance of introducing constraints into the gravity concept, has been able to give an interpretation of this term.

We may recall that in the production constrained case, the constraint

$$I_i = \sum_{j=1}^{n} I_{ij} = O_i \qquad (6.7)$$

must be satisfied. Also, we may remember that since in this single constrained case, an independent estimate of D_j is not available, the attraction variable D_j is replaced by its proxy $W_j^{(2)}$ in the general expression of the gravity model (equation 6.2). Thus

$$I_{ij} = KO_i W_j^{(2)} T_{ij}^{-1} \qquad (6.9)$$

and substituting in equation 6.7 we have,

$$\sum_{j=1}^{n} KO_i W_j^{(2)} T_{ij}^{-1} = O_i$$

This constraint can only be satisfied if a set of proportionality constants $K_i^{(1)}$ replaces the single constant K.

Then
$$K_i^{(1)} = \frac{1}{\sum\limits_{j=1}^{n} W_j^{(2)} T_{ij}^{-1}} \qquad (6.10)$$

Wilson[4] considers that the term $1/K_i^{(1)}$ can be associated with the rival attractiveness of other destination zones; and in the attraction constrained case, the constraint

$$I_j = \sum_{i=1}^{n} I_{ij} = D_j \qquad (6.8)$$

must be satisfied; since in this case an independent estimate of O_i is not available, the production variable O_i is replaced in equation 6.2 by the proxy variable $W_i^{(1)}$. The equation 6.2 becomes

$$I_{ij} = KW_i^{(1)} D_j T_{ij}^{-1} \qquad (6.18)$$

and substituting in equation 6.8 we have,

$$\sum_{i=1}^{n} KW_i^{(1)}D_jT_{ij}^{-1} = D_j$$

To satisfy this constraint, the constant K must be replaced by a set of constants $K_j^{(2)}$ given by

$$K_j^{(2)} = \frac{1}{\sum_{i=1}^{n} W_i^{(1)}T_{ij}^{-1}} \qquad (6.20)$$

The term $1/K_j^{(2)}$ can be considered as representing a measure of the competitiveness of origins for the constrained opportunities D_j.

6.5 Entropy maximizing methods

The work of Wilson[4] has produced an outstanding advance in urban modelling by supplying a new approach in deriving theories of spatial interaction. This approach draws heavily from concepts and techniques in statistical mechanics linked to the social physics approach. The entropy maximizing method gives a sound theoretical basis to an approach which has previously been based on empirical regularities and analogy.

Wilson[4] has shown that the hypotheses giving rise to traditional gravitational models can be formalized to give a family of spatial interaction models by means of entropy maximizing methods. He has demonstrated this feature in relation to the traffic distribution model (used in transportation studies) in the following way: In terms of a model simulating interaction between activities which are fixed in time and space, three constraints are needed:

$$\sum_{j=1}^{n} I_{ij} = O_i \qquad (6.54)$$

$$\sum_{i=1}^{n} I_{ij} = D_j \qquad (6.55)$$

$$\sum_{i=1}^{n} \sum_{j=1}^{n} I_{ij}c_{ij} = C \qquad (6.56)$$

where I_{ij} = number of individuals living in zone i and working in zone j (to be estimated)

O_i = total number of workers who live in zone i (given)

D_j = total number of jobs in zone j (given)

C = total expenditure on travel to work (given)

n = total number of zones (given)

c_{ij} = cost of travelling from zone i to zone j (given).

Equations 6.54 and 6.55 are identical with equations 6.7 and 6.8 respectively, introduced into the production–attraction constrained case of the gravity model. Equation 6.56 is a constraint upon the total expenditure on trips in the system being modelled and '... can be regarded as a behavioural constraint in the sense that it ensures that the method generates a pattern of flows which is consistent with observed expenditure patterns' (Cordey-Hayes and Wilson[7]).

This system can be specified by an origin—destination table as shown below:

Destination

Origin—destination table

We shall define a microstate of the system as an assignment of individual persons to the origin—destination table which does not violate any of the constraints on movements. A macrostate of the system is a distribution of movements regardless of the individual persons.

The basic assumption of this method is that the probability of the distribution $\{I_{ij}\}$ (macrostate) occurring is proportional to the number of microstates (assignments) which give rise to this particular distribution and which satisfy the constraint equations 6.54–6.56. Suppose

$$I = \sum_{i=1}^{n} \sum_{j=1}^{n} I_{ij} = \sum_{i=1}^{n} O_i = \sum_{j=1}^{n} D_j$$

is the total number of trips. The number of distinct arrangements of individuals which gives rise to the distribution $\{I_{ij}\}$ is defined to be $W(\{I_{ij}\})$ and is the number of ways in which I_{11} can be selected from I, I_{12} from $I - I_{11}$, . . . etc. and so,

$$W(\{I_{ij}\}) = \frac{I!}{I_{11}!(I - I_{11})!} \cdot \frac{(I - I_{11})!}{I_{12}!(I - I_{11} - I_{12})!} \cdots = \frac{I!}{\prod_{i=1}^{n} \prod_{j=1}^{n} I_{ij}!} \qquad (6.57)$$

and by maximizing the log of equation 6.57 subject to equations 6.54 to 6.56 using Lagrange's method of undetermined multipliers, Wilson[4] derives the following model:

$$I_{ij} = A_i B_j O_i D_j \exp(-\beta c_{ij}) \qquad (6.58)$$

where

$$A_i = \frac{1}{\sum\limits_{j=1}^{n} B_j D_j \exp(-\beta c_{ij})} \qquad (6.59)$$

and

$$B_j = \frac{1}{\sum\limits_{i=1}^{n} A_i O_i \exp(-\beta c_{ij})} \qquad (6.60)$$

The model in equations 6.58 to 6.60 has a similar form to the gravity model in equations 6.22 to 6.24, and a negative exponential function of travel cost $\exp(-\beta c_{ij})$, replaces the generalized travel function T_{ij}^{-1}.

This statistical theory is effectively saying that given the total number of trips, origins and destinations for each zone for a homogeneous person trip purpose category, given the costs of travelling between a pair of zones and given that there is some fixed total expenditure on transport in the region at the given point in time, then there is a most probable distribution of trips between zones. Also, this distribution is the same as the one obtained using the gravity model, though with the negative exponential function appearing as the preferred form of the deterrent function.

Thus, Wilson has demonstrated that the gravity model can be derived by his method of entropy maximization and that a whole family of spatial interaction models can be obtained by defining different types of constraints. Thus, the most important contribution that this methodology makes involves the role of the constraint equations. These constraint equations represent the amount of information known about the system. Therefore, the approach is sufficiently general to mean that appropriate models can be generated in situations where information about the problem is limited.

6.6 Problems and limitations in the application of interaction models

Problems and limitations in the application of elementary interaction models can be described briefly around three basic points:

(1) The need to introduce additional parameters
(2) The need for care in zoning.
(3) The need for care in calibration.

The need to introduce additional parameters

In practice, the use of only one parameter in the deterrent function has proved to be inadequate to describe the real situation, and so additional parameters have to be introduced to cope with these discrepancies. According to Harris[17] the need to introduce additional parameters into a model suggests that some observable variable that is influencing behaviour has been overlooked.

It is probable that because interaction models try to give aggregative explanation of urban processes and assume that people behave in an average sort of way, they under-represent a considerable important variation in population behaviour. One way of dealing with this kind of problem is to dissaggregate these models. For example, they could be dissaggregated by

(1)   Income groups in the population
(2)   Wage levels in different locations
(3)   Prices of house by location, etc.

The need for care in zoning

As Cripps[16] says '. . . the need to introduce additional parameters, not only is due to the failure to include enough variables to adequately explain behaviour, but is evidently also affected by the choice of zoning systems'. Generally, when we are using interaction models, we are interested in bringing out interzonal effects while interaction within the zone itself is either neglected or easily estimated. Therefore, in zoning the system, we should seek to maximize the amount of 'between zone interaction' by attempting to have the zones sufficiently small.

For example, in a transportation model, in order to represent trips between zones and disregard intrazonal trips, the size of zones of the area under study should be kept small as possible, according to the data and computation facilities available.

The need for care in calibration

According to Cripps,[16] parameters for gravity models are better estimated independently of the model by regression analysis with the observed data, but in practice, there are insufficient data, and so parameters have to be fitted internally by a trial and error process with its consequent dangers. David Bayliss,[1] Chief Transport Planner of the Greater London Council, points out that:

There is a basic problem in understanding spatial interaction models which no-one seems to have explained in the literature and yet is fundamental to any adequate general theory of spatial interaction models. This is the explication of the spectrum of durations between cause and effect. This complex overlapping is calibrated into the model parameters and thus any relative change in pace in the component phenomena is precluded. For example an affluent household may be able to change its location in a few months to take account of fresh employment opportunities, improved transportation or new educational needs. By contrast an old canal-side industry, perhaps because of title and tradition, can remain for a century after its locational raison d'etre (as recognised by the model) has evaporated. As culture, technology and institutional and legal frameworks change, so does the pattern of responsiveness.

References
1 CARROTHERS, G. 'An historical review of the gravity and potential concepts of human interaction'. *Journal of the American Institute of Planners*, vol. 22, no. 2, pp. 94–102.
2 REILLY, W. J. 'Methods for the study of retail relationships'. University of Texas, Bureau of Business Research Studies, Report no. 4, 1929, November. Subsequently incorporated in *The Law of Retail Gravitation*. 2nd Edition Pilsburry Publishers Inc., New York, 1953.
3 CONVERSE, P. D., HUEGY, H. W. and MITCHELL, R. V. *Elements of Marketing*. Prentice Hall, 1930 (7th Ed. 1965).
4 WILSON, A. G. 'A statistical theory of spatial distribution models'. *Transportation Research*, 1968, vol. 1, no. 3, pp. 253–270.
5 WILSON, A. G. 'Developments of some elementary residential locations models'. Centre for Environmental Studies, WP 22, 1968, December.
6 WILSON, A. G. 'Entropy'. Centre for Environmental Studies, WP 26, 1969, January.
7 CORDEY-HAYES, M. and WILSON, A. G. 'Spatial interaction'. Centre for Environmental Studies, WP 57, 1970, January.
8 LOWRY, I. S. *A Model of Metropolis*. Rand Corporation, Santa Monica, California, 1964.
9 STOUFFER, A. 'Intervening opportunities: a theory retailing mobility and distance'. *American Social Review*, 1940, vol. 5, no. 6.
10 SCHNEIDER, M. 'Gravity Models and Trip Distribution Theory'. *Papers and Proceedings of the Regional Science Association*, 1959, vol. V, pp. 51–56.
11 HUFF, D. L. 'A probabilistic analysis of shopping centre trade areas'. *Land Economics*, 1963, February.
12 MANCHESTER UNIVERSITY. 'Shopping centres in north west England'. Department of Town and Country Planning, Part 2, 1968.
13 PARRY-LEWIS, J. and TRAIL, A. C. 'An assessment of shopping models'. *Town Planning Review*, 1968, January.
14 CASEY, H. J. 'The law of retail gravitation applied to traffic engineering'. *Traffic Quarterly*, 1955, July, pp. 313–322.
15 TANNER, J. C. 'Factors affecting the amount of travel'. Road Research Laboratory, H.M.S.O., London 1961.
16 CRIPPS, E. L. 'Limitations of the gravity concept'. Gravity Models in Town Planning, Department of Town Planning, Lanchester College of Technology, Coventry, 1969, October.
17 HARRIS, B. 'Some problems in the theory of intra-urban location'. *Operations Research*. 1961, vol. 9 (Fall).
18 BAYLISS, D. Private communication from Mr. Bayliss to the author in July 1972.

7 Models of the Urban Spatial Structure: Classification and Selected Examples

7.1 Three dimensional classification

The separate examination of each of the characteristics of models involves difficulties in attempting to show how all these characteristics can be combined to form practical models of use in the planning process. To remedy this deficiency, selected examples of models of the urban spatial structure will be described here, with the aim of elucidating any general or particular lessons from them.

Alternative schemes for the classification of models of the urban spatial structure have been proposed. Harris[1] develops a six dimensional classification based on 'a sequence of dichotomies or antinomies which define some of the major dimensions of the strategy of model building'. Thus, he classifies models in the following way:

(1) Descriptive versus analytic
(2) Holistic versus partial
(3) Macro versus micro
(4) Static versus dynamic
(5) Deterministic versus probabilistic
(6) Simultaneous versus sequential.

Harris adds that 'the six dimensions outlined here are centred on, but not exclusively related to, the prediction or simulation phase of planning'.

Lowry[2] makes a very interesting classification of existing models according to their emphasis on:

(1) Land-use patterns
(2) Location patterns
(3) Land-use succession patterns
(4) Migration patterns.

In his survey of models, Lowry presents three examples which do not fit any of the four classifications given above; one is a hybrid of two strategies, and two approach the complete system of market interdependence, but with significant variations in emphasis (market demand and market supply).

Wilson[3] presents a list of six kinds of models resulting from different answers to the questions of time and the level of aggregation:

(1)   A deterministic comparative–static equilibrium model
(2)   A comparative–static equilibrium model which has a probabilistic
        component in that Monte Carlo methods are used to estimate values
        of variables at any point in time. (In neither of these models does time
        appear explicitly as a variable.)
(3)   A dynamic model in which time is treated as a discrete variable and
        the model is expressed in terms of difference equations. The system
        is regarded as deterministic
(4)   A dynamic model in which time is treated as a continuous variable, and
        the model is expressed in terms of differential equations. The system
        is regarded as deterministic
(5)   A dynamic model written in terms of stochastic difference equations
(6)   A dynamic model written in terms of stochastic differential equations.

Wilson points out that 'Systems described on large aggregate scales often behave
in more deterministic less probabilistic ways'.
    Any of the classification systems already outlined here defines a set of
convenient models on which to base a description of them, but for ease in
understanding it has been found more convenient to group selected examples
of models of the urban spatial structure using a three dimensional classification,
based on the following important features:

(1)   Degree of comprehensiveness
(2)   Type of relationship between variables
(3)   Level of outcome.

Graphically, this classification can be represented as shown in Figure 7.1.

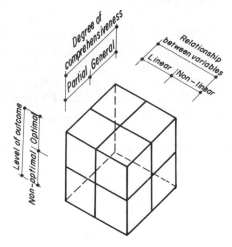

Figure 7.1   Three dimensional classification system for models

Degree of comprehensiveness
The degree of comprehensiveness is related to the number of activities that the model tends to simulate. A simple distinction between partial and general models can be considered.

Partial models
This type of model tends to simulate only one land use or activity of the system concerned. The approach of these models is based on the examination of the behaviour of a subsystem of the metropolitan area while holding the environment constant.

Partial models simulating variations in one activity or land use have been mainly developed in the study of retail behaviour (shopping models) and in the field of transport. Another sector of the spatial system where this type of model has been applied is in the housing market.

General models
Those models which attempt to simulate two or more land uses or activities are referred to as general models. They are built up of partial models, communicating with each other and interacting generally in a computer. Undoubtedly, the planner is interested in being able to model the total number of activities and interactions that take place in the urban spatial system by integrating several partial models. There are some problems inherent in this approach which can be overcome by careful planning as Harris[1] points out.

First it seems likely that the actual communication between subsystems is much more complex and diverse than at first appears to be the case. When designing partial models, there is a tendency to reduce rather than to increase the number of independent variables, and so we need to be careful and introduce as many variables as necessary, in order to allow perfect interaction with other partial models and with the 'constant' environment.

The second difficulty arises from the fact that partial models are apt to use variables not ordinarily predicted by other partial models. Consequently, there is a need to include in the general model a partial model which generates as output the variables needed as input by the other partial models.

A third difficulty arises from the need to ensure that the division of the total problem into subproblems is not exhaustive, but also realistic in the overall system sense.

Examples of general models are Lowry's 'A Model of Metropolis'[4] and Schlager's model 'A Land Use Plan Design Model'.[5]

Type of relationship between variables
The system of relationships between parameters, independent and dependent variables can be thought of as equations, and we may distinguish between linear and non-linear systems. There are some models which incorporate in their

structure both linear and non-linear systems at the same time, and consequently a clear classification of models between linear and non-linear is difficult to make.

Linear models
Models whose systems of equations have relationships based on proportionality, or on proportionality plus a fixed constant, are considered linear models. A linear model can be represented by the equation

$$y = a + bx \tag{7.1}$$

where y is the dependent variable
x is the independent variable
a and b are parameters.

A very simple model of this type may be, for example, a model that derives population from employment.

If we plot employment against population on a graph for the eight largest towns in central and north east Lancashire (where there is little commuting between towns), we get a fairly straight line as shown in Figure 7.2. Then we say that employment and population are related in a linear fashion.

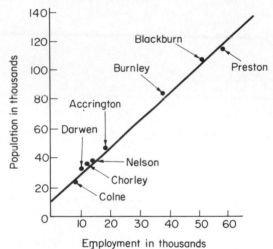

Figure 7.2 Linear relations between population and employment (Batty[6])

The most outstanding value of linear models is that we can relate two or more variables together. For instance, a linear model relating three variables could derive car ownership rates (dependent variable) from income levels and some index measuring the availability of public transport.

The general expression of a linear model which has n independent variables can be written as

$$y = a + b_1 x_1 + b_2 x_2 + + + b_n x_n = a + \sum_{i=1}^{n} b_i x_i \tag{7.2}$$

Non-linear models

Non-linear models are those models whose variables are related in a non-linear fashion. Non-linear models generally have equations of the following type

$$y = bx^{\alpha} \qquad (\alpha \neq 1) \qquad\qquad (7.3)$$

where y is the dependent variable
x is the independent variable
b and α are constants. α must be not equal 1, otherwise the equation becomes linear.

A model which deals with the growth of population over time can be represented by equation 7.3, where y is population, x is time and $\alpha > 1$ (see Figure 7.3).

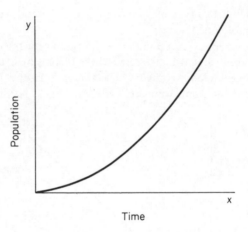

Figure 7.3 Non-linear relationship between time and population

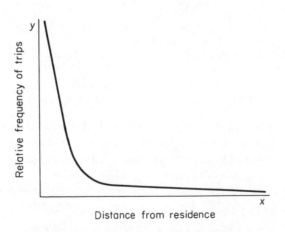

Figure 7.4 Non-linear relationship between distance and frequency of trips

Non-linear equations are very commonly used in models which deal with interaction of activities which take place over distance. We can use non-linear equations to show the relationship between distance and the number of journeys made to any point. Figure 7.4 shows how frequency of trips an individual makes, decreases as distance increases – assuming of course that the number of people or places 'available' to visit is the same at each distance.

Level of outcome
According to the level of outcome, it is necessary to make a division into two classes based on optimizing and non-optimizing models.

Optimizing models
The structure of an optimizing model involves some process in which the model is able to predict 'best' or optimal values of its independent variables. It is easy to see the relationship between optimizing models and decision or planning models, for both involve the search for an optimal solution.

Despite the rigorous nature of linear programming formulation and its intrinsic difficulties, the best known optimizing models have been built using this technique.

One of the most difficult features of this kind of model is related to the criteria of optimality which must be established before the model is operated. Although it may appear at first that this type of model is unsuitable for simulating human behaviour, there are some situations where this is possible. For example, the model proposed by Herbert and Stevens[7] to simulate the locational behaviour of different household types was based on a fundamental behavioural premise that households maximize their savings. Schlager[5] developed an optimizing model which simply sought an optimal configuration of land uses in terms of minimum cost location.

Non-optimizing models
This kind of model, as the name suggests, does not use any explicit process involving optimality. The difficulties of defining optimality in systems involving human behaviour force the majority of models to fall into this class. Furthermore, as Batty[8] says:

> Developments in spatial theory have not concentrated upon optimality in any general sense, and as many models reflect previously established theories, these models do not explicitly define optimality.

7.2 Selected examples
It is considered to be of little use to give a brief explanation of each of the many models developed, and that it will be better to describe and analyse the basic principles underlying the structure of some of them and to point out the main features. It is expected that the understanding of these principles will give

the reader a greater ability to deal with most of the models which are not described here.

The selected examples of models of the urban spatial structure described in the following chapters attempt to show how particular aspects are unified in specific models, showing how the models are of operational value in practice. The examples chosen are in no way a comprehensive selection, and few have gained a widespread acceptance in planning practice. According to the three dimensional classification defined before, the following types of models can be generated:

Partial, linear and non-optimal models
As an example of this type, the 'Probabilistic Model for Residential Growth' developed by Chapin and Weiss[9, 10] will be described here.

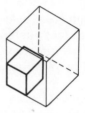

Partial, non-linear and non-optimal models
As an example of this type of model, that prepared by Lakshmanan and Hansen[11] will be used.

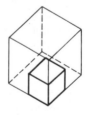

Partial, linear and optimal models
The 'Penn-Jersey Model' proposed by Herbert and Stevens[7] will be described in this category.

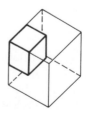

General, linear and non-optimal models
Hill's model[12] 'A Growth Allocation Model for the Boston Region', also called the EMPIRIC model, will be used as an example of this type of model.

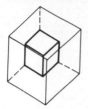

General, non-linear and non-optimal models
Lowry has developed an outstanding model called 'A Model of Metropolis'[4] which has stimulated a population explosion of successors with their corresponding improvements. One is due to Garin[13] which has been designated the Garin–Lowry model. This model is also described here.

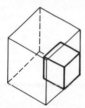

General, linear and optimal models
The model prepared by Schlager[5] called 'A Land Use Plan Design Model' will be used as an example of this type of model.

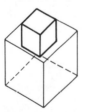

Other models
The difficulties which arise in dealing with non-linear equations in an optimizing procedure, have not permitted a full development of either partial or general models. Consequently, no examples related to these types of model will be presented.

Model name	Author (s)	City	Date	Activities and land uses.					Function			Theory		Solution methods			Treat-ment of time		Degree of comprehe-nsiveness		Type of relation-ship		Level of outcome		Ref.
				Industrial	Residential	Retail trade	Recreational	Public utilities uses	Projection	Allocation	Derivation	Behavioural	Social/physics	Analytic	Numerical	Simulation	Static	Dynamic	Partial	General	Linear	Non-linear	Optimal	Non-optimal	
Probabilistic model for residential growth	F. Chaplin, S. Weiss and T. Donnelly	Greensboro	1964		●					●			●			●		●	●		●			●	7·9
A retail market potential model	T. R Lakshmanan and W. G. Hansen	Baltimore	1964			●				●			●		●		●		●			●		●	7·11
The Penn-Jersey regional growth model	J. Herbert and B. J. Stevens	Originally for Philadelphia	1960		●					●		●			●			●	●		●		●		7·7
The EMPIRIC model	D. M. Hill	Boston	1965	●	●	●				●			●	●				●		●	●			●	7·12
A model of metropolis	I. S. Lowry	Pittsburgh	1964		●	●				●	●		●		●		●			●		●		●	7·4
A land use plan design model	K. J Schlager	S.E. Wisconsin	1965	●	●	●	●	●		●	●	●			●		●			●	●		●		7·5

Figure 7.5 Models of the urban spatial structure: main features

For each of the models described here, the main features are summarized in Figure 7.5.

It is important to notice that a clear classification of models is generally impossible; consequently, each model has been assigned to features, according to its major inclination or emphasis. For example, Lowry's 'A Model of Metropolis', although it uses behavioural concepts, also follows very strongly the social physics approach, and so it has been classified as a model based on this last approach.

References

1 HARRIS, B. 'Quantitative models of urban development: their role in metropolitan policy-making'. in PERLOFF, HARVEY, S. and WINGO, LOWDON JR. *Issues in Urban Economics*, Johns Hopkins, Baltimore, 1968.

2 LOWRY, I. S. 'Seven models of urban development: a structural comparation'. Special Report 97, Highway Research Board, Washington D.C., 1968.

3 WILSON, A. G. 'Models in urban planning: a synoptic review of recent literature'. *Abstract in Urban Studies*, 1968, November, pp. 249–276.

4 LOWRY, I. S. *A Model of Metropolis*. Rand Corporation, Santa Monica, California, 1964.

5 SCHLAGER, K.J. 'A land use plan design model'. *Journal of the American Institute of Planners*, 1965, May, pp. 103–111.

6 BATTY, M. 'Introductory model-building problems for urban and regional planning'. Urban Systems Research Unit, Department of Geography, University of Reading, 1970.

7 HERBERT, J. D. and STEVENS, B. H. 'A model for the distribution of residential activities in urban areas'. *Journal of Regional Science*, 1960 (Fall), 2/2 pp. 21–36.

8 BATTY, M. 'Recent developments in land use modelling: a review of British research'. Urban Systems Research Unit, Department of Geography, University of Reading, 1970.

9 CHAPIN, F. S. Jr. and WEISS, S. F. 'A probabilistic model for residential growth'. *Transportation Research*, 1968, vol. 2, pp. 375–390.

10 CHAPIN, F. S. Jr. 'A model for simulating residential development'. *Journal of the American Institute of Planners*, 1965, May, pp. 120–136.

11 LAKSHMANAN, T. R. and HANSEN, W. G. 'A retail market potential model'. *Journal of the American Institute of Planners,* 1965, May, pp. 134–143.

12 HILL, D. M. 'A growth allocation model for the Boston region'. *Journal of the American Institute of Planners*, 1965, May, pp. 111–120.

13 GARIN, R. A. 'A matrix formulation of the Lowry model for intra-metropolitan activity allocation'. *Journal of the American Institute of Planners*, 1966, November.

8 A Probabilistic Model for Residential Growth

8.1 Introduction

This model of residential growth was developed[1,2] at the Center for Urban and Regional Studies, University of North Carolina by F. Stuart Chapin, Jr., Shirley F. Weiss and Thomas G. Donnelly, in 1964.

8.2 Underlying concepts

The underlying conceptual basis of urban structure is based on the view that change in the urban system is characterized by complex decision chains related to the process of land development. To quote from the original statement of their model (Chapin and Weiss[1]):

> Land development is viewed as the consequence of many decisions and implementing actions of a public and private nature, in both the growing edges of metropolitan areas and in the renewal of central areas. Some are 'priming actions' in the sense that they trigger other 'secondary actions' which taken together produce the total pattern of land development.

This distinction between priming and secondary actions tends crudely to group variables involved in the land development process in a form that has a direct tie with factors which public policy decisions can influence.

Examples of priming actions considered in this study are:

Expressway locations
Route locations for rapid rail transit
Locations of major industrial installations
Developments involving large employment concentrations, etc.

Examples of secondary actions include the location decisions of small shop-keepers, institutions and organizations. The largest group in this category is made up of location decisions that produce residential communities. Although they are very complex to trace as individual decisions, they can be observed in the aggregate.

These secondary actions in the land development process produce a great number of location decisions from different decision making entities like firms, government, households and others. These decisions are seen as consisting of chains of decisions, some being the outcomes of others. In the residential development process, both consumers (households) and suppliers of land are seen as essential agents in such a process.

At the beginning of the process, when land is being prepared for development, financiers, developers, builders and sellers are interacting in various sequences until the land is ready to be sold. Subsequently, according to the opportunities emerging from this part of the residential development process, households enter into the process as the final consumers making their locational decisions, with each particular consumer outcome having a lesser or greater degree of impact on the subsequent chain of decisions.

This model of residential growth development is the outcome of a study whose objective was:

(1)   To perfect an approach for analysing the range of factors commonly associated with land development, to determine their influence individually and in various combinations as a mix on the distribution and intensity of development in a metropolitan area

(2)   To utilize these results in the formulation of a model for forecasting residential development in a metropolitan area.

Thus, the UNC study can be conveniently divided into two stages:

(1)   Identification of the important priming variables of residential growth, by techniques of multiple linear regression

(2)   Formulation of a model designed to predict the incidence of conversion of rural or vacant area to residential use as the population of the study increases.

8.3 Stage one: Identification of variables of residential growth

For this first stage, Chapin and Weiss did an extensive investigation on factors commonly held to be closely associated with *growth at the periphery*. The aim of this phase of the work was to identify variables that:

(1)   Were relevant conceptually to the land development rationale (according to Chapin and Weiss criteria), including factors that appear to both trigger (priming factors) and constrain (conditioning factors) development

(2)   Were available in measurable form in most local information systems or could be easily added without exorbitant expense

(3)   Could be coded in meaningful units in a grid co-ordinate system

(4)   Showed a range of variability sufficient for statistical analysis.

The method used to evaluate variables was a stepwise linear form of multiple regression.

An equation of the following form was used to relate a secondary action, in this case land in urban use or residential development y_i, to a series of priming actions x_{ij} in each zone i of the system:

$$y_i = \beta_0 + \sum_{j=1}^{m} \beta_j x_{ij} \qquad (i = 1, 2, \ldots n) \qquad (8.1)$$

where
y_i = the amount of residential development in zone i
$x_{i1}, x_{i2}, \ldots x_{im}$ = independent variables such as the sewerage facilities of zone i, the amenity of zone i, etc.
m = number of independent variables
n = number of zones
β_j = parameters associated with the independent variables
β_0 = another parameter of the model.

The dependent variable y_i, the number of independent variables and the particular time instants from which these variables were drawn were varied, and eventually in the final tests seven strong independent variables emerged.

Four are well within the control of public officials:

(1) Accessibility to work areas
(2) Travel distance to major street
(3) Distance to nearest available elementary school
(4) Availability of sewerage (represents the combined influence of water systems and sewerage systems).

These four factors, according to the authors of this model, may be regarded as shaping residential development (priming factors).

The other three factors are qualities which the designers of the model considered as intrinsic to the residential site itself (conditioning factors). They are:

Marginal land not in urban use
Assessed value
Residential amenity.

This last factor, due to difficulties in measuring it, is not used in the model. Chapin and Weiss[1] remark that:

Measures must first be improved upon before this factor can be given explicit recognition.

The authors of this model considered that because the techniques used do not lead themselves to establishing cause-and-effect linkage, the study uses the term 'factor' in preference to 'determinant' of land development.

8.4 Stage two: Formulation of the model

In this second stage of the study, Chapin and Weiss formulate a model whose function is simply one of *allocation* of units of new development to the site experiencing growth. Based on a measure of attractiveness, a given number of new residences are allocated to competing unoccupied land zones, using a random procedure based on the Monte Carlo method.

Level of aggregation

The study area is divided by a rectangular grid into cells (1000×1000 ft^2) of about 23 acres each. The cells in turn are divided into 'ninths' of about 2.5 acres, the unit of land development.

Treatment of time

The forecast period is divided into equal growth periods of 3—5 years. At the beginning of each growth period, the measure of attractiveness utilized by the model for the allocation procedure is 'reassessed' in such a way that each stage of the model process belongs to the corresponding stage of the city's development.

Constraints

Certain cells are not used in the model and they are 'sterilized' for varying reasons, basically because:

(1)   They are already developed
(2)   The land development plan has earmarked them for non-residential use
(3)   They must remain in the open-space system for some other reason.

This step of sterilizing grid cells creates one type of constraint on the use of land for residential purposes. A second type of constraint prevents the movement of the locations of supplier-generated residential development tagged at different density and different sale-rent levels. This type of constraint recognizes both public control and supplier offerings, and so cells are classified according to particular submarkets in order that the households in search for housing can find them in the list corresponding to their category.

Attractiveness

The UNC programme assigns to each fertile cell a 'measure of attractiveness' for development. This 'attractiveness' score is a linear combination of the initial assessed value modified on the basis of the four priming factors identified in the first stage of the study. At the threshold date of the forecast period, the measures of attractiveness are based on assessed land values.

For present purposes, it is assumed that land values represent an index of the following household location factors:

(1)   The price of the shelter package
(2)   A summary evaluation of the accessibility advantages of each cell for a particular set of activities relative to all other cells
(3)   A measure of its amenities, prestige value and the other living qualities the consumer considers important in choosing a place of residence in comparison to all other cells.

Chapin and Weiss expect to evaluate separately in the future these three location factors.

The index of attractiveness A_i of each cell, can be represented as

$$A_i = \sum_{j=1}^{m} \alpha_j \beta_j x_{ij} \qquad (i = 1,2, \ldots n) \qquad (8.2)$$

where x_{ij} = independent variable

β_j = parameter associated with the independent variable

α_j = weight used to scale the independent variables to values suitable for use in the model

n = number of cells

m = 5, corresponding to the four priming variables and the assessed land value.

Owing to the fact that the model uses a random simulation procedure based on the Monte Carlo method to allocate residences to sites, each undeveloped cell has to have assigned a probability of conversion to residential use during the following forecasting period which is proportional to that cell's attractiveness score. Then, the composite indices are transformed to probabilities P_i as follows:

$$P_i = \frac{\sum\limits_{j=1}^{m} \alpha_j \beta_j x_{ij}}{\sum\limits_{i=1}^{n} \sum\limits_{j=1}^{m} \alpha_j \beta_j x_{ij}} \qquad (8.3)$$

Allocation of households

The distribution of households in this model is made on a probabilistic rather than a deterministic basis, in recognition of the chance considerations operating in the residential development process, especially the factors of human caprice.

At each successive growth period, the model has a set of locations of differing attractiveness for development for particular classes of households, and exogenously to the model a set of households in search of land is also present. Theoretically this set of households has differing purses, differing living requirements and differing activity demands.

Then, discrete units of development are assigned to cells by random sampling without replacement from the resulting probability distribution. In place of distributing households *per se*, the model distributes the equivalent number of ninths at the prescribed residential density. The sampling process continues until enough ninths have been developed to accommodate the given increment of urban population. Once the model has allocated the given number of ninths for that particular growth period and before the next growth period is started, a complete 'reassessment' of attractiveness is done because it is assumed that the ninths already allocated will have an effect in the level of attractiveness of the remaining cells in the following period.

As the settlement, town or city, develops, changes in technology, life styles and tastes can be assumed, and certain preconditions with respect to growth introduced, such as a new major road is built, a public water system is constructed, a town school system is created, and so on. In whatever period, one or more of these elements is introduced and the model will take into account these changes, producing a new set of 'attractiveness' values for the various grid cells remaining for development.

The time lag effect of the decisions into the process of development is also taken into account by the model, and it is estimated from the regression analyses.

Data inputs
This model operates on four kinds of inputs:

(1)   A land supply
(2)   An attractiveness for development
(3)   A set of priming factors
(4)   The total number of residential units to be allocated to the terrain.

Land supply
This category of input involves three preprocessing analyses:

(1)   An inventory of land *available* for residential purposes at different residential densities
(2)   The land available for residential purposes is analysed in order to find out whether this inventory is *capable* of residential use
(3)   The inventory of land capable *and* available for residential use is differentiated between tract acreage and subdivided land, with prescribed increments of tract land shifted to the subdivided category at the beginning of each growth period used in the model.

Measures of attractiveness
This input is essential only for the threshold date for simulation runs. Changes in these measures are computed by the model at the beginning of each period based on the influence of priming factors. The measures used in the initial instance are simple weights based on assessed land values.

A set of priming factors
This third form of input consists of a schedule of public improvements which are related and specified by a particular plan alternative being tested with the model. This schedule specifies what elements of the programme being tested are going to be introduced in each growth period and its corresponding location in the area under study.

Number of residential units
The total number of residential units is given as input to the model as a series of matrices, one for each growth period, where it is specified how the household units are going to be distributed among usable and available residential sites, broken down by subdivided and acreage parcels, by value category and by density category. This series of matrices would be prepared exogenously from housing market analyses, in a forecast application of this model.

Basic simulation routine
The basic sequence of operations of the model during one growth period is the following:

(1) The inventory of land available and capable of residential development is introduced by the computer. It consists of density-value classes for each of the subdivided and the open space land categories. This step consists essentially of introducing a baseline description of undeveloped land in the area under study as it exists at the beginning of a growth period.

(2) A measure of relative attractiveness is assigned to each unit of land suitable for residential use. For the first growth period, assessed land values are used to establish a measure of attractiveness. At the beginning of each successive period, the fertile cells remaining are 'reassessed' on the basis of non-residential changes in land use that occurred in the preceding period.

(3) Changes anticipated in the location of employment opportunities and the assumed construction of selected programmed public improvements (priming actions) scheduled for the next growth period modify the relative value of land for residential use. This effect is estimated at this step.

(4) Density and housing-value constraints imposed by the zoning ordinance and the operations of the land market are introduced, and each fertile cell is 'reassessed' to obtain the *total* attractiveness for residential use. Then, this attractiveness is transformed into probability.

(5) Finally, households in the market for each class of housing during the growth period (expressed in units of land) are allocated to sites on a probabilistic basis using the Monte Carlo method.

8.5 Uses of the model

The principal use that can be made of the model is as an instrument for studying the effects that selected public policy decisions can be expected to have on the pattern of residential growth. If a fairly accurate estimate of the distribution of residential growth is needed instead of comparative analyses of different policy decisions, then the development process will need to be subaggregated to give the accuracy required.

8.6 Comments

Analysing this model, one finds that it is basically a consumer model rather than a producer model. The behaviour of land developers is not visibly reflected in the structure of the model. One finds that 'development' occurs only when households are assigned to a site. Speculative overbuilding or withholding of choice land from the market are phenomena not considered by the model.

Another point to note is the fact that the model only deals with growth areas and *new* residential development; it does not include replacement and renewal, or take account of movements within the area studied; Chapin and Weiss[2] make the following remark about their model:

> Household decisions are treated in very broad classes and involve only the simple growth situation found in fringe areas of the metropolitan community, omitting for the present, the situation of decreasing population.

A very interesting point is raised by Lowry[3] when he analyses this model specifically from the point of view of his theory of the market for urban land. He says:

> But it is not at all clear why the chances of development for each ninth are proportional to its attractiveness. If there are no constraining prices, one would expect the most attractive ninths to be developed first, and the least attractive ones to be developed last. If there are price constraints on residential choice, one would expect the prices to be collinear with attractiveness; . . . the market solution would not be a proportional distribution; indeed, it could not be determined at all without comparing demand prices offered for each ninth by competing user-groups.

Harris[4] makes the following comments about this model:

> Despite their many interesting features and their insights into consumer and entrepreneurial behaviour, these efforts have not attempted to provide a model or group of models which could be used for long term projection and for complete market simulation.

The assumption that land values represent an index of house price, an evaluation of the accessibility advantages, and a measure of amenity, prestige value and other determining consumer product characteristics was questioned. Consequently, in later work, Chapin[5] attempted to replace this unsatisfactory assumption with a more thorough analysis of household activity, patterns and taste norms involving sociological concepts.

It is interesting to note that one of the most remarkable features of this model is that it exhibits the only genuinely stochastic approach to residential location behaviour. This model also shows how linear models are constructed and how probabilistic methods can be used in model building.

8.7 Worked problem

In order to fix ideas and to clarify the structure of this model, the following application to a simple problem is given, based on a computation prepared by Batty.[6]

The task will be to produce a model of an imaginary town which is divided into four zones. The residential development of each zone of the town is known and it is measured as population.

Zone:	1	2	3	4
Population:	480	870	1020	720
Total population:	3090 units			

For the sake of simplicity, let us assume that after analysing which factors are relevant to residential development, only one factor — a composite index called 'employment potential' — is significant. Let us suppose that the variable employment potential is defined as:

$$x_{i1} = \sum_{j=1}^{n} E_j d_{ij}^{-\alpha} \tag{8.4}$$

where x_{i1} = employment potential of zone i
     E_j = employment at zone j
     d_{ij} = distance between zones i and j
     α = parameter
     n = 4 (number of zones).

Then, in order to calculate the employment potential of each cell, we need a statement of the employment of each zone and a matrix of distances between any two zones; these data are also known:

Zone	1	2	3	4
Employment	100	200	800	100

The town schematically and the matrix of distances are as shown below:

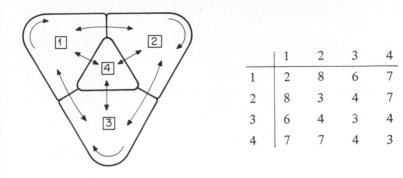

	1	2	3	4
1	2	8	6	7
2	8	3	4	7
3	6	4	3	4
4	7	7	4	3

Step 1: Construction of the employment potential index
This index is constructed using equation 8.4 and assuming $\alpha = 2$:

$$E_j d_{ij}^{-2} \qquad\qquad \sum_{j=1}^{4} E_j d_{ij}^{-2}$$

1	2	3	4	
$\dfrac{100}{4}$	$\dfrac{200}{64}$	$\dfrac{800}{36}$	$\dfrac{100}{49}$	$52.36 = x_{11}$
$\dfrac{100}{64}$	$\dfrac{200}{9}$	$\dfrac{800}{16}$	$\dfrac{100}{49}$	$75.80 = x_{21}$
$\dfrac{100}{36}$	$\dfrac{200}{16}$	$\dfrac{800}{9}$	$\dfrac{100}{16}$	$110.32 = x_{31}$
$\dfrac{100}{49}$	$\dfrac{200}{49}$	$\dfrac{800}{16}$	$\dfrac{100}{9}$	$67.22 = x_{41}$

Step 2: Fitting a regression line
We now fit to the data a regression line of the form

$$y_i = \beta_0 + \beta_1 x_{i1}$$

where y_i = residential development in zone i
x_{i1} = variable defined by equation 8.4 and already calculated in
step 1
β_0 and β_1 = parameters; these are going to be estimated in this step.

Applying linear regression techniques, the equation obtained is:

$$y_i^* = 104.35 + 8.74 x_{i1} + \epsilon_i$$

where y_i^* = predicted value of residential development
ϵ_i = error term or residual.

As a matter of interest, the coefficient of determination (R^2) for this hypothetical value is 0.8710, which is reasonable enough to support the relationship between y_i and x_{i1}.

A comparison of the observed and predicted values of residential development (measured as population) is given below (see also Figure 8.1):

Zones	1	2	3	4
Observed	480	870	1020	720
Predicted	562	767	1069	692

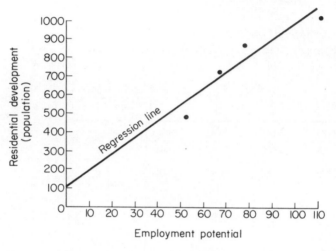

Figure 8.1　Graph showing the relationship between residential development and employment potential

Step 3: Construction of a cumulative distribution

These values are calculated in the following way:

Zone	y_i^*	$y_i^* / \sum\limits_{i=1}^{4} y_i^*$	P_i	Cumulative distribution
1	562	0.1819	18.19	0–17
2	767	0.2482	24.82	18–42
3	1069	0.3458	34.58	43–77
4	692	0.2239	22.39	78–99

From the cumulative distribution, we can see that to each zone a range of numbers has been given, with the total range being 0–99. The range of a particular zone reflects its probability of receiving a unit of development.

Range of numbers according to each zone is shown below.

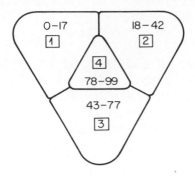

Step 4: Random sampling

For every unit of development that we are going to allocate, we pick up a random number from a table of two-digit random numbers, and see on which of the zones the number falls in and, consequently, the unit of development. As we have 3090 units of population to allocate, instead of drawing 3090 random numbers, we can assume that population locates in units of 10. Then, we have to draw only 309 random numbers.

When a large amount of random numbers are drawn, one would expect the number to fall in proportion to the ranges given by the cumulative distribution. If this exercise were done again, we would get a slightly different allocation following a structured pattern. Tocher[7] gives a clear discussion about this procedure.

Having done the random sampling, the following distribution has been found, and it is shown in comparison against the observed and deterministic distributions.

Zone	Observed	Deterministic	Probabilistic
1	480	562	580
2	870	767	780
3	1020	1069	1100
4	720	692	630

To show the fit of the observed, deterministic and probabilistic distribution to each other, a correlation matrix is presented below:

	observed	deterministic	probabilistic
observed	1.000	0.933	0.899
deterministic	0.933	1.000	0.986
probabilistic	0.899	0.986	1.000

The structure of the model has been outlined here and the important point to note concerns the use of a probabilistic method, and the emphasis on *simulating* the allocation of residential development.

References

1 CHAPIN, F. S. Jr. and WEISS, S.F. 'A probabilistic model for residential growth'. *Transportation Research*, 1968, vol. 2, pp. 375–390.

2 CHAPIN, F. S. Jr. 'A model for simulating residential development'. *Journal of the American Institute of Planners*, 1965, May, pp. 120–136.

3 LOWRY, I. S. 'Seven models of urban development: a structural comparation'. Special Report 97, Highway Research Board, Washington D.C., 1968.

4 HARRIS, B. 'Quantitative models of urban development: their role in metro-politan policy-making', in PERLOFF, HARVEY S. and WINGO, LOWDON JR. *Issues in Urban Economics*, Johns Hopkins, Baltimore, 1968.

5 CHAPIN, F. S. 'Activity systems and urban structure'. *Journal of the American Institute of Planners*, 1968, January.

6 BATTY, M. 'Introductory model-building problems for urban and regional planning', Urban Systems Research Unit, Department of Geography, University of Reading, 1970.

7 TOCHER, K. D. *The Art of Simulation*. The English Universities Press Ltd., London, Third impression, 1969.

9   A Retail Market Potential Model

9.1 Introduction

This model was developed[1] by T. R. Lakshmanan and Walter G. Hansen to explore possible equilibrium distributions for large retail trade centres in the Baltimore region (USA) in 1964. As part of a more comprehensive study which investigates the size, composition, location, etc. of a system of suburban towns (Metrotowns) displayed radially and in rings around the city of Baltimore, this model deals with the retail core of the town centres.

It is important to notice that the model does not generate patterns of location and size of the future retail development. The model only evaluates the performance of the different alternative patterns which are given as input to the model.

9.2 The model

The model describes a situation of overlapping competition between shopping centres and develops a mathematical framework to distribute the retail expenditure of a group of households between the competing shopping centres. The following statements are expressed by the model:[1]

(1)   The sales potential of a retail centre is directly related to its attractive power. The designers of this model used the size of the shopping centre as an index of attractiveness. Other suitable indices may be used, such as existing sales, number of department stores, parking space, etc. or a combination of these.

(2)   The sales potential of a centre is directly related to its proximity to the number and prosperity of the consumers.

(3)   The sales potential of a retail centre is related to how disposed it is to competing shopping facilities.

Mathematically, these statements can be represented by the following gravity submodel:

$$S_{ij} = C_i \frac{F_{ij}^{\beta}/d_{ij}^{\alpha}}{\dfrac{F_1^{\beta}}{d_{i1}^{\alpha}} + \dfrac{F_2^{\beta}}{d_{i2}^{\alpha}} + + + \dfrac{F_n^{\beta}}{d_{in}^{\alpha}}} = C_i \frac{F_{ij}^{\beta}/d_{ij}^{\alpha}}{\displaystyle\sum_{j=1}^{n} \dfrac{F_j^{\beta}}{d_{ij}^{\alpha}}} \tag{9.1}$$

where S_{ij} = consumer retail expenditures of population resident in zone i spent at zone j

C_i = total consumer retail expenditures of population resident in zone i

F_j = attractive power of retail centre in zone j

d_{ij} = spatial separation between zone i and zone j

α = an exponent applied to the distance variable

β = an exponent applied to the attraction variable; in the original formulation of this model by Lakshmanan and Hansen,[1] this exponent is not considered, and consequently, has an implicit value of 1 ($\beta = 1$)

n = number of zones.

In reality, not all the zones have centres of retail trade. In those non-shopping zones, obviously, the attractive power is set to zero ($F_j^\beta = 0$).

Analysing the submodel indicated by equation 9.1, we find that the amount of retail sales in any centre j is:

(1)   In direct proportion to the consumer expenditure on goods C_i, usually measured in monetary terms

(2)   In direct proportion to its attractive power (F_j^β)

(3)   In inverse proportion to distance of the consumers d_{ij}^α; in the original formulation, this distance is measured in terms of driving time

(4)   In inverse proportion to competition

$$\sum_{j=1}^{n} \frac{F_j^\beta}{d_{ij}^\alpha}$$

To obtain the total sales in retail centre j we add up the consumer retail expenditures available in all zones of the area under study that would probably be spent in zone j,

$$S_j = \sum_{i=1}^{n} S_{ij} = \sum_{i=1}^{n} C_i \frac{F_j^\beta / d_{ij}^\alpha}{\sum_{j=1}^{n} \frac{F_j^\beta}{d_{ij}^\alpha}} \tag{9.2}$$

where S_j = total sales in retail centre j.

A premise used by the model is that, within a metropolitan region, which is considered by the model as an economic and spatial entity, the total sales generated at all the retail centres must equal the total available consumer expenditures for retail goods. Mathematically, this premise can be expressed as

$$\sum_{j=1}^{n} S_j = \sum_{i=1}^{n} C_i \tag{9.3}$$

This formulation assumes that the sales made to visitors to the region are balanced by the purchases made by residents in retail establishments outside the region.

9.3 Calibration and evaluation of the model's performance

In this model, the calibration procedure takes place independently outside the context of the system and derives the parameters from actual trip-making behaviour obtained from the Baltimore Metropolitan Area Transportation Study.

The model was evaluated by comparing the actual current shopping patterns with the ones predicted by the model, in terms of

(1) Sales expressed in monetary units
(2) Shopping trips

in the Baltimore regions.

The consumer expenditures C_i per zones were the product of population of the particular zone and per capita shopping goods expenditures. The attractiveness of a retail centre F_j was expressed in terms of square feet of shopping goods floor space.

A comparison of the annual amount of sales generated by the model and the actual observed sales, was performed for six large retail centres and according to Lakshmanan and Hansen[1] it showed a good fit. An additional verification of the model's performance was made by comparing shopping trips. From an origin—destination survey data, the number of shopping goods trips that actually left every residential zone was obtained. These trips were distributed to the various retail centres by means of gravity submodels where shopping goods floor space was used as an attractor. A comparison between actual shopping person trips obtained by the origin—destination survey and those generated by the model also showed a good fit ($R^2 = 0.91$), according to the model builders.

The purchases made by workers and visitors in the central business district (CBD) were difficult to assess, and consequently a conclusive comparison between sales generated by the model and those actually observed was not possible. Lakshmanan and Hansen[1] concluded the evaluation of the model saying:

> Summing up, the comparison of the actual and estimated patterns of current shopping sales and trips in the Baltimore region demonstrates that the model performs reasonable well. The noticeable variations appear to be a measure of the inevitable abstraction in any model formulation as well as data problems.

9.4 Inputs

Framework
The model requires as input a description of the area under study in terms of the following components of the retail spatial structure:

(1)   Demand for shopping goods by zones
(2)   Supply of competing shopping good facilities
(3)   Some measure of the spatial separation between the retailers and the consumers.

This model is essentially a tool for estimating, for a future time horizon, the market potential of each retail centre of the area under study; consequently, projections of the above mentioned components of retail spatial structure for the future year are required. The projections used for the Baltimore region made the following assumptions:

(1)   Existing trends in the residential site selection process would continue.
(2)   Existing policies (zoning, public work, highway networks, etc.) in the region will continue.

Demand for shopping goods by zones
The demand for shopping goods is represented by the consumer purchasing power in the region, which is the product of the population of the region and per capita shopping expenditures. Thus projections for the future time period of population and per capita expenditures are required. They were found externally to the model by demographic and econometric models. It is clear that both the population and income projections used in the study of retail market potential for the Baltimore region imply the continuation of existing policies.

Supply of competing shopping goods facilities
It is important to notice that the model does not locate shopping centres to zones of the region under study. It simply locates or distributes the amount of trade flowing from any of the zones to the 'already' located centres. The locations of the shopping centres are exogenously determined and given as input to the model. In this way, the model estimates the sales levels of each retail centre for a given locational pattern of shopping centres. Then, given different alternatives of size and location of shopping facilities, the model is able to evaluate each of them, performing an evaluative function which allows the best of the proposed alternatives to be chosen. As can be seen, the use of this model to seek a solution to a system of shopping centres is a trial-and-error process.

To apply the model for a future time horizon, the size and location of the retail centres for that future point in time have to be introduced as input to the model; commonly they are given by general models of the urban spatial structure.

Some measure of the spatial separation
The interzonal network given in terms of driving time between the consumer's zone and the retailer's zone is one of the most important inputs, especially

since the model is highly sensitive to it. The application of this model for a future estimation requires the corresponding interzonal network for the particular time horizon.

9.5 Outputs

For each alternative given to the model as input, the model provides the following measures as output:

(1) The probable sales levels at each centre — 'existing' and 'future'
(2) The average trip length for shopping goods for the system as a whole
(3) The amount of trade flowing from any residential zone to any shopping centre.

9.6 Criteria for evaluation of alternatives

Minimum size
The model deals only with shopping centres of a certain minimum size, to form the cores of Metrotown Centres. Two minimum sizes related to location in the region were used for consideration of shopping centres as Metrotown Centre potential: In the more densely populated areas, the minimum size of retail centres was assumed to be 450,000–500,000 square feet of shopping floor space. In the areas of sparser development, the minimum size was postulated as 250,000–300,000 square feet of shopping floor space.

Individual criterion
The Baltimore study assumed that new shopping goods aggregations are viable when the return in annual sales per square foot was at least US $50. When the model shows that a retail centre will sell less than the minimum, the particular centre is reduced in size in the next run of the model. In this way, the scale at which shopping centres are viable is determined.

Aggregate criterion
The individual criterion of evaluation based on economic feasibility will only show which retail centres are viable in a future time for a particular size of centre chosen, and as Lakshmanan and Hansen[1] point out,

> It will not show whether the set of 'future' centres tested in any sub-region or in the entire region are a reasonable approximation of the probable commercial development as a result of market processes.

Because such an evaluation is difficult to make, the designers of this model suggest that some indications may be obtained by considering simultaneously the group or set of centres tested in a subregion for any of the alternatives studied. Two criteria were used:

(1)   Sales per square foot of shopping centre aggregated by subregions (transportation districts)

(2)   Average length of shopping trips for the region of study.

Under criterion (1), the sales per square foot of shopping centre were aggregated by subregions (transportation districts) for any of the alternatives studied. An upper limit for sales per square foot was fixed (say US $75), above which the customers of the particular shopping centre are considered poorly served. If high levels of sales per square foot of retail centre occur, then the shopping floor space should be increased either by extension of the actual centres or by the development of new ones nearby. Consequently, owing to these alterations in the alternatives studied, the evaluation procedure would be repeated.

Criterion (2) is based on the average length of shopping trips for the area under study, and can be considered as a gross measure of the 'system efficiency' of an alternative. The underlying assumption of this criterion is that:

If the assumed centres are tested at locations eccentric to population distribution, the average length of the shopping goods trip will increase (Lakshmanan and Hansen[1]),

and consequently, the efficiency of an alternative pattern of shopping centres was evaluated against the present-day average trip length level. In the Baltimore study, a 5—7 per cent variation from the current average trip length for the whole region was considered acceptable.

9.7 Equilibrium condition

Once the model has distributed the demand for shopping goods among the competing shopping centres, these results are examined. In the event that the demand exceeds (under certain criteria) the availability of shopping opportunities, the size of the centres is expanded or new centres are introduced into the system. Conversely, the size of the centres may be contracted or the centres deleted. For the system to be in equilibrium, there should be a balance between the demand for shopping goods of the predicted population and the location of future shopping centres.

9.8 Application of criteria

As has been indicated before, the development of alternative patterns of possible future retail development is a trial-and-error process. In the Baltimore study, two basic initial alternatives were tested: a 'concentration' alternative which assumed that most of the growth will take place within the densely settled inner beltway area, and a 'dispersion' alternative which located most of the growth in the outer beltway area. The preliminary evaluation of these two basic alternatives showed that their development was very unlikely in the future, and so composite patterns that combine features of both alternatives were proposed and tested.

Although the basic framework of the evaluation was the subregion, overlapping of services by centres situated in different subregions was contemplated by the model. The comparison between alternatives was easily expressed by two graphs for each subregion considered (Lakshmanan and Hansen[1]). Both these graphs are plots of sales per square foot versus size of centres for selected alternatives. For the projected time horizon, the two graphs were:

(1) Comparative success of centres in the subregion (Figure 9.1)
(2) Comparative 'system' performance in the subregion (Figure 9.2).

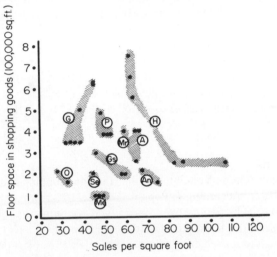

Figure 9.1 Comparative success of centres (Lakshmanan and Hansen[1])*

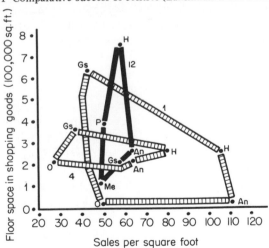

Figure 9.2 Comparative system performance (Lakshmanan and Hansen[1])*

* Reprinted by permission of the *Journal of the American Institute of Planners*, May 1965

In Figure 9.1, all alternatives for each centre are connected, showing the relationship between size and performance. In Figure 9.2, the plots of all the centres for each alternative are connected, giving a visual measure of the performance range of different centres within the subregion. From this graph we can see that alternative 12 gives better retail service than alternatives 1 or 4.

9.9 Applications of the model

Although in the Baltimore study, the continuation of existing policies was assumed, 'the model can be applied equally well with different assumptions of metropolitan policies and various evaluative criteria related to other forms of commercial organisation' (Lakshmanan and Hansen[1]).

One of the major applications of this model is to assess the impact of new shopping centres introduced into the retail system. It helps not only to decide the location of new developments but also their sizes, using among other measures, the drop in performance likely to occur in existing centres nearby and its own performance, neither of which is allowed to fall below a certain minimum level.

9.10 Comments

This model only considers one type of demand for shopping goods, which is residentially based. According to Pope,[2] about 15 to 20 per cent of a shopping centre's turnover is frequently 'work-based' and consequently, in any application of this model this limitation should be considered.

Research on shopping habits indicates that most customers patronize a variety of shopping centres — from the local neighbourhood retail centre which is visited almost daily, to the large shopping centres in the big cities where the customer goes only a few times a year. It is interesting to notice that this model, in theory at least, is able to represent these shopping habits. In the model every customer has some probability, however small, of interacting with every shopping centre in the region under study.

The sensitivity of the model to the interzonal network is important, and must be carefully projected. Although the model uses driving time as a measure of spatial separation, it is probable that a better and more comprehensive approach would be to use the cost in monetary terms between the consumer's zone and the retailer's zone as a deterrent for travel, because this economic approach can take into account more factors.

In relation to the optimality implications of this model Harris[3] stresses that considerable future investigation should be done in this direction due to:

> . . . the finding of the Lakshmanan and Hansen study that the most nearly 'balanced' distribution of shopping centres also corresponded with the minimum expenditure of travel effort by shoppers, given the alternatives studied.

The criticisms applied to models based on the social physics approach can generally be applied to this model; mainly the critical issue which centres around the validity of using parameters fitted for the current period at a future date. According to Pope,[2]

> There is a second major doubt surrounding the use of Gravity Models by planners for retailing studies. The relationship between length, frequency or destination of shopping trips, and spending per trip is rarely discussed because of the difficulty of collecting reliable data on spending. Retail gravity models assume a regular proportional fall off in spending with distance.

Much more work is needed on all these aspects since it is possible that:

> The apparently good fits which are being obtained at the moment on retail gravity models are a good fit for the wrong reasons: that calibration is indeed no more than fiddling sets of figures to fit each other (Pope[2]).

9.11 Worked problem

In order to fix ideas and to clarify the structure of this model, the following example will be given, based on a computation prepared by Batty.[4] Our problem is to find the sales generated in each retail centre of an imaginary town which is divided into three zones. Each zone has a shopping centre.

In order to find out how much trade each centre attracts, equation 9.2 will be used, and is presented below:

$$S_j = \sum_{i=1}^{n} S_{ij} = \sum_{i=1}^{n} C_i \frac{F_j{}^{\beta}/d_{ij}{}^{\alpha}}{\sum_{j=1}^{n} \dfrac{F_j{}^{\beta}}{d_{ij}{}^{\alpha}}}$$

As input, we need the following components of the retail spatial structure:

(1) Table of distances between zones. The schematic representation and the distance matrix are given below:

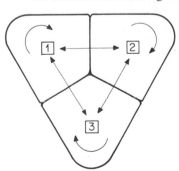

	1	2	3
1	2	10	15
2	10	3	12
3	15	12	2

(2)   Expenditures or demand for shopping goods by each zone (usually measured in monetary units).

(3)   Supply of competing shopping goods facilities expressed by the attractiveness of each zone. (This attractiveness can be measured by an index of the size of the retail centre, parking space facilities, etc.)

That is:

Zone	Expenditure (C_i)	Attractiveness $(F_j{}^\beta)$
1	1000	70
2	1500	100
3	800	160
Total:	3300	

For simplicity, let us assume that by calibration the values of the parameters have been found to be $\alpha = 2$ and $\beta = 1$. Now, to find out how much trade each shopping centre attracts, the following steps should be taken.

Step 1   Divide the attraction of each centre by the distance to each residential zone and add up by residential zones.

$\dfrac{F_j{}^1}{d_{ij}{}^2}$	retail centres			$\sum\limits_{j=1}^{3} \dfrac{F_j{}^1}{d_{ij}{}^2}$
	1	2	3	
1	$\dfrac{70}{2^2}$	$\dfrac{100}{10^2}$	$\dfrac{160}{15^2}$	$=$	19.2
2	$\dfrac{70}{10^2}$	$\dfrac{100}{3^2}$	$\dfrac{160}{12^2}$	$=$	12.9
3	$\dfrac{70}{15^2}$	$\dfrac{100}{12^2}$	$\dfrac{160}{2^2}$	$=$	41.0

residential zones

Step 2   Work out the relative proportion of attraction by means of the following expression:

$$\frac{F_j{}^1 / d_{ij}{}^2}{\sum\limits_{j=1}^{3} \dfrac{F_j{}^1}{d_{ij}{}^2}}$$

retail centres

		1	2	3		
residential	1	0.91	0.05	0.04	=	1.00
zones	2	0.05	0.86	0.09	=	1.00
	3	0.01	0.02	0.97	=	1.00

By adding up the rows of the above matrix we can check whether the relative proportion has been calculated correctly.

Step 3 The amount of trade flowing from any residential zone to any shopping centre (S_{ij}) is obtained by multiplying the demand for shopping goods for each zone C_i by the relative proportion of attraction influenced by each retail centre; that is,

$$S_{ij} = C_i \frac{F_j^{\,1}/d_{ij}^{\,2}}{\sum\limits_{j=1}^{3} \dfrac{F_j^{\,1}}{d_{ij}^{\,2}}}$$

retail centres

	S_{ij}	1	2	3		
residential	1	910	50	40	=	1000
zones	2	75	1290	135	=	1500
	3	8	16	776	=	800

By adding up the rows of the above matrix, we can perform a check by comparing whether these values equal the amount of expenditure C_i in the corresponding zone.

Step 4 To find out the sales generated in each shopping centre, we sum all the trade flowing into each centre, that is:

$$S_j = \sum_{i=1}^{3} S_{ij}$$

Practically, this is obtained by adding up each column of the above matrix:

retail centres

	1	2	3	$\sum\limits_{j=1}^{3} S_j$
$S_j =$	993	1356	951	= 3300

Step 5 Finally, we may perform a rough check on the calculations so far worked out by applying equation 9.3,

$$\sum_{j=1}^{3} S_j = \sum_{i=1}^{3} C_i = 3300$$

which expresses the fact that the total sales generated at all the retail centres must equal the total available consumer expenditures for retail goods.

References

1 LAKSHMANAN, T. R. and HANSEN, W. G. 'A retail market potential model'. *Journal of the American Institute of Planners*, 1965, May, pp. 134–143.
2 POPE, A. S. 'Gravity models in town planning: use in retailing exercises'. Department of Town Planning, Lanchester College of Technology, Coventry, 1969, October.
3 HARRIS, B. 'Quantitative models of urban development: their role in metropolitan policy making', in PERLOFF, HARVEY, S. and WINGO, LOWDON JR. *Issues in Urban Economics*, Johns Hopkins, Baltimore, 1968.
4 BATTY, M. 'Introductory model-building problems for urban and regional planning', Urban Systems Research Unit, University of Reading, 1970.

10   The Penn–Jersey Regional Growth Model

10.1 Introduction

The Penn–Jersey model proposed by John Herbert and Benjamin J. Stevens[1] was originally designed to simulate the locational behaviour of different household types in the Penn–Jersey Transportation Study. Although the model was eventually abandoned by that study in favour of other approaches, it is a remarkable proposal on which development resumed at the Institute for Environmental Studies, University of Pennsylvania, under the guidance of its designers.

Originally, the model was intended to link with other models; that is, the model was constructed as part of a larger model which was designed to deal with all types of land-use activity. This model is a simulation of residential location based on the economic theory that individual households tend to maximize their local advantage, and at the same time land is allocated to that group of households which can pay the highest price for it. This equilibrium location of households based on maximization of satisfaction is generated within the constraints posed by their budgets. Linear programming techniques are used to translate this process into an operational form.

10.2 Treatment of time

The total relevant period is subdivided into a number of short iterative periods. The shorter the iterative period is, the more interactions among land users is taken into account, but on the other hand the computational complexity increases. In order to obtain a balance between these two factors, the model envisages an iterative period of at least a year.

In a particular iterative period, the number of households to be located and the amount of land that is expected to be available for residential use is forecast exogenously.

10.3 Data

This model is probably one of the models that requires the greatest amount of data. It is necessary to obtain an inventory of households cross classified by incomes, patterns of consumption preferences and patterns of daily movement; an inventory of all residential sites in the region grouped into districts such that sites within a given district are homogeneous with respect to size of lot, type and quality of structure and neighbourhood amenities. Also, for each district, accessibility to alternative destination sets must be calculated.

10.4 Definitions

In order to gain a better understanding of the structure of this model, it has been considered convenient to identify fully the terms used in the model, giving the definitions proposed by its designers Herbert and Stevens:[1]

Household: A household is a person or group of persons with a common budget purchasing a single residential bundle.

Household group: A household group is a collection of households which have similar residential budgets and similar tastes with respect to residential bundles. (Herbert and Stevens assume that households that have similar tastes give rise to similar phenomena on the sites they occupy.)

House: A house is the physical structure to be occupied by a single household.

House cost: House cost is the dollar cost of constructing, operating and maintaining a house over a specified time period, computed on an annual basis.

Amenity level: The amenity level associated with a site is the level of psychic satisfaction which a household has an opportunity to enjoy because of certain characteristics of that site. (The site characteristics contributing to the amenity of a site, could be the characteristics of the existing households, level of public services and age of the area, planting on the site and views from the area.)

Amenity cost: The amenity cost associated with a particular site is the annual dollar cost of providing a specified amenity level on that site. (To a particular type of house offered to a particular type of household for each area, a 'premium' due to the amenity of that area has been attached. The amenity cost of a particular site will be the difference between the premium associated with its area and the maximum premium for that particular type of household and house.)

Trip set: A trip set consists of the number of each type of trip generated per year by a household. (Types of trips could be for example a trip to a particular type of employment, recreation, shopping, etc., but the origins and destinations in a set are not specified since it is assumed that the alternative trip sets considered by a household will be independent of that household's location.)

Trip pattern: The trips in a trip set when their origin and destination have been identified. (The destination will be forecast exogenously by a probability interaction model.)

Travel cost: Travel cost is the annual dollar cost to the household of carrying out a trip pattern.

Site: A site is the parcel of land assignable to a particular household.

Total site rent: Total site rent is the dollar value of the amount received annually by a site owner for the use of the *land* in the site. It is *exclusive* of the value of the house, amenity level and travel pattern associated with the site.

Unit site rent: The unit site rent on a site is the total site rent divided by the number of acres in the site.

Residential bundle: A residential bundle is a unique combination of a house, an amenity level, a trip set and a site of a particular size.

Market basket: A market basket is a unique combination of: a residential bundle and an 'other commodities' bundle, both consumed annually by a household.

Total household budget: A household's total budget is the dollar amount that a household allocates annually to the purchase of a market basket.

Residential budget: A residential budget is that part of a household's total budget that is allocated annually to the purchase of a residential bundle.

Region: A region is the geographical space within which the model is required to allocate a given number of households to a given supply of land.

Area: An area is a regional subdivision whose characteristics are homogeneous with respect to the costs of construction, amenity costs and the costs of transportation to other areas.

10.5 Conceptual framework

The model assumes using Alonso's theory* that the factor which a household considers in choosing an area in which to allocate are:

Its budget limitations or total budget
The items which constitute a market basket
The costs of obtaining those items.

Households which are grouped into homogeneous units or household groups are allowed to choose their location from a set of market baskets among which each household in that group is 'indifferent'. (The procedure used by the model to build the indifferences set of market baskets does not appear in the information provided, and so it is not possible to given any idea of how this is obtained.) The household will select from this set of market baskets the one which maximizes his 'savings' or rent-paying ability.

---

* One of the important points of Alonso's theory is its first method of economic analysis which is clearly summarized by Batty:[2] 'The individual or household has a fixed budget determined by its income. This budget is assumed to consist of purchases of three goods – residential space or housing, transportation and a composite good (all other purchases). Alonso assumes that different combinations of each of these goods will give rise to different utilities or satisfaction. It is then possible to construct indifference surfaces giving equivalent utility, and utility can then be maximized within the constraints imposed by the budget equation.'

To introduce the idea of 'savings' or rent-paying ability, it is helpful to recall that a household has a residential budget which it uses for the purchase of the following items:

A house
An amenity level
A trip set
A site of a particular size

which form a residential bundle in a particular area. If land were free, the household would save the cost of the last item, and this would be a measure of the savings enjoyed by the household because of the locational advantages of the area.

This means that for a particular area, the difference between the residential budget assigned to a particular residential bundle and the cost of the bundle *exclusive* of the site in it is the maximum amount the household can pay in that area for that site; and it will be the maximum amount that the landowner could extract from the household as site rent. This difference is the definition of the household's rent-paying ability for that site in that area. In reality, there is little doubt that these savings would be drawn off as rent from the household due to the land market process.

Although a household is 'indifferent' among the market baskets in its indifference set, it seems reasonable to suppose that such savings would have a positive marginal utility for the household; and so a rational household will select from its indifference set the market basket which will maximize its savings. The solution is found by a linear programme which assigns households to sites so as to maximize aggregate 'rent-paying ability' of the region's population; in terms of the classical location theories, this would be the equilibrium location.

10.6 Mathematical formulation
Before we describe the mathematical formulation of this model, it will be useful to give a short explanation of linear programming and the concepts of 'primal' and 'dual' solutions.

Linear programming
Linear programming refers to techniques for solving a general class of optimization problems, in which a large number of simple conditions have to be satisfied at the same time. They are characterized by a linear function we would like to optimize (the objective function) and a set of linear constraints. Thus, linear programming problems are those in which:

(1)   The objective can be expressed as a linear function of variables
(2)   The constraints can be expressed as a linear function of variables.

We shall illustrate the fundamentals of the linear programming techniques by means of a very simple example:

A manufacturer produces two types of products: type I and type II, each of which requires a different proportion of three ingredients: A, B and C, as follows

Product	Ingredient A	Ingredient B	Ingredient C
type I	1	2	1
type II	1	1	2

Availability of the ingredients is restricted as shown below

Ingredient A: 4000 units
Ingredient B: 7000 units
Ingredient C: 7000 units

Profit per unit output is

Product type I :   £5
Product type II: £4

We are interested in determining which is the combination of products that the manufacturer should produce in order to maximize his profit.

We can express all the information given as follows,

Ingredient	One item of product type I	type II	Total availabilities
A	1	1	4000
B	2	1	7000
C	1	2	7000
Profit per unit	5	4	Maximize

Let us now rephrase the problem in mathematical form. If we let:

x_1 = number of units of product type I we shall produce
x_2 = number of units of product type II we shall produce

we can express the constraints posed by the availability of ingredients by inequalities. Let us consider the restrictions imposed by the availability of ingredient A: This ingredient is used

$$(1)x_1 + (1)x_2 \text{ units,}$$

since one (1) unit is required for each unit of product type I and x_1 units of product type I are produced; additionally, one (1) unit is required for each unit of product type II and x_2 units of product type II are produced. Thus, the total ingredient A used is the sum of the units required to produce each product. The total amount of ingredient A used cannot be greater than 4000 units. Mathematically this means that

$$x_1 + x_2 \leqslant 4000 \tag{10.1}$$

The same reasoning applied to the other ingredients will give us the following inequalities:

Availability of ingredient B:
$$2x_1 + x_2 \leqslant 7000 \tag{10.2}$$

Availability of ingredient C:
$$x_1 + 2x_2 \leqslant 7000 \tag{10.3}$$

Obviously, negative quantities cannot be produced, thus, we impose a further two restrictions on the problem:

$$x_1 \geqslant 0 \tag{10.4}$$

$$x_2 \geqslant 0 \tag{10.5}$$

Subject to the above restrictions, the manufacturer's objective is to maximize profit. Thus, if the variable z represents the total profit, the objective can be formulated as

$$\text{maximize } z = 5x_1 + 4x_2 \tag{10.6}$$

Summarizing, the problem can be expressed algebraically as:

$$\text{maximize } z = 5x_1 + 4x_2 \tag{10.6}$$

subject to
$$x_1 + x_2 \leqslant 4000 \tag{10.1}$$

$$2x_1 + x_2 \leqslant 7000 \tag{10.2}$$

$$x_1 + 2x_2 \leqslant 7000 \tag{10.3}$$

$$x_1, x_2 \geqslant 0 \qquad \text{(10.4) and (10.5)}$$

Although there are several ways of solving a linear programming problem, we shall solve this one using the graphical method. This is possible because we are dealing here with only two variables. If we would have more than three variables, this method could not be employed because graphical representation in spaces of more than three dimensions is not possible.

Graphical method

To start, we shall plot on a graph the set of points which satisfies the constraints of the problem. To do so, we use a two dimensional graph ($x_1 x_2$ co-ordinate system) where we represent each of the linear constraints by a line. This is shown in Figure 10.1. If we analyse this figure carefully, we shall see that by limiting a region (the feasible region) we have determined the set of points which represents all the feasible solutions to the problem. This region has been obtained by representing the constraints as equalities. The inequality sign helps us to determine which side of the graph (half-plane) is an admissible area. For example consider the point ($x_1 = 0, x_2 = 0$), that is the origin. We substitute this point

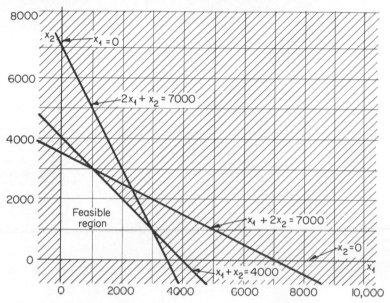

Figure 10.1 Graph relating the set of points which satisfies the constraints

(0, 0) in each of the constraints in turn, and we see if it satisfies the inequality. Thus, in the constraint $2x_1 + x_2 \leq 7000$, we have $2(0) + (0) < 7000$, indicating that the constraint is satisfied; Therefore, the set of points satisfying the inequality $2x_1 + x_2 \leq 7000$ consists of all the points lying *on* or *below* the line $2x_1 + x_2 = 7000$.

It now remains to be seen which of these solutions best suits the manufacturer's policy. That is, we must find the point or points in the region of feasible solutions which give the largest value of the objective function.

Now, for a fixed value z, $z = 5x_1 + 4x_2$ is a straight line. Any point on this line will give the same value of z. For each different value of z, we obtain a different line. We may draw a series of these lines or iso-profit lines on a graph. All points on an iso-profit line yield an equal profit. This is shown in Figure 10.2.

We can see that the iso-profit lines are parallel to each other and have a higher value the further they are from the origin. Now, we should try to find the iso-profit line with the largest value of z which has at least one point in common with the region of feasible solutions. To do so, we can superimpose on the graph in Figure 10.1 a series of iso-profit lines. This is shown in Figure 10.3.

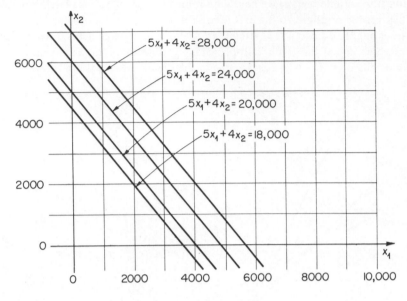

Figure 10.2 Iso-profit lines

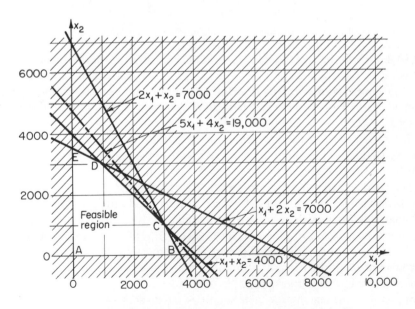

Figure 10.3 Graphical solution to a linear programming problem

We can see that the largest value iso-profit line that has a point in common with the feasible region is the one yielding a profit of £19,000. The only feasible point on this line is point C ($x_1 = 3000, x_2 = 1000$). Thus, the optimal solution is to produce 3000 units of product type I and 1000 units of product type II, which yields a profit of £19,000.

Algebraic method

For a problem with more than three variables (which applies to most practical problems), a graphical method of solution cannot be used and an alternative method is required. There are several algebraic methods, but we do not intend to explain these methods here because they go beyond the scope of this book. There are very many texts on linear programming which are very good on this topic: Vadja,[3] Loomba,[4] Wagner,[5] and Hadley,[6] However, we shall present here the formulation in equation form of the manufacturer's problem already solved by the graphical method, in order to understand the further possibilities of linear programming.

In general, we are more skilful at dealing with equalities than with inequalities. Therefore, it is desirable to convert the inequalities into equations, so that a system of simultaneous linear equations is obtained. We can do this easily by introducing some additional variables, which are called slack variables. For the availability of ingredient A:

$$x_1 + x_2 \leqslant 4000 \tag{10.1}$$

If a non-negative slack variable x_{s1} is added, an equation is obtained which is equivalent to the inequality constraint:

$$x_1 + x_2 + x_{s1} = 4000 \tag{10.7}$$

where $$x_{s1} \geqslant 0$$

The variable x_{s1} represents the amount of ingredient A that is available but not used. It is easily seen that if the manufacturer decides not to produce anything, that is $x_1 = 0$ and $x_2 = 0$, equation 10.7 indicates that $x_{s1} = 4000$.

In the same way, we can add slack variables to the other two constraints where: x_{s2} represents the amount of ingredient B that is available but not used; and x_{s3} represents the amount of ingredient C that is available but not used.

Thus, the problem can be formulated in equation form as follows:

Maximize $\qquad z = 5x_1 + 4x_2$ $\qquad\qquad\qquad$ (10.6)

subject to $\qquad x_1 + x_2 + x_{s1} = 4000$ $\qquad\qquad$ (10.7)

$\qquad\qquad\qquad 2x_1 + x_2 + x_{s2} = 7000$ $\qquad\qquad$ (10.8)

$\qquad\qquad\qquad x_1 + 2x_2 + x_{s3} = 7000$ $\qquad\qquad$ (10.9)

$\qquad\qquad\qquad x_1, x_2, x_{s1}, x_{s2}, x_{s3} \geqslant 0$ $\quad$ (10.4), (10.5), (10.10), (10.11), (10.12)

When solving this problem by any algebraic method, we shall get the following values as the optimal solution:

$$x_1 = 3000$$
$$x_2 = 1000$$
$$x_{s1} = 0$$
$$x_{s2} = 0$$
$$x_{s3} = 2000$$
$$z = 19,000$$

The values $x_{s1} = 0$ and $x_{s2} = 0$ indicate that at this solution, all the A and B ingredient availabilities are used; $x_{s3} = 2000$ shows that there is a surplus availability of 2000 units of ingredient C. Thus, we can see that we have obtained additional information about the solution to the problem, which is not easily grasped from the graphical method.

The dual problem

The problem as stated above is generally described as the primal. There is, however, a meaningful reciprocal method of formulating it that is of great practical utility; it is called the dual. The dual theorem of linear programming asserts that to every maximization problem in L.P. there corresponds a specific symmetric problem of minimization involving the same data as the original problem. Thus, the two problems have characteristics which give remarkable symmetry, as shown below

Primal problem

Maximize	$z = 5x_1 + 4x_2$	(10.6)
subject to ·	$x_1 + x_2 \leqslant 4000$	(10.1)
	$2x_1 + x_2 \leqslant 7000$	(10.2)
	$x_1 + 2x_2 \leqslant 7000$	(10.3)
	$x_1, x_2 \geqslant 0$	

Dual problem

Minimize	$g = 4000y_1 + 7000y_2 + 7000y_3$	(10.13)
subject to	$y_1 + 2y_2 + y_3 \geqslant 5$	(10.14)
	$y_1 + y_2 + 2y_3 \geqslant 4$	(10.15)
	$y_1, y_2, y_3 \geqslant 0$	(10.16)
		(10.17)
		(10.18)

The relationship between the variables in the primal and the dual may be easily grasped in tabular form as presented in Figure 10.4. The formulation of the dual problem in this example can be seen as the determination of the portion of the profits which is attributable to each of the scarce resources, because it is argued that profits that the manufacturer accrues are directly attributable to the scarce resources that are available. Thus, the dual problem requires us to find the very smallest valuation of the manufacturer's scarce resources which completely accounts for all the profits obtained for the outputs.

	x_1	x_2		
y_1	1	1	$\leq$	4000
y_2	2	1	$\leq$	7000
y_3	1	2	$\leq$	7000
	$\geq$	$\geq$		Min.
	5	4	Max	g / z

Figure 10.4 Primal–dual matrix

Analysing the constraints of the dual problem, we see that y_1, y_2 and y_3 represent the value assigned to each unit of availability of A, B and C ingredient respectively. Also, we can see that due to the fact that the total profit is going to be completely apportioned to the scarce input resources, these total input values must be at least as great as the corresponding unit profits; that is

$$y_1 + 2y_2 + y_3 \geq 5 \qquad (10.14)$$

$$y_1 + y_2 + 2y_3 \geq 4 \qquad (10.15)$$

Because it is nonsense to give negative values to the scarce resources, we see that there is a non-negativity restriction on the variables; that is

$$y_1, y_2 \text{ and } y_3 \geq 0 \quad (10.16), (10.17) \text{ and } (10.18)$$

The objective function of the dual formulation represents the assumption that the manufacturer wishes to determine values of y_1, y_2 and y_3 such that the total value assigned to the scarce resources is minimized,

minimize $$g = 4000y_1 + 7000y_2 + 7000y_3 \qquad (10.13)$$

When solving the dual problem by any of the methods available, we find the following results:

$$y_1 = 3$$

$$y_2 = 1$$

$$y_3 = 0$$

$$g = 19,000$$

$y_1 = 3$ indicates the marginal value of a unit increase in the ingredient A; in other words, for each unit of extra ingredient A availability, the profit could be increased by £3, and therefore it would pay the manufacturer to provide this extra availability if it could be obtained for less than £3 per unit. A similar interpretation can be given to $y_2 = 1$; that is the profit could be increased by £1 for each unit of extra B ingredient availability; Thus, the manufacturer could afford to pay up to £1 per unit of extra availability of ingredient B.

The fact that $y_3 = 0$ indicates that ingredient C is not scarce; this has already been seen in the solution to the primal problem since we have found that there is surplus availability of 2000 units of ingredient C.

It is not surprising that $g = 19,000 = z$ because this feature is a property of the dual problem. In fact, because of the properties of the primal and dual problems, it is a matter of indifference which of the two problems is solved. From the methodological view point, it may be simpler to solve the dual than the primal, or vice versa, depending on the number of variables and constraints involved.

As we have pointed out before, the utility of the dual is both interpretative and methodological. We shall stress again that the interpretative utility is based on the fact that the dual variable indicates the marginal value of a unit increase in the corresponding resource; in other words, the dual variables are measures of the effect of incremental changes in the constraints on the objective function.

Notation

The notation used in the linear programming formulation of this model, is the following:

U　areas which form an exhaustive subdivision of the region. Areas are indicated by the superscripts $K = 1, 2, \ldots U$

n　household groups indicated by subscripts $i = 1, 2, \ldots n$

m　residential bundles indicated by subscripts $h = 1, 2, \ldots m$

b_{ih}　is the residential budget allocated by a household of group i to the purchase of residential bundle h

c_{ih}^K　is the annual cost to a household of group i of the residential bundle h in area K, *exclusive* of site cost

s_{ih}　is the number of acres in the site used by a household of group i if it uses residential bundle h

L^K　is the number of acres of land available for residential use in area K in a particular iteration of the model

N_i　is the number of households of groups i that are to be located in the region in a particular iteration

X_{ih}^K　is the number of households of groups i using residential bundle h, located by the model in area K.

When dealing with the dual problem, the solution variables X_{ih}^K are replaced by:

r^K the annual rent per unit of land in area K
v_i the annual subsidy per household for all households of group i.

The primal problem

The primal linear programming formulation has the following form:

Maximize

$$Z = \sum_{K=1}^{U} \sum_{i=1}^{n} \sum_{h=1}^{m} X_{ih}^K (b_{ih} - c_{ih}^K) \tag{10.19}$$

subject to

$$\sum_{i=1}^{n} \sum_{h=1}^{m} s_{ih} X_{ih}^K \leqslant L^K \quad (K = 1, 2, \ldots U) \tag{10.20}$$

$$\sum_{K=1}^{U} \sum_{h=1}^{m} - X_{ih}^K = -N_i \quad (i = 1, 2, \ldots n) \tag{10.21}$$

and all

$$X_{ih}^K \geqslant 0 \qquad \begin{matrix} (K = 1, 2, \ldots U) \\ (i = 1, 2, \ldots n) \\ (h = 1, 2, \ldots m) \end{matrix}$$

The objective function (equation 10.19) refers to the maximization of the total savings in location rents. Constraint equation 10.20 prevents the consumption of land in each area from exceeding the land available; and constraint equation 10.21 will force the model to locate the projected number of households of each group. This means that the model will have to allocate *all* the projected households, even though some households may have negative or zero rent-paying ability in all areas. The fact that constraint equation 10.21 has a minus sign on both sides is only with the objective of facilitating the interpretation of the dual variables.

The dual problem

The interpretation of the dual problem clarifies considerably the operation of the allocation model. The dual problem takes the following formulation:

Minimize

$$Z' = \sum_{K=1}^{U} r^K L^K + \sum_{i=1}^{n} v_i (-N_i) \tag{10.22}$$

subject to:

$$s_{ih} r^K - v_i \geqslant b_{ih} - c_{ih}^K \quad (K = 1, 2, \ldots U) \tag{10.23}$$
$$(i = 1, 2, \ldots n)$$
$$(h = 1, 2, \ldots m)$$

all

$$r^K \geqslant 0 \qquad (K = 1, 2, \ldots U)$$
$$v_i \gtrless 0 \qquad (i = 1, 2, \ldots n)$$

A proof of the dual variable v_i being sign unrestricted can easily be found in Hadley[6] (page 237).

As can be seen, the objective function of the dual problem, equation 10.22 (neglecting for the moment the second summation), is to minimize total land rent paid to landlords, but at the same time, subject to the constraint equations (10.23) that prevent the unit rent of each site from falling below the unit rent-paying ability of any household that might locate on that site. This means that the individual landowner can receive at least as much per unit as the highest bidder for his land is willing to pay.

The use of the subsidy variable v_i enables households with no rent-paying ability to effect a residential location. Because unit rent-paying ability depends upon both total rent-paying ability and size of site purchased, 'poorer' households using small sites may be the highest bidders per unit of land in a particular area, and then, in some cases 'subsidies' in the model may be assigned to 'wealthy' households.

The use of subsidy variable v_i sometimes presents a problem: suppose, for example, that all of one household group is unable to locate in areas where aggregate rent-paying ability is maximized (due to capacity constraints), then the remaining households of the group have to be subsidized in order that they can be allocated elsewhere, but because of the nature of linear programming the same subsidy must be given to *all* the household group, and this may lead to excessively high rents in the most favourable areas. Herbert and Stevens suggest that this problem may be solved by adjusting the zoning of the system in order to relieve the excess demand on zones. In order to find the zones where the land constraints are reached, the model should be allowed to run and then re-run with the zones relaxed.

10.7 Uses of the model

The model is applicable to test policy decisions concerning zoning, transportation, redevelopment, public housing, etc. Different types of redevelopment can be easily allocated since the model provides rent levels for each zone, allowing the corresponding studies to be made. The alteration in transportation costs can be tested by multiple runs of the model. Also the introduction of direct or indirect subsidies can be easily experimented with in the model.

10.8 Comments

This model shows a direct attempt to simulate markets, and it focuses on residential activity from the demand side. By varying assumptions about public policy, values held by firms and households about location and movement, etc., a large number of alternatives of change can be generated for study.

An interesting comment about this model is given by Harris:[7]

> One of the main advantages of a programming type of market simulation model based on a genuine preference analysis and a market-clearing

concepts, like this model, is the output of values of the dual variables which gauge the intensity of demand for land and provide inputs to other submodels dealing with industrial and commercial location and with public policy determinations. Equally important, the dual variables applying to household types may be interpreted as needed adjustments in their preference anticipations in the current market, and thus, provide a basis for comparing the benefits conveyed under different plans.

The rigorous nature of the linear programming formulation is partially relaxed by the effect of the subsidy variable, but there remain several other problems that the authors of the model are trying to solve.

Lowry,[8] commenting on the fact that in the latest version of the model 'rent-paying ability' is replaced by 'bid rent' (a budget residual covering the entire residence package of site and structure – but not the transport cost), remarks:

> This modification was in part a response to certain mechanical difficulties in the linear program which threatened the integrity of the solution. Linear programming, an algorithm designed for continuous variables, does not readily cope with an assignment problem involving groups of households and groups of residential sites.

Though this model has proved difficult to calibrate, there is little doubt that the model builders gained good insights into the mechanisms of the urban development.

REFERENCES

1 HERBERT, J. D. and STEVENS, B. H. 'A model for the distribution of residential activities in urban areas'. *Journal of Regional Science,* 1960, (Fall) 2/2 pp. 21–36.
2 BATTY, M. 'Spatial theory and information systems'. Urban Systems Research Unit, Department of Geography, University of Reading, 1970, March.
3 VAJDA, S. *An Introduction to Linear Programming and the Theory of Games.* Methuen, Wiley, 1960.
4 LOOMBA, N. P. *Linear Programming: An Introductory Analysis.* McGraw-Hill, 1964.
5 WAGNER, H. M. *Principles of Operations Research.* Prentice-Hall International Inc., 1969.
6 HADLEY, G. *Linear Programming.* Addison-Wesley Publishing Company, Third printing 1969.
7 HARRIS, B. 'Quantitative models of urban development: their role in metropolitan policy-making', in PERLOFF, HARVEY, S. and WINGO, LOWDON JR. *Issues in Urban Economics*, Johns Hopkins, Baltimore, 1968.
8 LOWRY, I. S. 'Seven models of urban development: a structural comparation'. Special Report 97, Highway Research Board, Washington D.C., 1968.

11 The EMPIRIC Model

11.1 Introduction
The EMPIRIC model was devised by Donald M. Hill[1] for the Boston Regional Planning Project in order to develop a comprehensive development plan for the Greater Boston Region (USA), in 1965.

11.2 Function of the model
The model is designed to distribute or allocate externally supplied growth forecasts of activities such as population and employment among the zones or subdivisions of the region under study. This process of allocation takes place as local changes occur in the quality of public services and transportation networks as well as changes over time in the activity totals. Although the model for the Boston region only deals with population and employment, other activities can easily be incorporated into the model.

The predicting capabilities of the model are based on:

(1)   Existing patterns of urban development
(2)   Externally forecast regional growth
(3)   Exogenous policy considerations concerning transportation, open space, regional growth, zoning policies and public utilities.

11.3 Treatment of time
The model is operated recursively in a series of short steps, where each step depends upon the results of previous steps. The model can be applied in this manner over several consecutive 5- or 10-year intervals.

11.4 Level of categorization
For the study of the Boston Metropolitan region, the model distinguishes two classes of population:

(1)   White collar population
(2)   Blue collar population

and three classes of employment:

(1)   Retail and wholesale employment
(2)   Manufacturing employment
(3)   All other employment.

The model can be considered a general one because it covers several types of activities simultaneously.

11.5 Some terms explained

To describe the model, it is convenient to explain some terms:

Subregions: are the territorial subdivisions of the region under study.

Located variables: are those urban activities such as population and employment that the model is going to allocate or distribute among the subregions.

Locator variables: are those variables (e.g. transit accessibilities, sewage facilities, etc.) which by their presence or absence influence the amount of one or more located variables in each subregion.

11.6 Underlying concept

Hill[1] points out that:

> The underlying concept of the model is that the development patterns of urban activities are interrelated in a systematic manner which provides a reasonable basis for their prediction.

He also argues that there are stable relationships in the development patterns of urban activities and by a statistical analysis of the individual decisions made during a period of 5 or 10 years, the structure of these relations can be found and used for prediction purposes. These arguments are typical of a social physics approach.

In order to evaluate the extent of the interrelations between variables of the urban spatial structure, and to identify the influential locator variables, four methods of study were followed (Hill[1]):

(1)   A graphic analysis of a large number of relationships between sub-regional growth rates of population and employment, and a large number of causal (locator) variables which were thought to be important.

(2)   An investigation of the changes and trends in population and employment that took place during 1950–60 decade.

(3)   An analysis of population and employment data (using factor analysis techniques) to determine to what extent variables can be grouped according to their tendency to locate in proximity to one another, or to exhibit similarities in their influence on the locational tendencies of other variables.

(4)   The development of multiple regression equations which demonstrate the relationships between growth rates of population and employment

and a large number of variables that have significant effects upon locations of population and employment.

In evaluating the extent of the interrelationship between variables, the model imposes the restriction that the interrelationships must be expressed so that the influences of variables are additive. This restriction implies that the model incorporates a linear form.

11.7 The mathematical formulation

The findings of the four studies mentioned above provided the insight necessary to formulate the model as a set of simultaneous linear equations for each sub-region; one equation for each located variable. The model is expressed by the following equation system:

$$\Delta R_i = \sum_{\substack{j=1 \\ j \neq i}}^{N} a_{ij} \Delta R_j + \sum_{k=1}^{M} b_{ik} (Z_k \text{ or } \Delta Z_k) \qquad (11.1)$$

where i or $j = 1,2, \ldots i, j, \ldots N$: number of the located variable

$k = 1,2, \ldots k, \ldots M$: number of the locator variable

ΔR_i or ΔR_j = change in the level of the ith or jth located variable over the calibration or forecast time interval

Z_k = level of locator variable k at the beginning of the calibration or forecast time interval

ΔZ_k = change in the level of the kth locator variable over the calibration or forecast time interval

a_{ij}, b_{ij} = coefficients expressing the interrelationships among variables.

The equation system (11.1) states that the change in the subregional share of a located variable in each subregion is proportional to:

(1)   The change in the subregional share of all other located variables in the subregion
(2)   The change in the subregional share of a number of locator variables in the subregion
(3)   The value of the subregional shares of other locator variables.

This model is particularly flexible in the sense that it permits the inclusion of many different types of locator variables such as:

Intensities of land use
Quality of water service
Quality of sewage disposal service
Automobile and transit accessibilities, etc.

11.8 Functional structure

Introduction

The model can be conveniently divided into two stages for its application:

(1) Calibration stage: determination of a set of coefficients to enable the model to reproduce known development patterns with minimum error
(2) Allocation stage: distribution of externally supplied growth forecasts of the various activities.

Calibration stage

At this first stage, if we analyse the equation system (11.1) expressed below

$$\Delta R_i = \sum_{\substack{j=1 \\ j \neq i}}^{N} a_{ij} \Delta R_j + \sum_{k=1}^{M} b_{ik} \, (Z_k \text{ or } \Delta Z_k)$$

We can see that the values of all the variables may be obtained from data related to two past points in time. (The Baltimore Study used the years 1950 and 1960.) Only the values of the parameters a and b are not known, and these may be determined by means of regression analysis which deals with simultaneous equations.

Then, we may say that the objective of the calibration process was to determine a set of values for the coefficients a and b, such that the 1960 development patterns of a subregion were reproduced with minimum error. It is important to stress that there is one equation system (11.1) for every subregion of the study area.

Allocation stage

At this stage, the objective is to estimate the change in the level of every located variable for every subregion over the forecast period ΔR_i. We shall denote the variables related to the forecast period with a prime ($'$); the equation system (11.1) related to a forecast period may be expressed as

$$\Delta R_i' = \sum_{\substack{j=1 \\ j \neq i}}^{N} a_{ij} \Delta R_j' + \sum_{k=1}^{M} b_{ik} \, (Z_k' \text{ or } \Delta Z_k') \tag{11.2}$$

Analysing equation system 11.2, we can see that the values of the locator variables for the forecast period (Z_k' and $\Delta Z_k'$), can be obtained directly from the projected values determined exogenously and from data sources. In the Baltimore Study, the base year for the projection was 1960 and the projected year was 1970.

By using the values for the parameters a and b obtained during the calibration period, the system of equations (11.2) can be solved simultaneously to estimate future change in the level of each located variable for each subregion $\Delta R_i'$. These forecasts are simultaneous, that is, each change in share influences the others.

It is important to notice that the values obtained by solving equation system 11.2 do not directly estimate the levels of the located variables (e.g. population, employment) to be assigned to every subregion at the target date; they only estimate the *change* in the subregion's share of the regional total for that particular located variable, during the forecast period.

These changes in shares are added into the shares held by each subregion at the beginning of the forecast period, to obtain a relative value for the subregional share at the end of the forecast interval. To obtain the absolute values, these relative values are multiplied by the externally supplied forecast control figure.

11.9 Validation of the model

Several tests were performed to validate the model for the Baltimore region; one investigated the effect on forecast accuracy of varying the length of the historical forecast period. Other tests involved measuring the sensitivity of model forecast values to the lengths of future forecast periods and the size and number of subregions.

11.10 Comments

According to Hill:[1] 'The research development, calibration and test work has been successful and the model is practical and operational'.

Lowry,[2] calling districts the territorial subdivisions of the region, makes the following comment in relation to the equation system 11.1:

> The logic of these equations is puzzling. Since each district's population and employment variables are expressed as changes in shares, the fitted parameters fix relationships among these changes in shares without regard for the magnitude or even the sign of changes in the total regional volumes of the relevant activities. The fitted equations tell nothing about the relationships among changes in volumes for the activities within a district. (Further on she adds). The model does not comment on the pattern of inter-district flows necessary to produce these net changes.

In relation to the location of shopping centres, we may point out here that models of this type

> . . . do not adequately account for the known tendency of retail trade centres to 'peak' in selected locations and that they therefore predict an excessively uniform distribution (Harris[3]).

In this model, the manufacturing industry, which is considered as a single homogeneous one, is also located by the model. A deficiency of this model clearly indicated by Lowry[2] is that it does not have a set of land-use accounts through which the different activities compete for the same land.

This model is based on extremely simple concepts, and it is outstanding in the sense that it covers all main activities of urban location. Due to its recursive process, the model can be considered a dynamic one; and when used for fore-casting, current trends do not continue but are changed by later events. The fact that a very large number of locator variables may be introduced makes the model extremely flexible.

References

1 HILL, D. M. 'A growth allocation model for the Boston region'. *Journal of the American Institute of Planners*, 1965, May, pp. 111–120.
2 LOWRY, I. S. 'Seven models of urban development: a structural comparation'. Special Report 97, Highway Research Board, Washington D.C., 1968.
3 HARRIS, B. 'Quantitative models of urban development: their role in metro-politan policy-making', in PERLOFF, H. S. and WINGO, L. Jr. *Issues in Urban Economics*, Johns Hopkins, Baltimore, 1968.

12 A Model of Metropolis

12.1 Introduction

This model was developed in the USA by Ira S. Lowry[1] during 1962–63 as part of a modelling system to generate alternatives and aid decision making in the Pittsburgh Comprehensive Renewal Program (CRP).

The model has a very well-defined structure as we shall see from the description that follows, and the fact that the interaction submodels employed are so strongly coupled together has enriched the model with aesthetic qualities. Batty[2] referring to this model remarks:

> The Lowry model is the most complete for it is extremely well documented and it is one of the simplest model to construct in terms of its data requirements.

It is probably all these qualities that have led to its adoption by planning authorities in Britain and other countries (Goldner[3]). The object of this model, as stated by its author[1] was:

> The development of an analytical model capable of assigning urban activities to sub-areas of a bounded region in accordance with those principles of locational interdependence that could be reduced to quantitative form.

Thus, this model was developed to explain the geographical patterns of residential development and the associated service centres within the city of Pittsburg. It simulates the pattern of total development as it exists at a particular point in time: A given level and geographical distribution of basic employment within a city is input, and the model generates as output the rest of the city, as a geographical distribution and levels of retail employment and of total households. In other words, if the particular point in time happens to be in the future, we find that given information about the future location of basic employment, the future activity and population serving ratios calculated from population and employment projections, the future transport network and the future pattern of constraints, the model will predict location for population and non-basic employment consistent with these exogenous variables.

The urban spatial structure is seen as comprising three groups of activities:

(1)   A basic sector (roughly industrial and manufacturing activities)
(2)   A retail sector (population-serving activities)
(3)   A household sector (residential activity).

The basic sector

This includes industrial, business and administrative activities, whose locations are assumed to be unconstrained by local circumstances of population distribution, market areas, etc. Thus, the employment levels and locations of the basic sectors must be assumed as 'given', and so, determined outside the model.

It is important to point out that the model considers all industries, including those producing *intermediate* products for industries serving local markets, as located in relation to *other influences*, such as resource availabilities, interregional transportation routes, site features, agglomeration economies, etc. They are in fact a residual remaining after the 'retail' industries (considered as population-serving activities) have been identified.

The retail sector

This covers all those activities dependent directly on local resident population and purchasing power; that is, all activities for which a local market or service area can be identified for *final* products or services. The employment levels and locations in this sector are treated as endogenous variables whose variables are determined inside the model.

The household sector

This consists of the resident population, on which the retail sector depends and which itself depends on the total employment level (both basic and retail) available. It is assumed that the location of households is powerfully influenced by the distribution of employment. Therefore, both the population size and distribution are also determined within the model.

12.2 Level of categorization

This model is able to handle different levels of categorization of the variables considered; and for the Pittsburgh Study, employment and services activities are the only ones that are categorized, but only at a very general level. This is due to constraints of computer capacity and limitations of data.

The retail sector or population-servicing activity is broken down into three cluster types:

(1) 'Neighbourhood' clusters, consisting of food, drug and petrol service stations, personal-service establishments, and elementary schools.

(2) 'Local' clusters, containing a wider range of retail businesses, repair and professional services, municipal administration, churches, etc.

(3) 'Metropolitan' clusters, consisting predominantly of financial institutions, large department stores, public lodgings, business services, etc.

Employment is classified into two broad categories: basic and retail; and the latter group is further categorized into three classes according to the types of shopping establishments: neighbourhood, local or metropolitan service employment.

12.3 Level of aggregation

The model used one-mile square grid cells as zones or tracts. The city blocks falling within these cells were assembled so that block boundaries approximated the one-mile square.

12.4 Theory

This model attempts to simulate in a very empirical manner the *statistical regularities* in the geographical distribution of population, which in reality result from the combination of, and competition between, the many different forces operating within the urban system, without specifying these forces directly. Lowry[1] indicates that

> Rather than simulating detailed market processes in which individual establishments (households, business firms, and other activities) compete for sites, the model summarizes these processes by calculating the 'potential' of each location as a residential and/or retail site, given the pre-existing distributions of linked activities. . . . In planning the design of the Pittsburgh model, I have followed the guidance of the social physicists more than that of the location theorist.

Fleisher,[4] commenting about this model and referring to the allocation rules which operate between places of residence and places of work, and between shoppers and retail stores, said:

> They are obtained by fitting curves to origin and destination counts. The model, therefore, is essentially phenomenological; it refers neither to individual choices nor to collective rationales. Function is assigned to place by rules empirically devised and massively aggregated.

Although the model follows the social physics approach, it can be said that the model also uses behavioural concepts such as the assumption that residents in each area wish to minimize transportation costs.

12.5 Treatment of time

Lowry makes clear that the model has no time dimension; it generates what he calls 'an instant metropolis' in which the iterative sequences of the solution process are simply convenient substitutes for an analytical solution.

12.6 Formulation of the model

Notation
The following notation is used in the original model and will be employed here:

A = area of land (thousands of square feet)
E = employment (number of persons)
N = population (number of households)
T = index of trip distribution
Z = constraints.

In conjunction with these symbols, the following superscripts and subscripts appear:

U = unusable (land)
B = basic sector
R = retail sector
H = household sector
k = class of establishment within the retail sector (neighbourhood, local or metropolitan); also defines related class of 'shopping' trips
m = number of classes of retail establishments (k = 1, 2, ... m)
i, j = sub-areas of a bounded region, called tracts
n = number of tracts (i = 1, 2, ... n; j = 1, 2, ... n).

The structural parameters are indicated by:

a^k = retail employment coefficient related to class k or population serving ratio
b^k = retail employment scale factor related to class k
c^k, d^k = shopping trip weight factors related to class k, ($c^k + d^k = 1$)
e^k = retail employment density ratio related to class k
f = the reciprocal of the labour force participation rate or activity rate
g = population scale factor.

Mathematical structure
The model can be expressed in mathematical terms, as a set of nine simultaneous equations and three inequalities as constraints, which are replicated many times in the complete system. These equations are the following:

$$A_j = A_j^U + A_j^B + A_j^R + A_j^H \tag{12.1}$$

Given the area of each tract, and deducting the amount of land therein which is not usable by the activities concerned with the model, the remainder is available for use by the basic, retail and household sectors.

$$E^k = a^k N \tag{12.2}$$

Equation 12.2 treats employment in each class of retail trade as roughly a function of the number of households in the region.

$$E_j^k = b^k \left[\sum_{i=1}^{n} \left(\frac{c^k N_i}{T_{ij}{}^k} \right) + d^k E_j \right] \tag{12.3}$$

Equation 12.3 calculates the market potential (measured by retail employment) of any given location, which can be defined as a weighted index of the number of households in the surrounding areas and the number of persons employed nearby. b^k is a scale factor which adjusts the retail employment in each tract to the regional total determined in equation 12.2; then,

$$b^k \sum_{j=1}^{n} \left[\sum_{i=1}^{n} \left(\frac{c^k N_i}{T_{ij}^{k}} \right) + d^k E_j \right] = E^k \tag{12.3.1}$$

and so,

$$b^k = \frac{E^k}{\sum\limits_{j=1}^{n} \left[\sum\limits_{i=1}^{n} \left(\frac{c^k N_i}{T_{ij}^{k}} \right) + d^k E_j \right]} \tag{12.3.2}$$

and substituting this expression in equation 12.3 we have the market potential equation in an expanded form:

$$E_j^k = \frac{E^k \sum\limits_{i=1}^{n} \left(\frac{c^k N_i}{T_{ij}^{k}} \right) + d^k E_j}{\sum\limits_{j=1}^{n} \left[\sum\limits_{i=1}^{n} \left(\frac{c^k N_i}{T_{ij}^{k}} \right) + d^k E_j \right]} \tag{12.3.3}$$

This equation (12.3.3) is the potential submodel which is used to allocate retail employment category k, to each tract.

$$E^k = \sum_{j=1}^{n} E_j^k \tag{12.4}$$

Equation 12.4 determines the total amount of service employment for each class of retail trade.

$$E_j = E_j^B + \sum_{k=1}^{m} E_j^k \tag{12.5}$$

The total working population (both basic and service) for each zone, is calculated by equation 12.5.

$$A_j^R = \sum_{k=1}^{m} e^k E_j^k \tag{12.6}$$

Equation 12.6 indicates the amount of land in each tract which will be occupied by the retail sector. The employment-density coefficient e^k is exogenoulsy determined.

$$N = f \sum_{j=1}^{n} E_j \tag{12.7}$$

Equation 12.7 indicates that the region's population of households may be regarded as a function of total employment; where f is actually the reciprocal of the labour force participation rate, that is, the average number of households required to supply one worker. Lowry, in his experimental runs, used a multiplier in order to speed convergence during the solution process.

$$N = fE^B \left(1 - f \sum_{k=1}^{m} a^k\right)^{-1}$$ (12.7.1)

Equation 12.7.1 and the multiplier concept will be further analysed when we deal with the derivation process of the model.

$$N_j = g \sum_{i=1}^{n} \frac{E_i}{T_{ij}}$$ (12.8)

Equation 12.8 calculates the number of households (or dwelling units) in each tract as a function of that tract's accessibility to employment opportunities. The coefficient g is a scale factor whose value is determined by the requirement that the sum of tract populations must equal the total population N of the region as determined by equation 12.7; that is,

$$g \sum_{j=1}^{n} \sum_{i=1}^{n} \frac{E_i}{T_{ij}} = N$$ (12.8.1)

then,

$$g = \frac{N}{\sum\limits_{j=1}^{n} \sum\limits_{i=1}^{n} \frac{E_i}{T_{ij}}}$$ (12.8.2)

and substituting this expression in equation 12.8 we obtain,

$$N_j = \frac{N \sum\limits_{i=1}^{n} \frac{E_i}{T_{ij}}}{\sum\limits_{j=1}^{n} \sum\limits_{i=1}^{n} \frac{E_i}{T_{ij}}}$$ (12.8.3)

Equation 12.8.3 is the potential submodel used to allocate population (or dwelling units) to each zone or tract.

$$N = \sum_{j=1}^{n} N_j$$ (12.9)

The total population derived by the solution process is given by equation 12.9:

$$E_j^k \geqslant Z^k \quad \text{or else} \quad E_j^k = 0$$ (12.10)

Equation 12.10 imposes a minimum-size constraint Z^k expressed in terms of employment, in order to limit the dispersion of retail employment.

$$N_j \leqslant Z_j^H A_j^H$$ (12.11)

The constraint equation 12.11 imposes a maximum-density constraint Z_j^H, in order to prevent the system from generating excessive population densities in locations with high accessibility indices.

$$A_j^R \leqslant A_j - A_j^U - A_j^B \qquad (12.12)$$

Finally, equation 12.12 indicates that the amount of land set aside for retail establishments by equation 12.6, must not exceed the amount available.

Functional structure

The functional structure of the Lowry model is represented in Figure 12.1 and can be described as follows:

A level and location of industrial activity (measured by basic employment) is estimated externally and provided to the model; from this level, the model derives its related population which is then allocated spatially over the area under study.

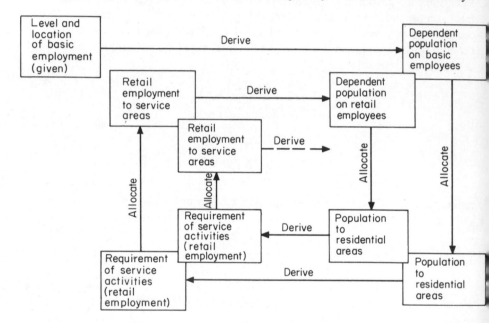

Figure 12.1 Functional structure of the Lowry model

It then derives the related requirement of service activities (measured by retail employment) and allocates them to service areas. Now, from this level and location of service employment, the model derives its dependent population related to this new employment force. Then this additional population is allocated, and at the same time demands for services, which in turn, create more jobs, and so on. The model iterates in this way until a stable solution is achieved for a given input of basic employees.

From this description, we can observe that the model performs two basic functions:

(1)   The model *derives* dependent population and service employment

(2)   Households and retail employment are *allocated* to zones of the area
      under study.

In order to facilitate the study of the model, each function will be analysed in
turn.

Derivation function
The essential derivation function concept of this model can be represented by
Figure 12.2, which exhibits the causal structure of the model. It shows the
relationships by which, from a given quantity of basic employment, the model
derives its dependent population (dependants and their families) who need
service. This service or retail activity, of course, represents employment

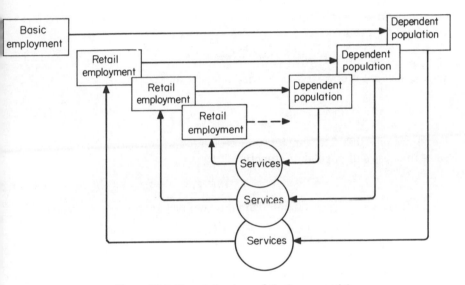

Figure 12.2 Causal structure of the Lowry model

opportunities in itself. The model then derives this retail employment and its
dependent population. This new dependent population, in turn, asks for service.
This cycle is continually repeated until the total population, retail and basic
employment are in mutual equilibrium.

The model partitions employment into basic and retail categories. It is
assumed that the location of basic employment is independent of the location
patterns of other activities such as service employment and population, but that
these other activities are locationally dependent upon basic employment. Therefore, the model assumes that households and services can be uniquely derived
from basic employment. This assumption implies some form of economic base
theory. Batty[5] says:

The economic base of any region can be defined as that sector of the production process whose location is solely governed by factors external to the region of study. In essence, such production is export-oriented, producing commodities which are consumed outside the region.

To introduce this concept, consider a region whose total economic activity measured by employment E is divided into basic employment E^B and retail employment E^R.

Then,
$$E = E^B + E^R \tag{12.13}$$

Supposing that the retail employment is divided into m classes, we have
$$E = E^B + E^1 + E^2 + + + E^m \tag{12.14}$$

Assuming some linear relationship f between total employment E and total population N
$$N = fE = f(E^B + E^1 + E^2 + + + E^m) \tag{12.15}$$

the coefficient f is obviously an activity rate; in other words
$$f = \frac{N}{E} \tag{12.16}$$

We also assume that retail employment is oriented to population, and is therefore some function a of population.
$$E^k = a^k N \qquad (k = 1, 2, \ldots m) \tag{12.17}$$

the coefficient a is a population-serving ratio defined as
$$a^k = \frac{E^k}{N} \tag{12.18}$$

Now, substituting retail employment defined from equation 12.17 into equation 12.15, we get
$$N = f(E^B + a^1 N + a^2 N + + + a^m N) \tag{12.19}$$

$$N = f(E^B + N \sum_{k=1}^{m} a^k) \tag{12.20}$$

Rearranging equation 12.20 gives
$$N - fN \sum_{k=1}^{m} a^k = fE^B \tag{12.21}$$

$$N(1 - f \sum_{k=1}^{m} a^k) = fE^B \tag{12.22}$$

$$N = fE^B (1 - f \sum_{k=1}^{m} a^k)^{-1} \tag{12.23}$$

Dividing both sides of equation 12.23 by N/E, that is f, and rearranging, we have

$$E = E^B (1 - f \sum_{k=1}^{m} a^k)^{-1} \qquad (12.24)$$

Equations 12.23 and 12.24 are the usual statement of the economic base method, and show the concept of the multiplier. Equation 12.23 corresponds to equation 12.7.1 already outlined in the mathematical structure of this model.

$$(1 - f \sum_{k=1}^{m} a^k)^{-1}$$

is the multiplier which scales basic employment to total employment; that is, knowing the level of basic employment of a region we can derive the total employment by means of this multiplier.

Allocation function
The allocation function takes place during each cycle of the derivation process. One cycle of this process (see Figure 12.3) will be analysed to see how geographical location is handled by the model.

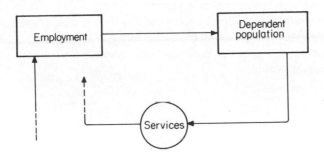

Figure 12.3 One cycle of the derivation process

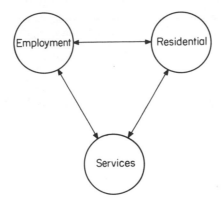

Figure 12.4 Spatial interaction between the major activities

Each cycle deals with three major activities: employment, residential and service activities. Interaction between them takes place in the system, and can be considered to be of three types: (see Figure 12.4)

(1)   Between employees and residences
(2)   Between households and services
(3)   Between employees and services.

As has been indicated before, at the beginning of a derivation cycle the geographical location and level of the employment activity is known. The model then derives the number of dwelling units and the level of services required which are going to be allocated to zones of the system; that is, the model has to allocate *households* and *retail stores*. Each of them will be described in turn.

Residential location
The model considers that the pattern of residential location is influenced by the location of employment opportunities. In the model, the location of services does not affect the places of residence because the retail stores appear only when and where the residential development asks for it.

A basic criterion of locational choice used by the model is proximity to the place of employment. In order to arrange population around workplaces, the model makes use of a potential submodel of interaction already introduced in the set of basic equations:

$$N_j = \frac{N \sum_{i=1}^{n} \frac{E_i}{T_{ij}}}{\sum_{j=1}^{n} \sum_{i=1}^{n} \frac{E_i}{T_{ij}}} \qquad (12.8.3)$$

This potential submodel allocates population (or dwelling units) to each zone of the area under study, with regard to the total employment population of each tract and its spatial distribution. This distribution is represented in the equation by the trip distribution index for residential location T_{ij}.

Trip distribution index for residential location
From the statistical analysis of the data, Lowry found that the empirical distribution of worktrips by distance from residence may be fitted rather well with a negative power function,

$$\frac{dP}{dr} = ar^{-x} \qquad (12.25)$$

where a and x are parameters to be calibrated and r is the distance from residence to workplace. He has analysed this function for different classes of employees, as shown in Figure 12.5.

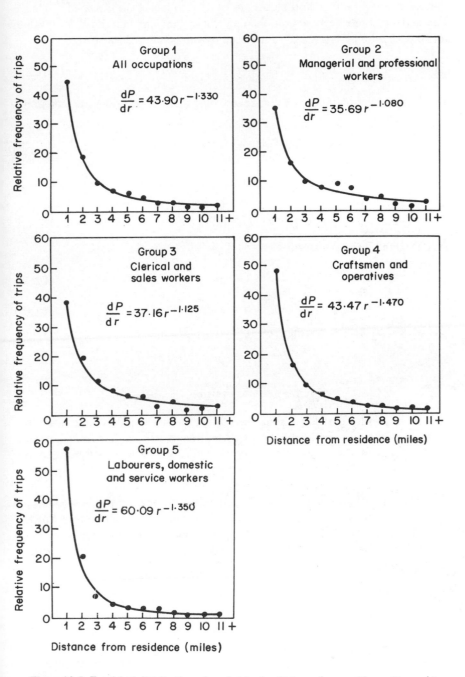

Figure 12.5 Empirical distribution of work trips by distance from residence (Lowry[1])

The model generates households by reversing the journey-to-work into a work-to-residence trip, so that workplaces can be used to locate the places of residence. Due to its level of categorization, the model uses the same functional form values for all occupations. The actual values used by the functional form are

$$\frac{dP}{dr} = r^{-1.33} \qquad (12.26)$$

The trip distribution index is obtained knowing that the point density function G is expressed as

$$G = \frac{dP/dr}{2\pi r} = \frac{ar^{-x}}{2\pi r} = \frac{a}{2\pi}r^{-(1+x)} \qquad (12.27)$$

the trip distribution index T_{ij} is the inverse of the point density function G:

$$T_{ij} = \frac{1}{G} = \frac{2\pi}{a}r^{1+x} \qquad (12.28)$$

Doing the following transformation,

$$\frac{2\pi}{a} = a' \qquad (12.29)$$

$$1 + x = x' \qquad (12.30)$$

we can express the trip distribution index as,

$$T_{ij} = a'r^{x'} \qquad (12.31)$$

Maximum-density constraints
In order to prevent the model from generating excessive population densities in the vicinity of major employment centres, limiting values are determined outside the model and imposed as constraints on the allocation process. Although Lowry used the same limiting value for all the tracts, each zone may have its own value, according to the zoning ordinance density limits or other factors.

Every time the model allocates a given number of households to a tract, its total is tested against the maximum-density constraint Z_j^H. In all cases in which this constraint is not satisfied, the excess population of the 'saturated' zone is distributed among all other tracts in proportion to their population potentials.

Retail location
The model assumes that the retail sector is governed by the principle of profit maximization, and so the service firm will seek to locate where it can attract the maximum patronage. This patronage is supplied by the interaction with the employment centres and the residential areas. A potential submodel of interaction is used to allocate retail activities to zones.

$$E_j^k = \frac{E^k \sum_{i=1}^{n} \left(\frac{c^k N_i}{T_{ij}^k} \right) + d^k E_j}{\sum_{j=1}^{n} \left[\sum_{i=1}^{n} \left(\frac{c^k N_i}{T_{ij}^k} \right) + d^k E_j \right]}$$
(12.3.3)

This submodel corresponds to the set of basic equations. The parameters c^k and d^k used in this potential submodel are weight factors which indicate the level of influence of the interaction between retail stores and households and between services and employees respectively.

The proportions used by the model are (Lowry[1]):

	households	employees
neighbourhood	0.90	0.10
local	0.70	0.30
metropolitan	0.50	0.50

According to the potential formula 12.3.3, the number of customers attracted to any given tract (measured as retail employment) depends on the spatial distribution of residence and employment with respect to the tract considered, and also on this same distribution with respect to all other tracts containing retail activities. In this submodel, the trip distribution index T_{ij}^k takes account of the spatial interaction between households and services.

The interaction between employees and retail stores is assumed to take place within the zone in which the workplace is located, and therefore, no allocation function is required.

Trip distribution index for service location
Lowry found that the best approximations to the empirical distribution of retail patronage by distance from residence were reciprocals of a quadratic function,

$$\frac{dP}{dr} = (a - br + cr^2)^{-1}$$
(12.32)

where a, b and c are parameters to be calibrated, and r is the distance from residence to services. Some of these distributions are shown in Figure 12.6.

The actual values that were used for the parameters, according to the different levels of retail activity, (Lowry[1]) are

	a	b	c
neighbourhood shopping	0.5107	0.7400	0.2699
local shopping	0.0116	0.0012	0.0202
metropolitan shopping	0.0664	0.0442	0.0156

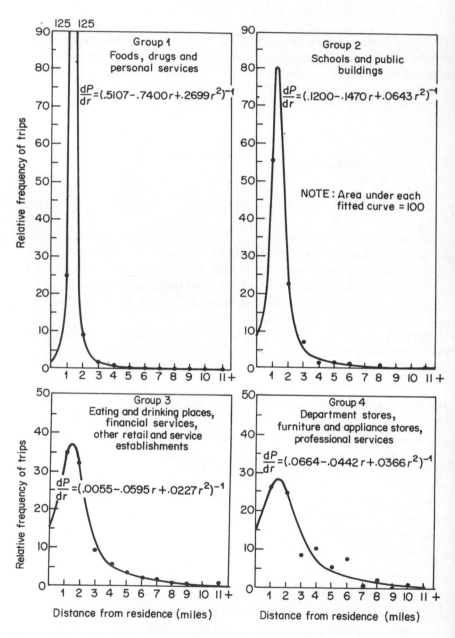

Figure 12.6 Empirical distribution of retail patronage by distance from residence (Lowry[1])

The point density function G is expressed as

$$G^k = \frac{dP/dr}{2\pi r} = \frac{(a - br + cr^2)^{-1}}{2\pi r} \qquad (12.33)$$

then, $\qquad T_{ij}{}^k = \frac{1}{G^k} = 2\pi r(a - br + cr^2) \qquad (12.34)$

and so the trip distribution index for service location class k $(T_{ij}{}^k)$ can be expressed as

$$T_{ij}{}^k = a' - b'r + c'r^2 \qquad (12.35)$$

Minimum-size constraints
Because the model algorithm does not have the property of bringing together retail activities to reflect the external economies of scale, Lowry identifies a lower employment threshold and excludes retail development below this limit. The minimum number of employees within a zone for each class of retail activity, which were used in the model (Lowry[1]), are

neighbourhood facilities   30
local facilities   250
metropolitan facilities   20,000

Once the model has allocated the service activity, this is considered as a provisional solution which is tested against the minimum-size constraints Z^k. The tract with the smallest service value which does not satisfy the constraint has its retail employment level set to zero and the service activity in all other zones is rescaled (increased). This process is repeated until the retail employment in all the tracts is zero or satisfies the minimum-size constraint.

12.7 Solution of the system
The importance of the Lowry model lies in the way derivation and allocation are built into one system. The solution method is illustrated in Figure 12.7, and a brief description of it is given below:

Input data
The following data are given as an input to the model:
The level, categorization and allocation of the basic employment.
An inventory of land, classified as unusable, basic or residential; strictly related to the grid pattern chosen.
The interzonal network. From this network, distances are calculated and used to determine the trip distribution indices. In the Pittsburgh model, air distances were used.
Structural parameters: retail employment coefficients, weight factors, retail employment density ratios, labour force participation rate, etc.
Constraints: on densities of residential development, on the minimum size of a 'cluster' of retail activities, and on the amount of land available in each zone.

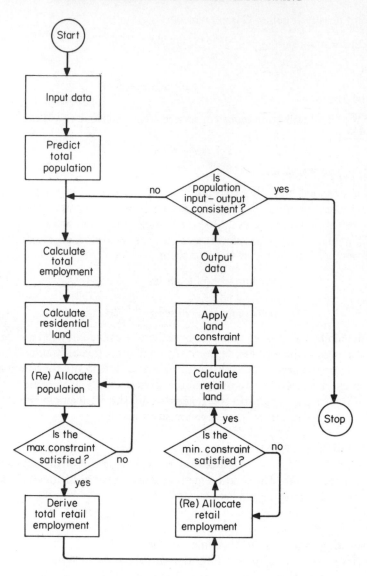

Figure 12.7 Original formulation of Lowry's model (based on Reference 1)

Predict total population
Given the basic employment E^B, the model predicts the total population N^* by way of the following formula

$$N^* = fE^B(1 - f\sum_{k=1}^{m} a^k)^{-1} \qquad (12.7.1)$$

Calculate total employment
By means of the formula

$$E_j = E_j^B + \sum_{k=1}^{m} E_j^k \qquad (12.5)$$

the total employment for each tract is calculated. For the first iteration, the retail employment is set to zero ($E_j^k = 0$), because no service activity haş been derived yet.

Calculate residential land
Using the following equation:

$$A_j^H = A_j - A_j^U - A_j^B - A_j^R \qquad (12.1)$$

The land available for residential development assigned to each tract is calculated. For the first iteration, land use for services is set to zero ($A_j^R = 0$), because no retail activities have emerged yet.

(Re)allocate population
By means of the following potential submodel

$$N_j = \frac{N \sum_{i=1}^{n} \dfrac{E_i}{T_{ij}}}{\sum_{j=1}^{n} \sum_{i=1}^{n} \dfrac{E_i}{T_{ij}}} \qquad (12.8.3)$$

Population (measured as number of households) is (re)allocated to zones of the area under study.

The total population N is obtained by means of equation 12.7. For the first iteration $E_j = E_j^B$ because no retail activities has emerged yet. Thus,

$$N = f \sum_{j=1}^{n} E_j^B$$

Is the maximum constraint satisfied?
At this point, the population for each tract N_j is tested against a maximum-density constraint Z_j^H by way of the equation

$$N_j \leqslant Z_j^H A_j^H \qquad (12.11)$$

and if this constraint is violated, the surplus population is reallocated until the constraint is satisfied.

Derive total retail employment
Applying the following equations:

$$N = \sum_{j=1}^{n} N_j \tag{12.9}$$

$$E^k = a^k N \tag{12.2}$$

the total retail employment by each class of service activity is derived.

(Re)allocate retail employment
The following potential submodel

$$E_j^k = \frac{E^k \sum\limits_{i=1}^{n} \left(\dfrac{c^k N_i}{T_{ij}^{\ k}} \right) + d^k E_j}{\sum\limits_{j=1}^{n} \left[\sum\limits_{i=1}^{n} \left(\dfrac{c^k N_i}{T_{ij}^{\ k}} \right) + d^k E_j \right]} \tag{12.3.3}$$

is employed to (re)allocate retail employment by each category k to zones.

Is the minimum constraint satisfied?
At this stage, the minimum-size constraint is tested to ensure that retail employment in any zone E_j^k is greater than some minimum size limit Z^k,

$$E_j^k \geqslant Z^k \tag{12.10}$$

If the constraint is not satisfied, the retail employment of tract j is set to zero $E_j^k = 0$ and its value reallocated.

Calculate retail land
By means of the equation

$$A_j^R = \sum_{k=1}^{m} e^k E_j^k \tag{12.6}$$

we calculate the land for retail activities needed for each tract.

Apply land constraint
The land for retail activities A_j^R for each tract is tested against the amount of space actually available on it; that is, we test this equation

$$A_j^R \leqslant A_j - A_j^U - A_j^B \tag{12.12}$$

if $A_j^R > A_j - A_j^U - A_j^B$, we set $A_j^R = A_j - A_j^U - A_j^B$; in other words, we allow overcrowding, but at the same time, the available land for residential use is driven to zero $A_j^H = 0$. In this way, retail uses have priority over residential uses. If households have been allocated to such a tract, they will be removed by the residential-density constraint on the next iteration. This overcrowding indicates that the model does not impose a 'maximum-density' constraint on the distribution of retail employment.

Output data
The values of the different variables obtained during the iteration are calculated.
Total population N is estimated using the following equations:

$$E_j = E_j^B + \sum_{k=1}^{m} E_j^k \qquad (12.5)$$

$$N = f \sum_{j=1}^{n} E_j \qquad (12.7)$$

Is population input–output consistent?
At this point, the total population N used by the model as an independent
variable is compared with the total population N^* predicted by the model. If they
are different, the derived values obtained during the iteration are fed back as
independent variables and the model is run in this iterative fashion until they
converge on a stable value. In the Pittsburgh Study, only three iterations were
needed to obtain consistency between input and output.

12.8 Uses of the model
Although the model can really be used at a coarse level to test large scale changes
or very different alternative plans, it has very real advantages of feasibility,
especially for impact analysis. Policies which can be tested include the effects of
introducing green belts, trading estates and large changes in the transportation
network such as a new motorway (for this last policy, some other measurement
of spatial separation should be used instead of the aerial distance employed by
Lowry in the Pittsburgh Study). Possible unforeseen changes can be tested for
their likely impact; for example, the establishment of a large new factory, or airport; a long term change in activity rate or unemployment.

More interesting and relevant policies affecting different income groups and
focusing more directly on specific issues such as particular types of urban
renewal, subsidies and so on, must wait for more sophisticated models. As
Lowry[1] points out about his model:

> Properly adapted, it should be useful for the projection of future patterns
> of land development and for the testing of public policies in the field of
> transportation planning, land-use controls, taxation and urban renewal.

12.9 Comments
One of the difficulties of model building is that cities are probably in a state of
constant disequilibrium, since there are substantial time lags between cause and
effect. Because Lowry's model is not formulated directly so as to simulate the
way growth and change actually occur through time, a whole range of further

assumptions has to be made: the service centres spring up exactly in order to meet the demand for goods, employees are in equilibrium with the number of jobs and location of workplaces, all at a single point in time. There is no question of delayed response to particular changes in time — or shops lagging behind residential development. The distribution of population generated by employment to the various areas is based on the assumption that residents in each area wish to minimize transportation costs; this assumption ignores social values which can influence locational behaviour as well as economic market conditions.

In relation to the location of retail centres, it may be objected that models of this type '. . . do not adequately account for the known tendency of retail trade centres to "peak" in selected locations and that they therefore predict an excessively uniform distribution' (Harris[6]). All these features indicate that it is a 'demand' model which does not incorporate a model of the supply side for houses and other constructions; also that it is a static equilibrium model. Although Lowry applies this model in a static form, he indicates some means by which the Pittsburgh model can be easily adapted to a semi-dynamic fashion.

This model will have limitations when used for forecasting if some of the underlying processes change in the future, because the parameters fitted from current data may be quite irrelevant. One of the weaknesses of this model is that it does take the industrial location as given exogenously. Harris[6] commenting on this aspect says

> For the Pittsburgh economy with its large-scale site-oriented manufacturing industries, this assumption is not unreasonable.

According to Massey and Cordey-Hayes,[7] the Lowry model despite all its criticisms is at present the most widely accepted urban spatial model in practice. All the weaknesses mentioned above are being dealt with by a new generation of models based on Lowry's underlying principles. Goldner,[3] in a paper outlining the model's history, states the reasons for the model's success:

> Somehow, the conceptual framework of what has come to be known as the 'Lowry model', has stimulated a population explosion of successors, each with meaningful elaborations. The development of the original model has had this effect because: the promise of meaningful operationality was a prime stimulus; the simplicity of the causal structure had substantial appeal; and the opportunity to enlarge and embellish the framework encouraged further work.

One of the most employed versions and one which has been intensively developed in Britain for urban and regional planning is due to Garin.[8] Owing to its widespread use, we will examine Garin's fundamental contribution to the Lowry model in the next chapter.

References

1 LOWRY, I. S. *A Model of Metropolis*. Rand Corporation, Santa Monica, California, 1964.
2 BATTY, M. 'Recent developments in land use modelling: a review of British research'. Urban Systems Research Unit, Department of Geography, University of Reading, 1970.
3 GOLDNER, W. 'The Lowry model heritage'. *Journal of the American Institute of Planners*, 1971, vol. 37, no. 2.
4 FLEISHER, A. 'Comments on a model of Metropolis'. *Journal of the American Institute of Planners*, 1965, May, pp. 175–176.
5 BATTY, M. 'Spatial theory and information systems'. Urban Systems Research Unit, Department of Geography, University of Reading, 1970.
6 HARRIS, B. 'Quantitative models of urban development: their role in metropolitan policy-making', in PERLOFF, H. S. and WINGO, L. Jr. *Issues in Urban Economics*, Johns Hopkins, Baltimore, 1968.
7 MASSEY, D. B. and CORDEY-HAYES, M. 'The use of models in structure planning'. *Town Planning Review*, 1971, vol. 42, January, no. 1.
8 GARIN, R. A. 'A matrix formulation of the Lowry model for intrametropolitan activity allocation'. *Journal of the American Institute of Planners*, 1966, November.

13 The Garin–Lowry Model

13.1 Introduction

Garin[1] has improved the Lowry model in two ways: by explicitly incorporating spatial submodels into the framework, and by expressing the fundamental Lowry algorithm in vector and matrix format. By the use of matrix algebra, Garin has been able to calculate the state of equilibrium of the system in one operation by inverting the matrix.

The Garin–Lowry model is conceptually much more satisfying than the original formulation, although the model does not include the constraints which Lowry imposed: neither the minimum-size constraint for retail employment nor the maximum-density constraint for residential development. In addition, the inversion of a matrix for a large size zonal system presents problems of computer storage and time cost. Modifications which incorporate constraints to the Garin–Lowry model have been developed and are widely used, especially in Britain.

13.2 Functional structure

To illustrate the way in which spatial interaction submodels are introduced into the system, a brief description of the functional structure of the Garin–Lowry model is given below and it is represented diagrammatically in Figure 13.1. From a level and distribution of basic employment, the model first allocates basic employees to residential zones. Then, the population associated with these basic employees is found. This population demands service from retail employees, which are allocated in service centres. In turn, these retail employees are allocated to residential areas and the associated population requires to be serviced. Further increments of population and service employment are derived and allocated, until this process converges, that is, until further increments of population and retail employment are small enough to be ignored. Some important features of the derivation and allocation functions in the Garin–Lowry model, are outlined below.

Derivation function

Here, the economic base method and the multiplier concept will be derived in a different way, which is more applicable to the operation of the Garin–Lowry model.

Given basic employment E^B, we can derive basic population $N(1)$, multiplying by the labour force participation rate f,

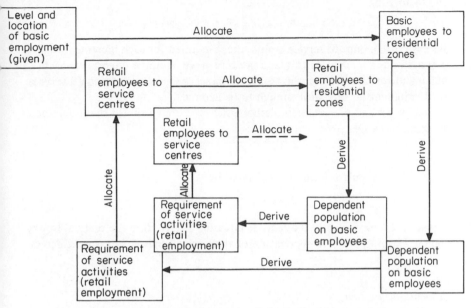

Figure 13.1 Functional structure of the Garin–Lowry model

$$N(1) = fE^B \tag{13.1}$$

The amount of retail employment $E^R(1)$ to serve the basic population $N(1)$ is found by applying the retail employment scale factor a. For simplicity, no categorization of the retail activity will be considered.

$$E^R(1) = aN(1) = afE^B \tag{13.2}$$

The population $N(2)$ related to the retail employment $E^R(1)$ can be calculated applying the participation rate f,

$$N(2) = fE^R(1) = faN(1) = af^2E^B \tag{13.3}$$

The service employment required by this population is

$$E^R(2) = aN(2) = a^2f^2E^B \tag{13.4}$$

$E^R(2)$ has also its associated population $N(3)$. Then by recursion, we can find

$$E^R(m) = a^m f^m E^B \tag{13.5}$$

The total employment of the system is found by adding up all the increments of employment.

$$E = E^B + E^R(1) + E^R(2) + + + E^R(m) \tag{13.6}$$

$$E = E^B + afE^B + a^2f^2E^B + + + a^m f^m E^B \tag{13.7}$$

and factorizing

$$E = E^B(1 + af + a^2f^2 + + + a^m f^m)$$ (13.8)

Because the amount of service employment required for each increment of population is a fraction of this, and because as we continue the process each increment gets smaller, we can expect the process to have a limiting value when further increments are small enough to be ignored.

If $af < 1$,* and $m \to \infty$, then mathematically it can be shown that equation 13.8 can be expressed as

$$E = E^B(1 - af)^{-1}$$ (13.9)

and so, total population can be calculated by

$$N = fE = fE^B(1 - af)^{-1}$$ (13.10)

Equation 13.10 is exactly the same as equation 12.7.1 from the original Lowry model, except that no categorization of the service employment is considered.

Allocation function

The Garin–Lowry model allocates the increments of employment and population by means of interaction submodels of the potential type of the following form

$$I_{ij} = K \frac{A_j}{T_{ij}}$$ (13.11)

where I_{ij} = interaction between zone i and zone j
         A_j = attractiveness of zone j
         T_{ij} = trip distribution index
         K = scaling constant.

Garin, improving Lowry's structure, uses these kinds of submodels in a way that allows them to represent explicitly the interactions of the activities of the system as flows, thereby taking into account the journeys from work to home and from home to services. In order to clarify this feature, a brief description of the residential and service locations is given below.

---

* We assume that $af < 1$ because

$$af = \frac{E^R}{N} \frac{N}{E} = \frac{E^R}{E}$$

If $E^R/E = 1$ then $E^R = E$ which means that we do not have basic employment, and so this case is not applicable to the model.
    If $E^R/E > 1$ then $E^R > E$ which is absurd because service employment can never be greater than total employment.

Residential location
The way·in which potential submodels are employed by the Garin–Lowry model
to allocate increments of employees to residential zones can be described using
the following submodel:

$$I_{ij}^{wh} = K \frac{N_j}{d_{ij}^{\alpha}}$$ (13.12)

where I_{ij} = number of trips between working zone i and residential zone j
N_j = population in zone j
d_{ij} = distance between zone i and zone j
α = parameter
K = scaling constant
wh = work to home trips.

If equation 13.12 gives us the number of trips between working zone i and
residential zone j, then to get the proportion of trips from zone i to any zone j
(P_{ij}^{wh}), we compute,

$$P_{ij}^{wh} = \frac{\text{number of trips from zone } i \text{ to zone } j}{\text{number of trips from zone } i \text{ to all zones}}$$ (13.13)

$$P_{ij}^{wh} = \frac{KN_j/d_{ij}^{\alpha}}{K\dfrac{N_1}{d_{i1}^{\alpha}} + K\dfrac{N_2}{d_{i2}^{\alpha}} + K\dfrac{N_3}{d_{i3}^{\alpha}} + + + K\dfrac{N_n}{d_{in}^{\alpha}}}$$ (13.14)

$$P_{ij}^{wh} = \frac{K N_j/d_{ij}^{\alpha}}{K \sum_{j=1}^{n} \dfrac{N_j}{d_{ij}^{\alpha}}} = \frac{N_j/d_{ij}^{\alpha}}{\sum_{j=1}^{n} \dfrac{N_j}{d_{ij}^{\alpha}}}$$ (13.15)

This proportion can be considered as the probability that an employee working
in zone i lives in zone j.

The number of trips from working zone i to residential zone j, can be found
by multiplying the number of trips generated in zone i (equivalent to the number
of employees working in zone i, E_i), by the proportion of them going to
residential zone j,

$$I_{ij}^{wh} = E_i P_{ij}^{wh}$$ (13.16)

Then, the number of work to home trips between zone i and zone j produced
due to increments in the working labour force related to iteration number z can
be obtained in the following way:

$$I_{ij}^{wh}(z) = E_i(z)P_{ij}^{wh} = E_i(z) \frac{N_j/d_{ij}^{\alpha}}{\sum_{j=1}^{n} \dfrac{N_j}{d_{ij}^{\alpha}}}$$ (13.17)

where $E_i(z)$ is the increment in employment in zone i related to iteration z.

Now, to obtain the increments in the number of employees living in zone j related to iteration z, $L_j(z)$, we add up all the work to home trips, $I_{ij}^{wh}(z)$ arriving at zone j,

$$L_j(z) = \sum_{i=1}^{n} I_{ij}^{wh}(z) = \sum_{i=1}^{n} E_i(z) P_{ij}^{wh} = \sum_{i=1}^{n} E_i(z) \frac{N_j/d_{ij}^{\alpha}}{\sum_{j=1}^{n} \frac{N_j}{d_{ij}^{\alpha}}} \qquad (13.18)$$

From here we can see how the potential submodel allows us to allocate employment increments to residential zones.

The total number of employees living in zone j can be obtained by adding up all the increments related to each of the m iterations:

$$L_j = \sum_{z=1}^{m} L_j(z) \qquad (13.19)$$

Retail location

The same basic potential submodel used for residential location is employed to allocate retail employees to service centres; but here the level of attractiveness is given by the service employment in zone $i(E_i^R)$, as follows:

$$I_{ij}^{hs} = K \frac{E_i^R}{d_{ij}^{\lambda}} \qquad (13.20)$$

where I_{ij} = number of trips between residential zone j and service zone i
E_i^R = retail employment in zone i
d_{ij} = distance between zone i and zone j
λ = parameter
K = scaling constant
hs = home to service trips.

The proportion of home to service trips from residential zone j to service zone i can be obtained,

$$P_{ij}^{hs} = \frac{\text{number of trips from zone } j \text{ to zone } i}{\text{number of trips from zone } j \text{ to all zones}} \qquad (13.21)$$

$$P_{ij}^{hs} = \frac{K E_i^R/d_{ij}^{\lambda}}{K \sum_{i=1}^{n} \frac{E_i^R}{d_{ij}^{\lambda}}} = \frac{E_i^R/d_{ij}^{\lambda}}{\sum_{i=1}^{n} \frac{E_i^R}{d_{ij}^{\lambda}}} \qquad (13.22)$$

This proportion can be considered as the probability that a household living in zone j will go shopping to zone i.

If we know that the increment of service employment related to iteration z requested by the population of zone j is $D_j(z)$ [where $D_j(z) = afL_j(z)$], we can distribute this value between the different service zones i by multiplying this level of retail activity by the probability that it will be supplied by centre i, that is

$$E_{ij}^R(z) = D_j(z)P_{ij}^{hs} = D_j(z)\frac{E_i^R/d_{ij}^{\lambda}}{\sum\limits_{i=1}^{n}\dfrac{E_i^R}{d_{ij}^{\lambda}}} \qquad (13.23)$$

where $E_{ij}^R(z)$ is the increment in the number of service employees working in zone i demanded by population living in zone j and related to iteration z, in other words, the additional demand made by the population of zone j for services in zone i. This value can be converted into home to service trips if required.

To find the z increment of service employment working in zone i, $E_i^R(z)$, we add up all the service employees working in zone i demanded by all the residential zones,

$$E_i^R(z) = \sum\limits_{j=1}^{n} E_{ij}^R(z) = \sum\limits_{j=1}^{n} D_j(z)P_{ij}^{hs} \qquad (13.24)$$

To obtain the increments in service employment for each iteration z, we sum over all service entres i,

$$E^R(z) = \sum\limits_{i=1}^{n} \sum\limits_{j=1}^{n} E_{ij}^R(z) \qquad (13.25)$$

The service employment of the system can be calculated by adding up the increments in retail employment for all iterations,

$$E^R = \sum\limits_{z=1}^{m} E^R(z) = \sum\limits_{z=1}^{m} \sum\limits_{i=1}^{n} \sum\limits_{j=1}^{n} E_{ij}^R(z) \qquad (13.26)$$

As can be seen, the total retail employment of the system is equivalent to the sum of all the demands made by the population for services.

13.3 Solution of the system

Garin has improved the Lowry model by explicitly incorporating spatial interaction submodels into the framework. Figure 13.2 illustrates the major features of the solution method of the Garin–Lowry model in its expanded form. A brief description of it is given below following the flow chart shown in Figure 13.2.

Input data
All the relevant data already outlined in the Lowry model are given to the model as input.

Predict total retail employment
Given the basic employment E^B, the total labour force in the system can be calculated by means of equation 13.9,

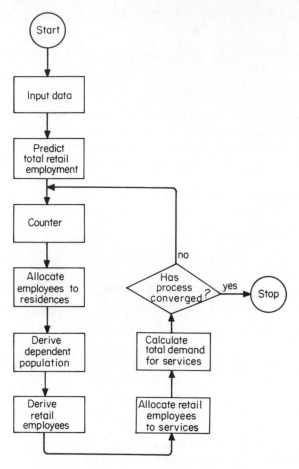

Figure 13.2 The Garin–Lowry model (based on Garin[1] and Batty[2])

$$E* = E^B(1 - af)^{-1}$$

Then, the predicted total retail employment can be found as a residual

$$E^{R*} = E* - E^B \qquad (13.27)$$

Counter
The index z indicates the iteration number. At the beginning of each cycle, this counter is increased by one.

Allocate employees to residences
The allocation of employees to areas of residence is performed by means of equation 13.18

$$L_j(z) = \sum_{i=1}^{n} I_{ij}^{wh}(z) = \sum_{i=1}^{n} E_i(z)P_{ij}^{wh}$$

Starting the first iteration $z = 1$, basic employment E_i^B is substituted for $E_i(1)$ in equation 13.18, that is

$$L_j(1) = \sum_{i=1}^{n} E_i(1)P_{ij}^{wh} = \sum_{i=1}^{n} E_i^B P_{ij}^{wh} \qquad (13.18.1)$$

Derive dependent population
To obtain the population $N_j(z)$ associated with the increment in employees living in zone j, $L_j(z)$, we apply the activity rate f

$$N_j(z) = fL_j(z) \qquad (13.28)$$

Derive retail employees
The increments of service employees corresponding to iteration z, $D_j(z)$, are found applying the population serving ratio a,

$$D_j(z) = aN_j(z) \qquad (13.29)$$

Allocate retail employees to services
The allocation of retail employees to service centres is performed by equation 13.24,

$$E_i^R(z) = \sum_{j=1}^{n} E_{ij}^R(z) = \sum_{j=1}^{n} D_j(z)P_{ij}^{hs}$$

Calculate total demand for services
The total demand for service employment corresponding to all iterations can be found applying equation 13.26

$$E^R = \sum_{z=1}^{m} E^R(z) = \sum_{z=1}^{m} \sum_{i=1}^{n} E_i^R(z) = \sum_{z=1}^{m} \sum_{i=1}^{n} \sum_{j=1}^{n} E_{ij}^R(z)$$

where m represents the number of iterations already performed.

Has process converged?
At this point, we compare the total demand for services E^R calculated from equation 13.26, with the total retail employment E^{R*} derived using equation 13.27 at the beginning of the solution process. If there is no convergence, we have to calculate an additional increment of service employment. To do so, we repeat the cycle. For example, after the first iteration, we can find the increment of population associated with $E_i^R(1)$ and derive its corresponding service requirements $E_i^R(2)$. To perform this task, $E_i^R(1)$ is substituted for $E_i(2)$ in equation 13.18, and the cycle is repeated in this iterative way until the process converges.

Once the process has converged, we can also obtain as output of the model, the total work to home trips in the system by the following equation:

$$I_{ij}^{wh} = \sum_{z=1}^{m} I_{ij}^{wh}(z) \qquad (13.30)$$

and the total service demand in the system can be calculated by

$$E_{ij}^{R} = \sum_{z=1}^{m} E_{ij}^{R}(z) \qquad (13.31)$$

13.4 Matrix formulation

Garin[1] has shown that the iterative process used by Lowry to generate retail employment could be replaced by elementary matrix operations to obtain an exact rather than an approximate solution.

Matrix notation

$e^b = (E_1^B, E_2^B, \ldots E_n^B)$; 1 x n vector of basic employment

$e(z) = [E_1(z), E_2(z), \ldots E_n(z)]$; 1 x n vector of employment whose value has been calculated during iteration $z - 1$; then by definition $e(1) = e^b$

$p(z) = [N_1(z), N_2(z), \ldots N_n(z)]$; 1 x n vector of population associated with employment vector $e(z)$

F = labour participation or activity rate diagonal matrix

$$F = \begin{bmatrix} f_1 & & & 0 \\ & f_2 & & \\ & & - & \\ 0 & & & f_n \end{bmatrix}$$

A = population serving ratio diagonal matrix

$$A = \begin{bmatrix} a_1 & & & 0 \\ & a_2 & & \\ & & - & \\ 0 & & & a_n \end{bmatrix}$$

H = work to home trip probability distribution matrix

$$H = \begin{bmatrix} P_{11}^{wh} & P_{12}^{wh} & & P_{1n}^{wh} \\ P_{21}^{wh} & & & \\ & & & \\ & & & \\ P_{n1}^{wh} & & & P_{nn}^{wh} \end{bmatrix}$$

S = home to service trip probability distribution matrix,

$$S = \begin{bmatrix} P_{11}^{hs} & P_{12}^{hs} & - & - & P_{1n}^{hs} \\ P_{21}^{hs} & & & & - \\ - & & & & - \\ - & & & & - \\ - & & & & - \\ P_{n1}^{hs} & - & - & - & P_{nn}^{hs} \end{bmatrix}$$

I = unit matrix

$$I = \begin{bmatrix} 1 & & & & 0 \\ & 1 & & & \\ & & - & & \\ & & & - & \\ 0 & & & & 1 \end{bmatrix}$$

Solution of the system (matrix formulation)

To develop the solution method in matrix format, we will follow the main steps already shown in Figure 13.2.

Iteration 1

Allocate employees to residences and derive dependent population
The allocation is performed multiplying the basic employment vector $e(1)$ by the journey to home probability distribution matrix H. To generate the basic population vector $p(1)$, the distribution already obtained is multiplied by the activity rate matrix F,

$$p(1) = e(1)HF \tag{13.32}$$

Derive retail employees and allocate them to services
To derive retail employees, the population vector $p(1)$ is multiplied by population serving ratio matrix A and the allocation is performed by multiplying this value, in turn, by the journey to service probability matrix S, that is,

$$e(2) = p(1)AS \tag{13.33}$$

but from equation 13.32 $p(1) = e(1)HF$, then

$$e(2) = e(1)HFAS \tag{13.34}$$

Iteration 2
The population vector $p(2)$ associated with retail employment vector $e(2)$ is found in similar fashion as indicated for the first iteration:

$$p(2) = e(2)HF = e(1)HFAS\ HF \qquad (13.32.1)$$

the same can be said about the increment of retail employment vector $e(3)$,

$$e(3) = p(2)AS = e(1)\ (HFAS)^2 \qquad (13.34.1)$$

Iteration 3

$$p(3) = e(3)HF = e(1)\ (HFAS)^2 HF \qquad (13.32.2)$$

$$e(4) = p(3)AS = e(1)\ (HFAS)^3 \qquad (13.34.2)$$

In general
Examination of the previous iterations, reveals the following recurrence relations

$$p(z) = e(1)\ (HFAS)^{z-1} HF \qquad (13.32.3)$$

$$e(z) = e(1)\ (HFAS)^{z-1} \qquad (13.34.3)$$

Calculate total demand for services
The total demand for services, vector e, can be found by summing all the increments vector $e(z)$, that is

$$e = e(1) + e(2) + e(3) + + + e(z) \qquad (13.35)$$

$$e = e(1) + e(1)\ (HFAS) + e(1)\ (HFAS)^2 + + + e(1)\ (HFAS)^{z-1} \qquad (13.36)$$

$$e = e(1)[I + HFAS + (HFAS)^2 + + + (HFAS)^{z-1}] \qquad (13.37)$$

The same procedure can be applied to obtain total employment vector p

$$p = p(1) + p(2) + p(3) + + + p(z) \qquad (13.38)$$

$$p = e(1)[I + HFAS + (HFAS)^2 + + + (HFAS)^{z-1}]HF \qquad (13.39)$$

Equation 13.37 and 13.39 present the expanded form in matrix formulation of the Garin–Lowry model.

Obviously, to obtain a better convergency we must allow $z \to \infty$; and because we know that $e(1) = e^b$ and $(HFAS)^0 = I$, we express equations 13.37 and 13.39 as

$$e = e^b \sum_{z=0}^{\infty} (HFAS)^z \qquad (13.40)$$

$$p = e^b \sum_{z=0}^{\infty} (HFAS)^z HF \qquad (13.41)$$

Garin[1] has shown that $(HFAS)^z \to 0$ as $z \to \infty$. In such a case the matrix series contained in equations 13.40 and 13.41 above, converges to $(I-HFAS)^{-1}$.

Therefore

$$e = e^b (I - HFAS)^{-1} \qquad (13.42)$$

$$p = e^b (I - HFAS)^{-1} HF \qquad (13.43)$$

Equations 13.42 and 13.43 present the analytic or contracted form of the Garin–Lowry model.

13.5 Comments

The Garin–Lowry model is conceptually much more satisfying than the original formulation. This model has been extensively used in Britain, where it has been improved in several ways. For example, the Cheshire Model[3] examines some aspects of the Garin–Lowry model and presents some developments:

(1) Improvements in the allocation formulae used within the allocation models. For example, the improvements being introduced into the residential allocation equations are:

(a) The introduction of a variable W_i to represent the 'intrinsic attractive power' of a zone for the location of residences. 'Intrinsic' here represents those attributes of an area which make it attractive for residential development but which are unrelated to its proximity to workplaces.

(b) The introduction of the concept of competition amongst residence zones, through a term which represents the total attractive power of all residence zones i as perceived from a fixed employment zone j.

(c) The introduction of methods of handling *within the equation system* constraints on the population capacities of some zones.

(d) The disaggregation of the locational characteristics through considerations of wage levels and house type.

Similar developments are introduced into the service allocation equations.

(2) Design of an hierarchical model which is based on a spatial system comprising a set of interlinked and nested subregions, zones and data units.

(3) Improved operational definitions; for example, the classification of basic and service employment and the formulation of criteria to define zone size.

(4) The adoption of a strategy and data study that lead toward improved aggregate models, which are used both to forecast aggregate levels of employment and to determine the coefficients that relate aggregate employment to aggregate population.

Batty[2] gives a very interesting review of the modifications developed in Britain in relation to the Garin–Lowry model.

13.6 Worked problem

In order to fix ideas and to clarify the structure of the Garin–Lowry model, an application to a simple problem is given, based on a computation of the expanded form prepared by Batty.[4] The task will be to produce a model of an imaginary town which is divided into four zones. The following set of data will be used.

Input data

The four-zone town and the matrix of distances are as follows:

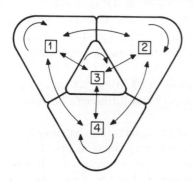

	1	2	3	4
1	2	8	6	7
2	8	3	4	7
3	6	4	3	4
4	7	7	4	3

Zone	Basic employment	Retail employment	Total employment	Population
1	70	30	100	480
2	100	100	200	870
3	300	500	800	1020
4	50	50	100	720
Total	520	680	1200	3090

The activity rate f and the population serving ratio a is required for the model, then applying equations 12.16 and 12.18 respectively, we have

$$f = \frac{N}{E} = \frac{3090}{1200} = 2.575$$

$$a = \frac{E^R}{N} = \frac{680}{3090} = 0.220$$

Preceding calculations

Before we start the iterative process, we need to compute the probabilities of residential location P_{ij}^{wh} and service centre location P_{ij}^{hs}. These probabilities do not change from iteration to iteration.

To obtain the probability distribution of residential location, we apply equation 13.15

$$P_{ij}^{wh} = \frac{N_j/d_{ij}^{\alpha}}{\sum\limits_{j=1}^{n} \dfrac{N_j}{d_{ij}^{\alpha}}}$$

Assuming that $\alpha = 2$ from the calibration, we proceed as follows

$$P_{11}^{wh} = \frac{480/2^2}{\dfrac{480}{2^2} + \dfrac{870}{8^2} + \dfrac{1020}{6^2} + \dfrac{720}{7^2}} = 0.68$$

In the same way we calculate all the probabilities; their values in matrix form are

P_{ij}^{wh}	1	2	3	4	$\sum\limits_{j=1}^{n} P_{ij}^{wh}$
1	0.68	0.08	0.16	0.08	1.00
2	0.04	0.53	0.35	0.08	1.00
3	0.06	0.24	0.50	0.20	1.00
4	0.06	0.10	0.37	0.47	1.00

The probability distribution of service centre location can be obtained in the same fashion, using equation 13.22

$$P_{ij}^{hs} = \frac{E_i^R/d_{ij}^{\lambda}}{\sum\limits_{i=1}^{n} \dfrac{E_i^R}{d_{ij}^{\lambda}}}$$

Assuming that $\lambda = 2$, the final form of this matrix is

P_{ij}^{ns}	1	2	3	4
1	0.31	0.01	0.01	0.02
2	0.07	0.25	0.10	0.05
3	0.58	0.71	0.84	0.79
4	0.04	0.03	0.05	0.14
$\sum\limits_{i=1}^{n} P_{ij}^{hs}$	1.00	1.00	1.00	1.00

Predict total retail employment
The total employment is found applying equation 13.9

$$E^* = E^B(1 - af)^{-1}$$

$$E^* = 520[1 - (0.220)(2.575)]^{-1} = 1200$$

and the retail employment is obtained using equation 13.27

$$E^{R*} = E^* - E^B$$

$$E^{R*} = 1200 - 520 = 680$$

In this particular case, this information could have also been obtained directly from the data.

Iterative process

Counter
We set our index z to one ($z = 1$), and start the first cycle or iteration.

Allocate employees to residences
This step is performed using equation 13.18

$$L_j(1) = \sum_{i=1}^{n} E_i(1) P_{ij}^{wh} = \sum_{i=1}^{n} I_{ij}^{wh}(1)$$

To obtain these values, we first calculate $I_{ij}^{wh}(1)$ using equation 13.16

$$I_{ij}^{wh}(1) = E_i(1) P_{ij}^{wh}$$

these values are shown in the following matrix

$I_{ij}^{wh}(1)$	1	2	3	4
1	48	5	11	6
2	4	53	35	8
3	18	72	150	60
4	3	5	19	23

and then, to obtain $L_j(1)$, we just sum over columns in the above matrix

Zone	1	2	3	4
$L_j(1) = \sum_{i=1}^{4} I_{ij}^{wh}(1)$	73	135	215	97

Derive dependent population
Applying equation 13.28

$$N_j(1) = fL_j(1)$$

where $f = 2.575$. We obtain the associated population $N_j(1)$

Zone	$L_j(1)$	$N_j(1) = fL_j(1)$
1	73	188
2	135	348
3	215	554
4	97	249

Derive retail employees
By means of equation 13.29

$$D_j(1) = aN_j(1)$$

and knowing that $a = 0.220$, we calculate the number of service employees required

Zone	$N_j(1)$	$D_j(1) = aN_j(1)$
1	188	41
2	348	77
3	554	122
4	249	55

Allocate retail employees to services
This allocation is performed using equation 13.24

$$E_i^R(1) = \sum_{j=1}^{4} D_j(1) P_{ij}^{hs} = \sum_{j=1}^{4} E_{ij}^R(1)$$

These values can be obtained practically if we first calculate $E_{ij}^R(1)$ by means of equation 13.23

$$E_{ij}^R(1) = D_j(1) P_{ij}^{hs}$$

These calculations are presented in the following matrix:

$E_{ij}^R(1)$	1	2	3	4
1	13	1	1	1
2	3	19	12	3
3	24	55	103	44
4	1	2	6	7

and then, to obtain $E_i^R(1)$, we sum over rows in the above matrix:

Zone	$E_i^R(1) = \sum_{j=1}^{4} E_{ij}^R(1)$
1	16
2	37
3	226
4	16

Calculate total demand for services
Using equation 13.26

$$E^R = \sum_{z=1}^{1} \sum_{i=1}^{4} E_i^R(z)$$

we have,

$$E^R = 16 + 37 + 226 + 16 = 295$$

Has process converged?
Comparing E^R (= 295 employees) with E^{R*} (= 680 employees), we see that additional increments of service employment are needed and so we repeat the cycle.

Iteration 2
We have now to find the increment of service employment $E_i^R(2)$ required to service the population associated with service employment $E_i^R(1)$. This iteration and the following ones will be notated in less detail than the first iteration for obvious reasons.

Allocate employees to residences

$I_{ij}^{wh}(2)$	1	2	3	4
1	11	1	3	1
2	1	20	13	3
3	13	54	113	46
4	1	2	6	7
$L_j(2)$	26	77	135	57

Derive dependent population and retail employees

Zone	$L_j(2)$	$N_j(2) = fL_j(2)$	$D_j(2) = aN_j(2)$
1	26	67	15
2	77	198	44
3	135	348	77
4	57	147	32

Allocate retail employees to services

$E_{ij}^R(2)$	1	2	3	4	$E_i^R(2) = \sum_{j=1}^{4} E_{ij}^R(2)$
1	5	0	1	0	6
2	1	11	8	1	21
3	9	31	65	25	130
4	0	0	4	5	9

Calculate total demand for services

$$E^R = (16 + 37 + 226 + 16) + (6 + 21 + 130 + 9)$$
$$E^R = 295 + 166 = 461$$

Has process converged?

$$E^R = 461 \text{ but } E^{R*} = 680, \text{ then,}$$

Iteration 3

Allocate employees to residences

$I_{ij}^{wh}(3)$	1	2	3	4
1	4	0	1	1
2	1	11	7	2
3	8	31	65	26
4	1	1	3	4
$L_j(3)$	14	43	76	33

Derive dependent population and retail employees

Zone	$L_j(3)$	$N_j(3) = fL_j(3)$	$D_j(3) = aN_j(3)$
1	14	36	8
2	43	111	24
3	76	196	43
4	33	85	19

Allocate retail employees to services

$E_{ij}^R(3)$	1	2	3	4	$E_i^R(3) = \sum_{j=1}^{4} E_{ij}^R(3)$
1	2	0	1	0	3
2	1	6	4	0	11
3	5	17	36	18	76
4	0	1	2	1	4

Calculate total demand for services

$$E^R = 295 + 166 + (3 + 11 + 76 + 4)$$
$$E^R = 295 + 166 + 94 = 555$$

Has process converged?

$$E^R = 555 \text{ but } E^{R*} = 680, \text{ then,}$$

Iteration 4

Allocate employees to residences

$I_{ij}^{wh}(4)$	1	2	3	4
1	2	0	1	0
2	0	6	4	1
3	5	18	38	15
4	0	1	1	2
$L_j(4)$	7	25	44	18

Derive dependent population and retail employees

Zone	$L_j(4)$	$N_j(4) = fL_j(4)$	$D_j(4) = aN_j(4)$
1	7	18	4
2	25	64	14
3	44	113	25
4	18	46	10

Allocate retail employees to services

$E_{ij}^R(4)$	1	2	3	4	$E_i^R(4) = \sum_{j=1}^{4} E_{ij}^R(4)$
1	1	0	1	0	2
2	1	3	2	1	7
3	2	10	21	8	41
4	0	1	1	1	3

Calculate total demand for services

$$E^R = 295 + 166 + 94 + (2 + 7 + 41 + 3)$$
$$E^R = 555 + 53 = 608$$

Has process converged?

$$E^R = 608 \text{ but } E^{R*} = 680, \text{ then,}$$

Iteration 5

Allocate employees to residences

$I_{ij}^{wh}(5)$	1	2	3	4
1	1	0	1	0
2	0	4	2	1
3	2	10	20	9
4	0	0	1	2
$L_j(5)$	3	14	24	12

Derive dependent population and retail employees

Zone	$L_j(5)$	$N_j(5) = fL_j(5)$	$D_j(5) = aN_j(5)$
1	3	8	2
2	14	36	8
3	24	62	14
4	12	31	7

Allocate retail employees to services

$E_{ij}^R(5)$	1	2	3	4
1	1	0	0	0
2	0	2	1	1
3	0	6	12	5
4	0	0	1	1

$E_i^R(5) = \sum_{j=1}^{4} E_{ij}^R(5)$

1
4
23
2

Calculate total demand for services

$$E^R = 295 + 166 + 94 + 53 + (1 + 4 + 23 + 2)$$
$$E^R = 608 + 30 = 638$$

Has process converged?

$$E^R = 638 \text{ but } E^{R*} = 680, \text{ then,}$$

Iteration 6

Allocate employees to residences

$I_{ij}^{wh}(6)$	1	2	3	4
1	1	0	0	0
2	0	3	1	0
3	1	6	11	5
4	0	0	0	2
$L_j(6)$	2	9	12	7

Derive dependent population and retail employees

Zone	$L_j(6)$	$N_j(6) = fL_j(6)$	$D_j(6) = aN_j(6)$
1	2	5	1
2	9	23	5
3	12	31	7
4	7	18	4

Allocate retail employees to services

$E_{ij}^R(6)$	1	2	3	4	$E_i^R(6) = \sum_{j=1}^{4} E_{ij}^R(6)$
1	0	0	0	0	0
2	0	1	1	0	2
3	1	4	6	3	14
4	0	0	0	1	1

Calculate total demand for services

$$E^R = 295 + 166 + 94 + 53 + 30 + (2 + 14 + 1)$$
$$E^R = 638 + 17 = 655$$

Has process converged?

$$E^R = 655 \text{ and } E^{R*} = 680$$

Further iterations could make the predicted and derived totals equal, but for the purpose of this example we are going to consider iteration 6 as the last one. Also it is to be noticed that some slight arithmetical errors in the previous calculations are due to rounding.

Outputs of the model

If we tabulate the employments and population derived at each iteration and located at each zone, we can see how quickly the system is converging.

Employment

Zone	Basic	$E_i^R(1)$	$E_i^R(2)$	$E_i^R(3)$	$E_i^R(4)$	$E_i^R(5)$	$E_i^R(6)$	Total
1	70	16	6	3	2	1	0	98
2	100	37	21	11	7	4	2	182
3	300	226	130	76	41	23	14	810
4	50	16	9	4	3	2	1	85
Total	520	295	166	94	53	30	17	1175
Cumulative total	520	815	981	1075	1128	1158	1175	

A graph indicating the convergence between derived and predicted total employment is shown in Figure 13.3.

Population

Zone	$N_j(1)$	$N_j(2)$	$N_j(3)$	$N_j(4)$	$N_j(5)$	$N_j(6)$	Total
1	188	67	36	18	8	5	322
2	348	198	111	64	36	23	780
3	554	348	196	113	62	31	1304
4	249	147	85	46	31	18	576
Total	1339	760	428	241	137	77	2982
Cumulative total	1339	2099	2527	2768	2905	2982	

Figure 13.4 shows a graph where the population cumulative values are plotted.

Goodness of fit

The goodness of fit of the model's derivations to the real situation has been assessed using the correlation coefficient R and coefficient of determination R^2.

A comparison of the derived and observed values of total employment and population in each zone is given in the table below.

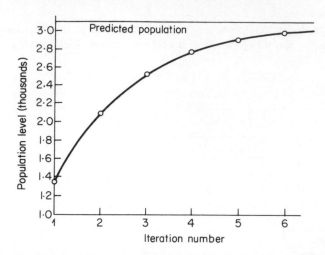

Figure 13.3 Convergence between derived and predicted total population

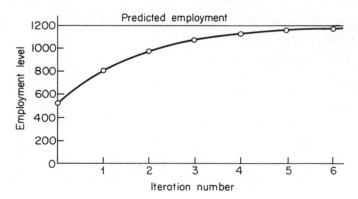

Figure 13.4 Convergence between derived and predicted total employment

Zone	Employment		Population	
	Observed	Derived	Observed	Derived
1	100	98	480	322
2	200	182	870	780
3	800	810	1020	1304
4	100	85	720	576
R^2	0.9994		0.9078	

These quite remarkable values of the coefficient of determination R^2 show that the model is an extremely powerful device for effecting good simulations. We should add to this feature the fact that only a limited set of data is necessary to operate the model.

Other outputs of the model

One of the outstanding features of Garin's improvement to the Lowry model is that relationships between activities are represented explicitly. This allows the model to predict trips between workplaces and zones of residence, as well as to estimate demands made by the population for services which can be converted into home to service trips if required.

At each iteration, the work to home trips $I_{ij}^{wh}(z)$ are presented in matrix form, as well as the service demand $E_{ij}^{R}(z)$.

Total work to home trips in the system can be calculated

$$I_{ij}^{wh} = \sum_{z=1}^{6} I_{ij}^{wh}(z) \tag{13.30}$$

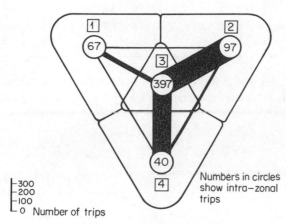

Figure 13.5 Work trips: numbers in circles show intra-zonal trips

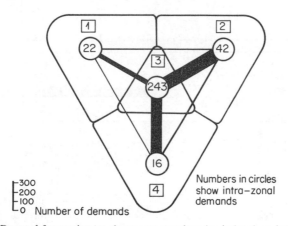

Figure 13.6 Demand for service employment: numbers in circles show intra-zonal demands

This trip matrix is given below,

I_{ij}^{wh}	1	2	3	4
1	67	6	17	8
2	6	97	62	15
3	47	191	397	161
4	5	9	30	40

To have an impression of the gross iteration between zones, trips in both directions between any pair of zones are summed

	1	2	3	4
1	67	12	64	13
2		97	253	24
3			397	191
4				40

Diagrammatically, this distribution of work trips can be represented as shown in Figure 13.5. The total service demand in the system can be calculated

$$E_{ij}^R = \sum_{z=1}^{6} E_{ij}^R(z) \tag{13.31}$$

This service demand matrix is given below

E_{ij}^R	1	2	3	4
1	22	1	4	1
2	6	42	27	7
3	42	123	243	103
4	1	4	14	16

The gross iteration between zones is

	1	2	3	4
1	22	7	46	2
2		42	150	11
3			243	117
4				16

This demand for service employment can be presented diagrammatically, as shown in Figure 13.6.

References

1 GARIN, R. A. 'A matrix formulation of the Lowry model for intra-metropolitan activity allocation'. *Journal of the American Institute of Planners*, 1966, November.

2 BATTY, M. 'Recent developments in land use modelling: a review of British research'. Urban Systems Research Unit, Department of Geography, University of Reading, 1970.

3 CORDEY–HAYES, M. and others. 'An operational urban development model of Cheshire'. Centre for Environmental Studies, Working Paper 64, 1970, October.

4 BATTY, M. 'Introductory model-building problems for urban and regional planning'. Urban Systems Research Unit, Department of Geography, University of Reading, 1970.

14   A Land-Use Plan Design Model

14.1 Introduction
This model has been prepared by Kenneth J. Schlager[1] for the Land-Use
Transportation Study of the Southeastern Wisconsin Regional Planning
Commission in 1965, and has been tested using data from the Waukesha area.
Schlager has called his model a 'Plan Design' model, which could be identified
as a decision model, according to the classification used here.

The process of evaluation of the different alternative programmes is done
endogenously by the model itself, using mathematical programming techniques.
The object is to minimize total public and private investment costs subject to
certain constraints. Only major land uses such as agriculture, industry, residential,
open space, etc. are handled by this model.

14.2 Underlying concepts
The underlying concepts of this model have their basis in the analytical studies
of Christopher Alexander[2] who indicates that difficulties in the design process
derive primarily from the inability of the human designer to manipulate
simultaneously a large number of interacting design relationships. Schlager[1]
remarks:

> While Alexander does not pursue the direct solution of selection problems
> by means of mathematical techniques, his definition provides useful
> criteria for the systematic formulation of such problems.

In relation to the following conditions connected to a 'selection problem'
pointed out by Alexander,[2]

(1)   'It must be possible to generate a wide enough range of possible
alternative solutions symbolically.'
(2)   'It must be possible to express all criteria for solution in terms of the
same symbolism.'

Schlager indicates that the first requirement is naturally achieved because all
land-use plans may be expressed symbolically by three sets of variables:

(1)   The type of land use (quality variables)
(2)   The density of land use (quantity variables)
(3)   The geographic location (location variables).

The land area under study is subdivided into a grid of 'zones' of equal area. The geographic co-ordinates of the zone determine the location variable. For each zone, the types and densities of land uses may be expressed as a measure of the activities in that zonal area.

The requirements of the second condition, which deals with the symbolic relationship between alternative forms and design requirements, are divided into two primary classes:

(1) Requirements that restrict the numerical value of a land use or a relationship between land uses *within* a grid zone. Examples of these requirements are the exclusion of flood plain areas from development in a given zone grid, or prevention of the simultaneous development of both industrial and residential land in the same grid zone.

(2) Requirements that restrict a relationship between land uses *between* grid zones; for example, the need to provide an elementary school within a specified distance (or time) of all residential units.

Then, given these design requirements in terms of restrictions on possible land-use relationships, and a set of demands or total needs (based on previously prepared forecasts for the area under study), the problem is to (Schlager[1]):

Synthesize a land use plan design that satisfies both the land use demands and design standards considering the current state of both natural and man-made land characteristics, at a minimal combination of public and private costs.

He tries to emphasize that minimal cost does not necessarily mean a cheap plan, but only to avoid unnecessary expenditure of precious resources.

14.3 The linear programming formulation

Schlager only gives an outline of the mathematical formulation of his model, but in the following analysis a more complete description of the linear programming will be attempted based on the information provided. The original notation will be modified and expanded in order to fulfil this intention.

The following notation will be used:

m = number of zones of equal area which form an exhaustive subdivision of the land area under study; zones are indicated by the subscripts $i = 1, 2, \ldots m$

n = number of land uses categories such as single family residential, multi-family residential, industrial, agricultural, etc. considered by the designer; Land uses categories are indicated by the subscripts $j = 1, 2, \ldots n$

x_{ij} = number of acres of zone i to be allocated to land use category j

c_{ij} = cost of developing an acre of zone i for allocation of land use category j; cost may be related to the topography and soil characteristics of the area

E_j = total demand for land use category j

d_j = service ratio coefficient which provides for supporting service land requirements, such as streets, which are necessary for development of land use category j

F_i = limit in the amount of area from zone i that can be allocated to land uses

G_{jk} = ratio of land use category j allowed relative to land use category k, with land uses categories j and k in the *same* zone

G_k^j = ratio of land uses categories j allowed relative to land use category k with land uses categories j and k in *different* zones.

The mathematical structure of this model can be identified as a 'transportation problem' which is solved using linear programming techniques. The linear programming formulation has the following form:

Minimize
$$Z = \sum_{i=1}^{m} \sum_{j=1}^{n} c_{ij} x_{ij} \tag{14.1}$$

subject to
$$\sum_{i=1}^{m} d_j x_{ij} = E_j \qquad (j = 1, 2, \dots n) \tag{14.2}$$

$$\sum_{j=1}^{n} x_{ij} \leqslant F_i \qquad (i = 1, 2, \dots m) \tag{14.3}$$

$$x_{ij} \leqslant G_{jk} x_{ik} \qquad \begin{array}{l}(i = 1, 2, \dots m) \\ (j = 1, 2, \dots k, \dots n)\end{array} \tag{14.4}$$

$$x_{ij} \leqslant G_k^j x_{hk} \qquad \begin{array}{l}(i = 1, 2, \dots h, \dots m) \\ (j = 1, 2, \dots k, \dots n)\end{array} \tag{14.5}$$

The objective function (14.1) relates to the cost of developing land for a given land use category. Constraint equations 14.2 ensure that the total demand requirement for each land-use category is satisfied by the model; that is, the allocations add up to the forecast total. Because only primary land uses such as residential, industrial, agricultural and recreational land are directly determined, service ratios incorporated in the d parameters account for secondary land uses as streets and parks.

Constraint equations 14.3 limit the use of land within a zone; it will usually reflect a density standard. Constraint equations 14.4 and 14.5 indicate restrictions on coexistent land uses within and between zones. This type of constraint will also reflect accessibility standards for employment and shopping areas. The introduction of more constraints will depend on the characteristics of the study, and of course, will have the effect of restricting the set of possible solutions. Constraints can be added as long as they are linear and continuous.

14.4 Inputs

Four main classes of input data are required:

(1) Costs of unimproved land and land development by land use and type of soil
(2) Forecast total demand for each land use
(3) Design standards (e.g. densities) and inter- and intra-zonal limitations on land-use relationships
(4) The current land inventory including land uses and soil types.

Land development cost data obtained by statistical analysis of recent land development generally are very expensive and difficult to obtain. Engineering cost estimates are usually preferable if competent professional experience is available. In the Waukesha area, separate cost estimates were prepared for each of three classes of soil. Assessed and equalized land value data on the basis of prices realized in recent land transactions were obtained for each of the zones. It is possible to consider redevelopment in the form of urban renewal, and for this approach, redevelopment cost would be required.

The aggregate demand for each primary land use activity is input to the model and may be obtained by applying design standards to forecasts of population and employment in the area under study.

The design standards reflect the plan objectives and restrict the set of acceptable plans, also they limit the land use relationships that may exist in the plan. Basically they are the densities assigned to each zone, the service ratios for the amount of secondary land (streets, parks) required to support the primary land uses, and the ratios of coexistent land uses within and between zones.

An inventory of both current land use activities and soil characteristics is one of the most important inputs. The soil inventory makes it possible to assign a development cost to each zone in the study area.

14.5 Limitations of the linear programming

Schlager introduces his model using linear programming techniques and points out two major limitations:

(1) Because land-use choices are by nature usually discrete, land-use variables should take discrete values rather than continuous ones. Linear programming solution could be rounded off to satisfy these natural discrete levels, but such a solution does not usually correspond with the associated discrete optimal combination.
(2) The need for both a linear objective function and linear constraints is the second limitation of linear programming.

The use of a linear objective function as an approximation to non-linear costs is not a severe one, because the inaccuracies introduced by this approximation are usually less than the errors of cost estimation. But linear constraint relationships provide an unsatisfactory substitute to design standards which are generally non-linear. If these design standards are not represented properly, the model loses most of its usefulness. In order to remove these limitations, the author of this model suggests the possible application of dynamic programming as a computational procedure to be used in the model.

14.6 Comments

Although many comments have been presented along the analysis of this model, two major points will be emphasized here.

The first one is related to the conceptual basis of minimizing costs. Cost can be an interesting factor to be employed in the objective function, if it is representative of all the elements that shape the urban spatial structure; but in the particular way that this model handles these elements, it is doubtful whether the representation required is manifested. There is little doubt that development cost is important, but to consider it as the basic factor which (under certain restrictions) defines an optimal allocation of different land uses, shows an opposite viewpoint from the comprehensive and systematic approach to planning advocated here.

The second point refers to an apparent absence of the dual problem. Many interesting features about relevant ways of introducing changes into the land-use plan could be obtained by the use and interpretation of the dual variables, which apparently are not considered in the framework of the model. Changes in the land-use plan can probably appear during the implementation stage, where dual variables could give a deeper insight in the nature of the changes required.

New models have been developed which attempt to overcome these deficiences. One is the model[3] for the Irvine New Town in Britain, which was carried out by the Israel Institute of Urban Studies and P.A. Management Consultants Ltd. in 1968. The purpose of the model was to maximize the value of the welfare goal function (objective function) within the given constraints, by the efficient allocation of population and dwelling units to the different zones and development stages of the plan.

The Irvine New Town model recognizes that there are criteria which are not measurable in financial terms, and thus the optimal plan cannot be easily obtained. Therefore, several alternative directives are specified for different levels of these criteria and for each alternative, and the best possible solution is found which is regarded as efficient. From the list of alternative efficient plans, that plan which best suits the planner's criteria is chosen. 'The selection of this plan is not simple, because the plans differ from one another, not only in the value of their goal function but also in other criteria which are unmeasurable. This process of selection requires the deep consideration not only of planners, but also most importantly of public authorities'.[3]

The construction of the welfare goal function included the following criteria for the residential areas:

The market value of housing
Construction costs of housing
Site development costs of residential areas
The alternative agricultural value of the land
Land value premia due to environmental conditions
The value of the time that the population will spend in travelling for all
purposes, etc.

The Irvine New Town model makes use of the dual variables, and thus it is
possible to indicate by how much the total value of the goal or objective function
increases as a result of marginal relaxation of the constraints. Since some of the
constraints are subject to the decision of the public authorities, the information
given by the dual variables allows the authorities to re-examine their former
decisions and modify them.

Another very interesting experience in England which used linear programming
techniques, was started towards the end of 1969 by the Greater London Council
in order to assist the overall planning of Greater London.[4] In this model, the
objective function is more safely regarded as an expression of one of the important factors which influence development. It is never considered the sole
important factor. Apart from those factors included in the constraints, other
important factors, such as the utilization of vacant land, the density of housing,
the total cost, the availability of land for redevelopment, etc., were also
included in the model by means of objective functions. It should be stressed that,
although many objective functions are contained in the model, only one can be
operative at any time.

Young[4] points out:

One use the model does *not* have is that of calculating what *will happen*
in the future. Its uses are, in fact, all concerned with calculating what
needs to happen if objectives are to be met.

The reader will find very easy to follow the description of the GLC model on
pages 5—15 of Reference 4.

References
1 SCHLAGER, K. J. 'A land use plan design model'. *Journal of the American
Institute of Planners*, 1965, May, pp. 103—111.
2 ALEXANDER, C. *Notes on the Synthesis of Form*. Cambridge: Harvard
University Press, 1964.
3 P.A. MANAGEMENT CONSULTANTS LTD. and ISRAEL INSTITUTE OF
URBAN STUDIES LTD. 'Irvine New Town planning study'. 1969, September.
4 YOUNG, W. 'Planning — a linear programming model'. *GLC Intelligence Unit
Quarterly Bulletin*, 1972, June, no. 19.

15 Appraisal

As we have seen, over the last 13 years considerable effort has been directed towards the development and application of new techniques, particularly by the application of mathematical models to the problems of urban spatial systems, which has been approached in the past largely by intuition and experience. Also, there has been an emphasis on the systems approach to planning, which has been mainly based on the acceptance of a systems structure framework allowing the comparatively easy elucidation of model concepts.

Although models have not played a decisive role in urban planning, they have been useful in the planning process where they have performed at least three major roles:

(1) In the understanding of the factors that influence land development
(2) As a predictive instrument to evaluate and test alternative plans
(3) As an optimizing tool.

The mere exercise of trying to simulate or produce a model of a system has a remarkable disciplining and clarifying effect, and increases rigour and order in the thought processes, especially because concepts have to be sharpened and quantified whenever possible. There is considerable hope that our understanding of the way cities work will be increased by the development of mathematical models. Certainly, urban spatial models have shown their value in helping our understanding of the effects of planning decisions. It has been indicated that urban spatial models can play an important part in clarifying possible alternative plans, but it has to be stressed that these alternatives have to be generated, and so the planner's imagination is the key feature necessary to produce the alternatives which are going to be tested. The simple fact that various alternatives are tested and their consequences assessed, in a way is a form of optimization. However, in cases where we use straightforward optimization techniques (such as mathematical programming, which requires a well-defined objective function which in urban spatial terms is very difficult to determine), the use of these optimization techniques other than for purely exploratory purposes is difficult to envisage at this stage of the model-building development.

Urban spatial models are so new that, to a considerable extent, all are research and training exercises. Even those models put up for the most practical and immediate needs are commonly seen later to have provided the necessary empirical investigation which gave planners more insight about the nature and relationship of urban phenomena and about the probable consequences of their actions. That is, their purpose has been mainly educational. There is little doubt that the use of mathematical models as an element in the planning process has enormously increased the planners' understanding of the urban spatial structure problems, and has forced them to deal explicitly and rigorously with many relationships within the urban spatial system that were previously ignored. In spite of all the weaknesses of the actual mathematical models, it can be said unequivocally that a tremendous amount has been learned from their use, and that by the experience gained from them, new models are being developed which will remedy their deficiencies.

As we have seen in this survey, the first land-use models were constructed about a decade ago in the United States. In a sense, most of them were too ambitious, and at the time, the difficulties of model building were not fully appreciated. In Britain, the first land-use models were constructed only six years ago. They were less ambitious and perhaps they have produced much better simulations in terms of performance than their counterparts in the United States. This may be attributed to limitations in the size of the system being simulated. British models have been mainly developed around the model first proposed by Lowry[1] in 1964 for the Pittsburgh City Region. Of course, there have been other models such as the Irvine New Town Model,[2] the GLC Planning Policy Model,[3] the Leicester Sub-Regional Model, etc., which are based on different formulations. It should be stressed here that British models have used improved spatial interaction models.

As has been pointed out in earlier chapters, good models have been developed and have been extensively used in planning contexts. Outside the transportation field, probably the best examples are found in the development of retail models capable of predicting the total sales in different shopping centres of a city for a given distribution of population. Residential location models have also made considerable progress, but models of industrial location have not received the same attention. Although most of the models so far developed have been partial models, some general models such as the Lowry model have been constructed. The results of using such models should be treated with great caution because they have generally been achieved when considerable approximations were made, due to the present state of the model building process.

Many urban spatial models have been built and we find them at different levels of development: some are already operational, others are mainly used for impact analysis and many others just for educational purposes. An example of an operational model can be found in the version of the Lowry model built by Cripps and Foot,[4] for which the original objective was to prepare a plan for the County of Bedford, and was later expanded to cover surrounding areas, particularly the new town of Milton Keynes. It is too soon to evaluate the validity of operational models, because it is becoming increasingly clear that the development and testing of such models are a long term process. For the study of the potential site for the third London Airport, Cripps and Foot[5] were able to provide decision makers with a substantial measurement of impact by using the Bedfordshire model. The use of models for educational purposes has been widely employed. For example, in England the model of Cambridge[6] was conceived as an educational programme and built by the sixth-year architectural students at the University of Cambridge. In the United States we find, for example, the CLUG (The Cornell Land Use Game) by Feldt[7] being used to teach planning principles to public officials and students.

One danger in urban planning today is the feeling sometimes held that mathematical models, such as the ones described in this survey, will actually solve problems. It should be remembered that they are only tools to *help* planners to solve them. One of the dangers of employing models is the use of parameters as a basis for prediction where these parameters are derived from observed data. This risk mainly applies to the social physics approach which, as we have seen, does not ask why things occur but merely looks at the result of what has happened without fully understanding how decisions are taken or how the various forces act. It is equally important to recognize that the building of a model provides an accurate description of the system under study only in terms of the input to the model: the outcome of a model will never be more accurate than the input.

It is my impression that the growth of urban spatial models on a broad scale will require more theory, and the availability of more and better organized data. There can be no adequate formulation of urban structure without better concepts and definitions. There is more need for carefully considered empirical investigation into behaviour decisions, that is, a need for a basic understanding of the physical processes that take place in the urban spatial system and a description of these processes in a theory specifically made to account for the phenomena involved. The use of sophisticated mathematical and computational techniques based on crude assumptions and inadequate theory can give rise to the justifiable fears that people may have in dealing with urban spatial models. Much of the more recent theoretical development still needs to be tested and justified empirically, and so models should be used with caution at the present time. There is also a circular effect in the relationship of models to theory, in that models can assist in the development of theory. Although a general theory of the urban spatial structure that would permit the deductive solution of large urban planning problems may never be developed, partial theories can help in modelling particular planning elements. Also lacking is a better co-ordination between partial models (residential, retail, etc.) so that they relate better to an overall planning strategy. Future work should be directed at this topic.

In the immediate future, there is clearly a great need for a development of scientific attitudes and growth of fundamental theory together with a need for more and better organized data. More information about the relationships between the different elements of the urban spatial system is necessary before these models can approach their final stages. There is a need to produce improved models, and the need for caution in the use of currently available ones. Future work should be directed towards this aim.

As a conclusion to this survey, it can be seen that the benefits accruing to our communities when these models are refined will be enormous. The work described in earlier chapters represents a considerable attack on the problem of modelling urban structure where significant breakthroughs have been made, but owing to the complexity and size of the urban system much work remains to be done in this field which is still in its infancy. Also, the systems approach to planning will allow the application of scientific thought to the problems of the urban spatial system in perhaps a more realistic way than at present. The new techniques will help planners in their task, but the planning team will need to acquire new skills in order to use the new tools provided by modern technology which are presently seen to be outside the traditional architectural approach.

References

1 LOWRY, I. S. *A Model of Metropolis*. Rand Corporation, Santa Monica, California, 1964.

2 P.A. MANAGEMENT CONSULTANTS LTD. and ISRAEL INSTITUTE OF URBAN STUDIES LTD. 'Irvine New Town planning study'. 1969, September.

3 YOUNG, W. 'Planning—a linear programming model'. *GLC Intelligence Unit Quarterly Bulletin* no. 19, 1972, June.

4 CRIPPS, E. L. and FOOT, D. H. S. 'The empirical development of an elementary residential location model for use in sub-regional planning'. *Environment and Planning 1*, 1969, pp. 81—90.

5 CRIPPS, E. L. and FOOT, D. H. S. 'The urbanisation effects of a third London airport'. *Environment and Planning 2*, 1970, pp. 153—192.

6 CAMBRIDGE UNIVERSITY. 'Cambridge: the evaluation of urban structure plans'. Land Use and Built Form Studies, WP 14, Cambridge, 1970, July.

7 FELDT, A. G. 'The Cornell land use game'. Ithaca, Center for Housing and Environmental Studies, Cornell University, p. 4, 1966.

Glossary

Algorithm A series of instructions or procedural steps for the solution of a specific problem.

Attributes Are the properties of an element.

Behaviourist approach A method of theory building where it is assumed that larger groups will act in ways which can be derived from an understanding of the individual unit.

Black box A system of whose structure we know nothing except that which we can deduce from its behaviour, thus, the interest is shifted to discover statistical relationships between the inputs and outputs, by manipulating the inputs.

Calibration The process of finding the parameter values of the model which make it fit the real world in the best possible way.

Closed system A system which does not interact with its environment.

Computer programming The devising of a series of operations to be performed by a computer.

Constraints Regulations, restrictions, limitations.

Correlation Denotes the relationship between measurable variates.

Correlation analysis Statistical methods for measuring the degree of relationships between variables.

Correlation coefficient A measure of the interdependence between two variates. It is usually a pure number which varies between -1 and $+1$ with the intermediate value of zero indicating the absence of correlation but not necessarily the independence of the variates.

Curve fitting An expression used to denote the fitting of a mathematical curve to any statistical data capable of being plotted against a time or space variable.

Cybernetics The science of the control of systems.

Decision theory The corpus of theoretical knowledge which bears on the process of optimization.

Dependent variable Its value is determined by the model and given by the model as output.

Determination coefficient If a dependent variate has multiple correlation R with a set of independent variates, R^2 is known as the coefficient of determination.

Deterministic model One which contains no random elements and for which, therefore, the future course of the system is determined by its position, etc. at some fixed point in time.

Difference equation An equation which relates the value of a variable in one period of time to its value in another period.

Differential equation An equation which relates the value of a variable at one moment to the rate of change of that variable at that moment.

Dynamic programming A type of mathematical programming that involves a multistage process of decision making, wherein each consecutive decision must take into account its effects on later decisions to arrive at an overall optimum return.

Element The 'smallest' part of a system. Also called entity. By listing its attributes we describe it.

Endogenous variable That variable whose value is generated by the model.

Entity The 'smallest' part of a system. Also called element. By listing its attributes, we describe it.

Entropy Conceptually entropy is a measure of uncertainty used in information theory, which is concerned with the problems of deriving maximum useful information from a given signal or data available.

Environment The set of all elements, a change in whose attributes affects the system and also of those elements whose attributes are changed by the behaviour of the system.

Exogenous variable That variable which, for reasons of convenience or cost, is not built into the basic statement of the model.

Feedback A process by which the result of a controlling operation is used as part of the data on which the next controlling operation is based, enabling a system to take correcting steps.

General systems theory A discipline which studies the things that systems have in common with the intention of writing down a general theory of systems behaviour.

Goal An end toward which processes are directed, the purpose for which the system has been organized and toward which everything is aimed.

Goodness of fit The goodness of agreement between an observed set of values and a second set which are derived wholly or partly on a hypothetical basis, that is to say, derive from the 'fitting' of a model to the data.

Grid A rectangular mesh on a plane formed by two sets of lines orthogonal to each other, each line of each set being at a constant interval from the adjacent lines.

Heuristic approach An exploratory approach to a problem which uses successive evaluations of trial and error to arrive at a final result.

Homeostasis A biological term denoting the principle that will bring correcting processes into play, so that the system does not go out of control.

Homeostat A mechanism for achieving stability; its sole objective is to settle down the system as quickly as possible to a stable condition after it has been disturbed.

Homomorphism Refers to a mapping which involve a many—one correspondence and where certain operational characteristics concerning the relationship of elements are preserved.

Independent variable Variable whose value is given as input to the model.

Information theory Concerns itself with the transmission of information by communication systems.

Isomorphism Is a mapping which not only involves a one—one correspondence of elements but which also preserves operational characteristics.

Iterative procedure A process for calculating a result by performing a series of trials repeatedly and in which successive approximations tend to approach an optimal solution.

Lag An event occurring at time $t + k$ $(k > 0)$ is said to lag behind event occurring at time t, the extent of the lag being k.

Least-squares method A technique of estimation by which the quantities being estimated are determined by minimizing a certain quadratic form in the observations and those quantities.

Level of aggregation Has usually been taken to mean the level of spatial aggregation.

Level of categorization Generally referred to as the degree of stratification of the variables other than land.

Linear function A mathematical expression for related variables that increase and decrease proportionately.

Linear programming Refers to techniques for solving a general class of optimization problems in which a large number of simple conditions have to be satisfied at the same time and where the relationships involved are linear.

Macro-analytic approach A method of theory building where the behaviour of the individual is deduced as being typical of group behaviour.

Mapping The process of equating one set, element by element, with another set.

Mathematical model A representation of some process or problem in mathematical form in which equations are used to simulate the behaviour of the system represented. The solution to the set of equations explains or predicts changes in the state of the system concerned.

Mathematical programming Methods for maximizing or minimizing linear and non-linear functions subject to linear and non-linear constraints.

Matrix A mathematical structure of cells, formed by rows and columns in which variables or numbers are located. This rectangular array of items may be operated on using prescribed rules involving mathematical operations such as addition, multiplication, etc.

Maximize To increase to the highest possible degree.

Micro-analytic approach A method of theory building where it is assumed that larger groups will act in ways which can be derived from an understanding of the individual unit.

Minimize To reduce to the smallest possible degree.

Model A model of a system is a representation of our understanding of the corresponding real world system.

Multiple correlation coefficient It measures the closeness of representation by the regression line. The coefficient is usually denoted by R.

Multiple regression The regression of a dependent variate on more than one independent variable.

Negative feedback When the correction takes place in the opposite direction to the original divergence and therefore does not allow the error to increase each moment.

Non-linear function A function whose variables do not increase linearly.

Non-linear programming Refers to techniques for solving a general class of optimization problems and is concerned with non-linear functions and constraints.

Objective An operational aim which is capable of both attainment and measurement.

Open system A system which interacts with its environment.

Operational research (OR) The application of scientific methods, techniques and tools to optimize the performance of systems.

Optimization The process of reaching the best decision.

Parameter A mathematical variable which takes on a constant value in a particular case.

Positive feedback When the correction acts in the same direction as the existing error, thereby increasing it.

Probability A numerical measure of certainty.

Property An external manifestation of the way in which an object or element is known, observed or introduced in a process.

Regression The estimation of one variable from the value of another variable (or set of independent variables in multiple regression) by means of a least-squares fit curve fitted to the data and expressed on a graph as a regression line or curve.

Regression curve A diagrammatic exposition of a regression equation. For two variables this can be shown on a plane with the independent variable X as abscissa and Y as ordinate.

Regression line In general this is synonymous with regression curve, but is sometimes (and rather ambiguously) used to denote a linear regression.

Resolution level Change in the level of viewpoint from which an individual system or group of systems can be viewed.

Set Any collection of objects or entities having at least one property in common.

Simulation A way of manipulating a model so that it imitates reality.

Social physics approach A method of theory building where the behaviour of the individual is deduced as being typical of group behaviour.

Stochastic The adjective 'stochastic' implies the presence of a random variable.

Stochastic model A model which incorporates some stochastic elements.

Structure The structure of a model is the pattern of relationship between its constituent variables as distinct from their values or coefficients associated with them.

System An assemblage of elements or parts that work together for the overall objective of the whole; this implies relationships between the elements and between their attributes.

Systems analysis Consists in clearly understanding the components of a system and their interrelationship and viewing individual operations within the system in the light of their implications for the system as a whole.

Systems approach Means looking at each component part in terms of the role it plays in the larger system.

Transformation Changing the elements of one set into those of the other in the process of mapping.

Urban spatial structure The outcome of a process which allocates population activities to sites.

Variable A quantity which may take any one of a specified set of values.

Variate A quantity which may take any of the values of a specified set with a specified frequency or probability. The variate is therefore often known as a random variable.

Variety The number of distinguishable elements within a set.

Weight The importance of an object in relation to a set of objects to which it belongs; a numerical coefficient attached to an observation in order that it shall assume a desired degree of importance in a function of all the observations of the set.

Bibliography

ABE, O. and KURAMATA, T. 'Computer Simulation of Residential Location'. *Proceedings of the Fifth International Conference of O.R.*, 1969, June, pp. 121–133.

ABEL, C. 'Urban chaos or self-organization'. *Architectural Design*, 1969, September, pp. 501–2.

ACKOFF, R. L. 'Games, decisions and organization'. *General Systems*, 1959, vol. 4, pp. 145–150.

ACKOFF, R. L. *Progressive Architecture*. 1967, August.

ACKOFF, R. L. *Scientific Method*. John Wiley and Sons, Inc., New York, 1968.

ACKOFF, R. L. and SASIENI, M. W. *Fundamentals of Operations Research*. John Wiley and Sons, Inc., 1968.

ALEXANDER, C. *Notes on the Synthesis of Form*. Cambridge: Harvard University Press, 1964.

APOSTEL, L. 'Towards the formal study of models in the non-formal sciences': the concept and role of the model' in *Mathematics and Natural Science*, ed. H. FREUDENTHAL, Dortrecht, Holland, 1961.

ASHBY, W. R. *An Introduction to Cybernetics*. Chapman & Hall Ltd. and University Paperbacks, London, reprinted 1970.

BATTY, M. 'Introductory model-building problems for urban and regional planning'. Urban Systems Research Unit, Department of Geography, University of Reading, 1970.

BATTY, M. 'Spatial theory and information systems'. Urban Systems Research Unit, Department of Geography, University of Reading, 1970.

BATTY, M. 'Models and projections of the space-economy'. *Town Planning Review*, 1970, vol. 41, 2.

BATTY, M. 'Recent developments in land use modelling: a review of British research'. Urban Systems Research Unit, Department of Geography, University of Reading, 1970.

BATTY, M. 'An approach to rational design, Part 1: the structure of design problems'. *Architectural Design*, 1971, July, p. 463. Part 2: 'Design problems as Markov chains'. *Architectural Design*, 1971, August, p. 498.

BECKERMAN, W. and ASSOCIATES. *The British Economy in 1975*. Cambridge, 1965.

BEER, S. *Decision and Control*. John Wiley and Sons, Ltd., London, 1966.

BEER, S. *Cybernetics and Management*. The English University Press Ltd., London, 1970.

BERNHART, A. P. 'The seven dimensional theory for the shaping of metropolis'. *Engineering Journal*, 1966, March, pp. 19–24.

BERRY, B. J. L. 'Cities as systems within systems of cities'. *The Regional Science Ass. Papers (US)*, 1964, vol. 13, pp. 147–163.

BERRY, B. J. L. 'The retail components of the urban model'. *Journal of the American Institute of Planners*, 1965, May, pp. 150–155.

BERTALANFFY, L. VON. *General Systems Theory*. George Braziller, New York, 1968.

BLUMENFELD, H. 'Are land use patterns predictable?'. *Journal of the American Institute of Planners*, 1959, May, pp. 61–66.

BLUNDEN, W. R. *The Land Use Transportation System*. Pergamon Press, 1971.

BODINGTON, S. 'Town planning considered as cybernetic modelling'. *Architectural Design*, 1970, March, pp. 150–151.

BOYCE, J. R. 'What is the systems approach?'. *Systems Approach*, 1969, November, pp. 118–121.

BROADBENT, T. A. 'An urban planners model: what does it look like?'. *Architectural Design*, 1970, August, pp. 408–410.

BROWN, R. C. 'The use and mis-use of distance variables in land-use analysis'. *The Professional Geographer*, 1968, vol. 20.

CAMBRIDGE UNIVERSITY. 'Cambridge: the evaluation of urban structure plans'. Land Use and Built Form Studies, WP 14, Cambridge, July 1970.

CAMBRIDGE UNIVERSITY. 'Urban system studies, demonstrations and seminars'. Land Use and Built Form Studies, Cambridge, July 1972.

CARROTHERS, G. A. 'An historical review of the gravity and potential concepts of human interaction'. *Journal of the American Institute of Planners*, vol. 22, no. 2, pp. 94–102.

CASEY, H. J. 'The law of retail gravitation applied to traffic engineering'. *Traffic Quarterly*, 1955, July, pp. 313–322.

CHADWICK, G. *A Systems View of Planning*. Pergamon Press, Oxford, 1971.

CHAPIN, F. S. 'Selected theories of urban growth and structure'. *Journal of the American Institute of Planners*, 1964, vol. 30, February, pp. 51–58.

CHAPIN, F. S. 'A model for simulating residential development'. *Journal of the American Institute of Planners*, 1965, May, pp. 120–136.

CHAPIN, F. S. *Urban Land Use Planning*. Urbana, Illinois, 1965.

CHAPIN, F. S. 'Activity systems and urban structure'. *Journal of the American Institute of Planners*, 1968, January.

CHAPIN, F. S. and WEISS, S. F. 'A probabilistic model for residential growth'. *Transportation Research*, 1968, vol. 2, pp. 375–390.

CHICAGO TRANSPORTATION STUDY. 'Final Report'. 1960, vol. II.

CHURCHMAN, C. W., ACKOFF, R. L. and ARNOFF, E. L. *Introduction to Operations Research*. John Wiley and Sons, Inc., New York, 1968.

CHURCHMAN, C. W. *The Systems Approach*. Dell Publishing Co. Inc., New York, 1968.

CHURCHMAN, C. W. 'Architecture and O.R.'. *Architectural Design*, 1969, September, p. 487.

CONVERSE, P. D., HUEGY, H. W. and MITCHELL, R. V. *Elements of Marketing.* Prentice Hall, 1930. (7th Ed. 1965).

CORDEY-HAYES, M. 'Structure plans and models'. *Architectural Design*, 1970, July, pp. 362–363.

CORDEY-HAYES, M. and others. 'An operational urban development model of Cheshire'. Centre for Environmental Studies, Working Paper 64, 1970, October.

CORDEY-HAYES, M. and WILSON, A. G. 'Spatial interaction'. Centre for Environmental Studies, WP 57, 1970, January.

COWAN, P. 'The accomodation of activities'. *Arena*, 1967, April, pp. 256–259.

COWAN, P. 'On irreversibility'. *Architectural Design*, 1969, September, pp. 485–486.

CREIGHTON, R. L., CARROLL, J. D. and FINNEY, G. 'Data processing for city planning'. *Journal of the American Institute of Planners*, 1959, May, pp. 96–103.

CRIPPS, E. L. 'Limitations of the gravity concept'. *Gravity Models in Town Planning.* Department of Town Planning, Lanchester College of Technology, Coventry, 1969, October.

CRIPPS, E. L. and FOOT, D. H. S. 'The empirical development of an elementary residential location model for use in sub-regional planning'. *Environment and Planning 1*, 1969, pp. 81–90.

CRIPPS, E. L. and FOOT, D. H. S. 'The urbanisation effects of a third London airport'. *Environment and Planning 2*, 1970, pp. 153–192.

DAVIES, R. L. 'Problems of variable selections and measurements'. *Gravity Models in Town Planning.* Department of Town Planning, Lanchester College of Technology, Coventry, 1969, October.

ECHENIQUE, M. 'Models: a discussion'. Land Use and Built Form Studies, WP 6, 1968, March.

ECHENIQUE, M. 'Urban systems: towards an explorative model'. Land Use and Built Form Studies, Cambridge, WP 7, 1968, November.

ECHENIQUE, M. 'The city scale'. *Architectural Design*, 1971, May, pp. 276–280.

ECHENIQUE, M., CROWTHER, D. and LINDSAY, W. 'A spatial model of urban stock and activity'. *Regional Studies*, 1969, 3/3, pp. 281–312.

EIDE PARR, A. 'The design of cities'. *Architectural Association Quarterly*, 1971, vol. 3, no. 3, p. 22.

FELDT, A. G. 'The Cornell land use game'. Ithaca, Center for Housing and Environmental Studies, Cornell University, p. 4, 1966.

FLEISHER, A. 'Comments on a model of metropolis'. *Journal of the American Institute of Planners*, 1965, May, pp. 175–176.

FOLEY, D. L. 'An approach to metropolitan spatial studies', in *Explorations into Urban Structure*, Philadelphia, 1964.

FORRESTER, J. *Urban Dynamics.* The M.I.T. Press, Cambridge, Massachusetts, 1969.

FURNESS, K. P. *Traffic Engineering Practice.* Editor E. Davies, Spon. 2nd Edition, 1968.

GARIN, R. A. 'A matrix formulation of the Lowry model for intrametropolitan activity allocation'. *Journal of the American Institute of Planners,* 1966, November.

GEORGE, F. H. 'The Use of Models in Science', in *Models in Geography,* ed. CHORLEY and HAGGET, London, 1967, pp. 43—56.

GOLDNER, W. 'The Lowry model heritage'. *Journal of the American Institute of Planners,* 1971, vol. 37, no. 2.

GOLDSMITH, E. 'Bringing order to chaos'. *The Ecologist Magazine,* 1970, vol. 1, part 2, pp. 16—19.

GUNN, P. 'Systems theory in architecture and planning'. Unpublished M.Sc. thesis, Queen's University, Belfast, 1971.

HANDLER, A. B. *Systems Approach to Architecture.* American Elsevier Publishing Co. Inc., New York, 1970.

HADLEY, G. *Linear Programming.* Addison—Wesley Publishing Company, Third printing 1969.

HAGGET, P. and CHORLEY, R. J. 'Models, paradigms and the new geography', in *Models in Geography,* ed. CHORLEY and HAGGET, London, 1967, pp. 19—41.

HALL, A. D. *A Methodology for Systems Engineering.* D. Van Nostrand Company, Inc., Princeton, New Jersey, reprinted 1968.

HANSEN, W. G. 'How accessibility shapes land use'. *Journal of the American Institute of Planners,* 1959, May, vol. 25, no. 2, pp. 73—76.

HARRIS, B. 'Plan or projection: an examination of the use of models in planning'. *Journal of the American Institute of Planners,* 1960, November, pp. 265—272.

HARRIS, B. 'Some problems in the theory of intra-urban location'. *Operations Research 9,* 1961 (Fall).

HARRIS, B. 'New tools for planning'. *Journal of the American Institute of Planners,* 1965, May, pp. 90—95.

HARRIS, B. 'The use of theory in the simulation of urban phenomena'. *Journal of the American Institute of Planners,* 1966, September, pp. 258—273.

HARRIS, B. 'The city of the future: the problem of optimal design'. *Regional Science Association Papers,* 1967, vol. 19, pp. 185—198.

HARRIS, B. 'Computer and urban planning'. *Socio-Economic Planning Sciences,* 1968, July, pp. 223—230.

HARRIS, B. 'Quantitative models of urban development: their role in metropolitan policy-making', in PERLOFF, HARVEY S. and WINGO, LOWDON Jr. *Issues in Urban Economics,* Johns Hopkins, Baltimore, 1968.

HEARLE, E. F. R. 'Are cities here to stay?'. Clearinghouse for Federal Scientific and Technical Information, U.S.G.R. & D.R. and AD—413102, 1963, July.

HERBERT, J. D. and STEVENS, B. H. 'A model for the distribution of residential activities in urban areas'. *Journal of Regional Science,* 1960 (Fall) 2/2, pp. 21—36.

HILL, M. 'A goal-achievements matrix for evaluating alternative plans'. *Journal of the American Institute of Planners,* no. 34, pp. 19—29.

HILL, D. M. 'A growth allocation model for the Boston region'. *Journal of the American Institute of Planners,* 1965, May, pp. 111—120.

HIRSCH, W. Z. *Elements of Regional Accounts.* Baltimore, Md., 1964.

HOWE, R. T. 'A theoretical prediction of work-trip patterns'. *Highway Research Board Bulletin,* 1960, no. 253.

HUFF, D. L. 'A probabilistic analysis of shopping centre trade areas'. *Land Economics,* 1963, February.

ISARD, W. *Methods of Regional Analysis.* Cambridge, Mass., 1960.

KAIN, J. F. 'A contribution to the urban transportation debate; an econometric model of urban residential and travel behaviour'. *Review of Economics and Statistics,* 1964, vol. 40.

KAIN, J. F. 'The journey to work as a determinant of residential location'. *Regional Science Association Papers and Proceedings,* vol. II.

KAIN, J. F. and QUILGEY, J. M. 'Evaluating the quality of the residential environment'. *Environment & Planning,* vol. 2, no. 1, pp. 23—32.

KANSKY, K. J. 'Travel patterns of urban residents'. *Transportation Science,* 1967, vol. 1, November, pp. 261—285.

KENDALL, M. G. and BUCKLAND, W. R. *A Dictionary of Statistical Terms.* Hafner Publishing Company, Second Edition, New York, 1967.

KILBRIDGE, M. and CARABATEAS, S. 'Urban planning models: a classification system'. *Ekstics,* 1967, vol. 24, pp. 480—485.

KILBRIDGE, M., O'BLOCK, R. and TEPLITZ, P. V. 'A conceptual framework for urban models'. *Management Science,* 1969, vol. 15, no. 6.

KRACHT, J. B. 'The application of models to the planning process with special emphasis on land use'. (Bibliography). Council of Planning Libraries, Exchange Bibliography 194, 1971, June.

KRAFT, G. and WOHL, M. 'New directions from passenger demand analysis and forecasting'. *Transportation Research,* 1967, vol. 1, no. 3.

LAKSHMANAN, T. R. and HANSEN, W. G. 'A retail market potential model'. *Journal of the American Institute of Planners,* 1965, May, pp. 134—143.

LANE, P. and PRESTWOOD SMITH. *Analytical Transport Planning.* Duckworth, England.

LATHROP, G. T. and HAMBURG, J. R. 'An opportunity-accessibility model for allocating regional growth'. *Journal of the American Institute of Planners,* 1965, May, pp. 95—103.

LEATHERS, N. J. 'Residential location and model of transportation to work: a model of choice'. *Transportation Research,* 1967, vol. 1, no. 2. pp. 129—155.

LEONTIEFF, W. *Input—Output Analysis.* Oxford University Press, 1967.

LICHFIELD, N. 'Cost-benefit analysis in city planning'. *Journal of the American Institute of Planners*, 1960, November, pp. 273–279.

LITTLE, A. D. 'Model of San Francisco housing market'. San Francisco Community Renewal C65400, Cambridge, 1966, January.

LOOMBA, N. P. *Linear Programming: An Introductory Analysis*. McGraw-Hill, 1964.

LOWRY, I. S. *A Model of Metropolis*. Rand Corporation, Santa Monica, California, 1964.

LOWRY, I. S. 'Location parameters in the Pittsburgh model'. *Papers and Proceedings of the Regional Science Association*, vol. II.

LOWRY, I. S. 'A short course in model design'. *Journal of the American Institute of Planners*, 1965, May, pp. 158–166.

LOWRY, I. S. 'Seven models of urban development: a structural comparation'. Special Report 97, Highway Research Board, Washington D.C., 1968.

MANCHESTER UNIVERSITY. 'Shopping centres in north west England'. Department of Town and Country Planning, Part 2, 1968.

MARCH, L. 'Urban systems: a generalised distribution function'. Land Use Built Form Studies, Cambridge, WP 24.

MASSER, I. 'Notes on an application of the Lowry model to Merseyside'. Unpublished paper, Dept. of Civic Design, University of Liverpool, 1970.

MASSEY, D. B. and CORDEY–HAYES, M. 'The use of models in structure planning'. *Town Planning Review*, 1971, vol. 42, no. 1.

MEIER, R. L. *A Communication Theory of Urban Growth*. M.I.T. Press, Cambridge, Mass., 1962.

MEIER, R. L. and DUKE, R. D. 'Gaming simulation for urban planning'. *Journal of the American Institute of Planners*, 1966, January, pp. 3–17.

M.I.T. 'Experiments in computer aided design'. *Architectural Design*, 1969, September, pp. 507–514.

MITCHELL, R. B. and RAPKIN, C. *Urban Traffic: A Function of Land Use*. New York, 1954.

McLOUGHLIN, J. B. 'Simulation for beginners: the planning of a sub-regional model system'. *Regional Studies*, 1969, December, 3/3, pp. 313–323.

McLOUGHLIN, J. B. 'Cities as open systems: a framework for analysis'. *Architectural Design*, 1970, June, pp. 313–314.

McLOUGHLIN, J. B. *Urban and Regional Planning*. Faber and Faber, London 1970.

McMILLAN, C. and GONZALEZ, R. F. *Systems Analysis: A Computer Approach to Decision Models*. Richard D. Irvin Inc., 1971.

NIEDERCORN, J. H. *An Econometric Model of Metropolitan Employment and Population Growth*. RM-3758-RC, Rand Corporation, Santa Monica, 1963, October.

OSOFSKY, S. 'The multiple regression method of forecasting traffic volumes'. *Traffic Quarterly*, 1959, vol. XIII, July.

P.A. MANAGEMENT CONSULTANTS LTD. and ISRAEL INSTITUTE OF URBAN STUDIES LTD. 'Irvine New Town planning study'. 1969, September.

PARRY-LEWIS, J. 'Invasion of Planning' and Comments by McLoughlin & Wilson. *Journal of Town Planning Institute*, 1970, March, pp. 100–106.

PARRY-LEWIS, J. and TRAIL, A. C. 'An assessment of shopping models'. *Town Planning Review*, 1968, January.

PASK, G. 'The architectural relevance of cybernetics'. *Architectural Design*, 1969, September, pp. 494–6.

POPE, A. S. 'Gravity models in town planning: use in retailing exercises'. Department of Town Planning, Lanchester College of Technology, Coventry, 1969, October.

PREST, A. R. and TURVEY, R. 'Cost-benefit analysis: a survey'. *Economic Journal*, 1965, vol. LXXV, pp. 683–735.

REILLY, W. J. 'Methods for the study of retail relationships'. University of Texas, Bureau of Business Research Studies Report, 1929, November, no. 4. Subsequently incorporated in *The Law of Retail Gravitation*. 2nd Edition, Pilsbury Publishers, Inc., New York, 1953.

RICHARDS, M. G. 'Applications in Transportation Planning', in *Gravity Models in Town Planning*. Department of Town Planning, Lanchester College of Technology, Coventry, 1969, October.

ROGERS, A. 'Matrix methods of population analysis'. *Journal of the American Institute of Planners*, 1966, January.

ROGERS, N. 'Model cities from city models.' *Industrial Engineering*, 1969, December, pp. 32–42.

SCHLAGER, K. J. 'A land use plan design model'. *Journal of the American Institute of Planners*, 1965, May, pp. 103–111.

SCHNEIDER, M. 'Gravity models and trip distribution theory'. *Papers and Proceedings of the Regional Science Association*, 1959, vol. V, pp. 51–56.

SESSOMS, H. D. 'New bases for recreation planning'. *Journal of the American Institute of Planners*, 1964, February, pp. 26–33.

SIMON, H. A. *The Sciences of the Artificial*. The M.I.T. Press, 1969.

SNELL, J. and SHULDINER, P. 'Analysis of urban transportation research'. North Western University Research Report, 1967.

STONE, R. *Mathematics in the Social Sciences*. Chapman and Hall, London, 1965.

STOUFFER, A. 'Intervening opportunities: a theory retailing mobility and distance'. *American Social Review*, 1940, vol. 5, no. 6.

STYLES, B. 'Principles and historical development of the gravity concept', in *Gravity Models in Town Planning*. Department of Town Planning, Lanchester College of Technology, Coventry, 1969, October.

TANNER, J. C. 'Factors affecting the amount of travel'. Road Research Laboratory, H.M.S.O. London 1961.

THOMPSON, D. L. 'Subjective distance'. *Journal of Retailing*, 1963, Spring.

TIEBOUT, C. M. 'The community economic base study'. The Committee for Economic Development, New York, 1962.

TOCHER, K. D. *The Art of Simulation*. The English Universities Press Ltd. London, Third impression 1969.

TOMAZINIS, A. R. 'A new method of trip distribution in an urban area'. *Highway Research Board Bulletin*, 1962, no. 347.

VAJDA, S. *An Introduction to Linear Programming and the Theory of Games.* Methuen, Wiley, 1960.

VOORHEES, A. M. 'The nature and uses of models in city planning'. *Journal of the American Institute of Planners*, 1959, vol. 25, no. 2, pp. 57–60.

WAGNER, H. M. *Principles of Operations Research.* Prentice-Hall International Inc., 1969.

WEBBER, M. M. 'Order in diversity: community without propinquity', in WINGO (ed.) *Cities and Space: The Future Use of Urban Land*, Baltimore, 1963, pp. 23–54.

WIENER, N. *Cybernetics.* The M.I.T. Press, New York, 1948.

WILLOUGHBY, T., PATERSON, W. and DRUMMOND, G. 'Computer aided architectural planning'. *Operational Research Quarterly*, 1970, vol. 21, no. 1, pp. 91–98.

WILSON, A. G. 'Mathematical models in planning'. *Arena Journal*, 1967, April, pp. 260–265.

WILSON, A. G. 'A statistical theory of spatial distribution models'. *Transportation Research*, 1968, vol. 1, no. 3, pp. 253–270.

WILSON, A. G. 'Models in urban planning: a synoptic review of recent literature'. *Abstract in Urban Studies*, 1968, November, pp. 249–276.

WILSON, A. G. 'Developments of some elementary residential locations models'. Centre for Environmental Studies, WP 22, 1968, December.

WILSON, A. G. 'Entropy'. Centre for Environmental Studies, WP 26, 1969, January.

WILSON, A. G. 'The use of analogies in geography'. Centre for Environmental Studies, Working paper, no. 32, 1969, March.

WILSON, A. G. 'New planning tools'. *Architectural Design*, 1969, September, p. 488.

WILSON, A. G. *Entropy in Urban and Regional Modelling.* Pion Limited, London, 1970.

WILSON, A. G., BAYLISS, D., BLACKBURN, A. J. and HUTCHINSON, B. G. 'New directions in strategic transport planning'. Centre for Environmental Studies, WP 36, 1969.

WILSON, A. G., HAWKINS, A. F., HILL, G. J. and WAGON, D. J. 'Calibration and testing of the SELNEC transport model'. *Regional Studies*, 1969, vol. 3, pp. 337–350.

YOUNG, R. C. 'Goals and goal setting'. *Journal of the American Institute of Planners*, 1965, August, p. 186.

YOUNG, W. 'Planning – a linear programming model'. *GLC Intelligence Unit Quarterly Bulletin*, 1972, no. 19.

Index